BESTSELLING BOOK SERIES

Puppies For Dummies, 2nd Edition

KT-495-986

Cheat Sheet

Routine Directions

Using familiar words helps your puppy feel like he's part of the group. Consider using the following:

- **Inside:** When bringing or calling your puppy inside
- **Outside:** When taking your puppy outside
- **Car:** When going on a car ride
- **Upstairs:** When going upstairs
- **Downstairs:** When going downstairs
- **Go to Sally:** Teach your puppy this command along with the names of everyone important to you
- **Walk:** When initiating a walk
- **Play:** When initiating play
- **Kitchen:** When going to the kitchen (this can be used for any other important room)

Sample Housetraining Schedule

This housetraining schedule is based on the needs of a healthy 4-month-old puppy. Vary the schedule according to your schedule and the age needs of your pup.

Period of Day/Time	Action
Wake up (7:00 a.m.)	Go outside immediately.
Breakfast (7:30 a.m.)	Go outside after breakfast.
Morning walk (8:00 to 8:30 a.m.)	Go outside after breakfast, before walk.
Late-morning walk (11:00 a.m.)	Potty before walk, if necessary.
Lunch (11:15 a.m.)	Young puppies must eat and go outside (if you work, hire a helper).
After-lunch outing (11:45 a.m.)	Go outside.
Afternoon (2:30 p.m.)	Go outside.
Dinner and walk (4:30 p.m.)	Go outside after dinner.
Early evening (7:00 p.m.)	Remove water.
Late evening (8:30 p.m.)	Go outside.
Before bed (11:00 p.m.)	Go outside.
Middle of the night	Go outside, if necessary.

Foundation Commands

- **Let's go:** This command says "I'm the leader, so follow me!" Say it whenever you're leading your puppy on leash.
- **Sit:** This direction is the human equivalent of "Say please." Direct your puppy to sit before giving him anything positive, from meals to treats, or when greeting strangers or friends.
- **Down:** Directing down helps your puppy calm down whenever you're going to be stationary for a while.
- **Stay:** This direction instills good impulse control. Direct your puppy to stay whenever you want him to be still.
- **Wait:** Use this direction for sudden stops or at curbs. It says "Stop and focus on me before proceeding."
- **Excuse me:** Teach your puppy to respect your space. Say this direction whenever your puppy is blocking you or is in your way. It's a passive way to say, "I'm the leader; watch me!"
- **No:** This direction is the human equivalent of "That's a bad idea" instead of "You're bad." Use it if you catch your puppy thinking about misbehaving.

For more direction on teaching and using these directions, read Chapters 13 and 14!

For Dummies: Bestselling Book Series for Beginners

Puppies For Dummies®, 2nd Edition

Cheat Sheet

Puppy First-Aid Kit Essentials

Here's a first-aid kit you can put together for your pup (see Chapter 21 for details). Set these things aside in a safe place or take them with you when you travel with your puppy:

- Strip of cloth to use as a muzzle
- Gauze pads
- A sheet or towel that can be used to carry your puppy in a supine position
- A few strips of cloth to tie around a bleeding wound
- A tourniquet rod (use only in severe emergencies)
- Hydrogen peroxide/ betadine solution
- The poison hotline number and a list of all poisonous plants
- Bacitracin
- Ice packs
- Snakebite kit, if you're in snake country
- Towels to wet in case of heatstroke
- Rectal thermometer
- Bowl and water jug (to be kept in your car) in case you get stranded
- A roll of vet wrap (pur- chased at your puppy's doctor) or bandage tape

Household Poisons

Following is a list of some of the more common poisons and plants found in and around your house. Keep your puppy away from these items! (Head to Chapter 20 for info on preventative and emergency care.)

Household Poisons	Common Plants	Outdoor Poisons
Acetaminophen	Azalea bush	Antifreeze
Acetone	Boxwood	Carbon monoxide
Ammonia	Cactus	Charcoal lighter fluid
Bleach	Columbine	Gasoline
Caffeine pills	Daffodil flower bud	Kerosene
Deodorants	Dumbcane	Lead
Furniture polish	Foxglove	Lime
Fly strips	Hemlock	Paint thinner
Ibuprofen	Honeysuckle	Phenol cleaners
Insecticides	Horse chestnut	Rat poison
Mothballs	Ivy	Strychnine
Rubbing alcohol	Lily of the valley	Turpentine
Soap	Lupine	Cocoa mulch
	Marijuana	
FOODS	Mistletoe	
Alcohol	Morning glory	
Chocolate	Oleander	
Grapes/raisins	Philodendron	
Illegal Drugs	Poinsettia	
Onions	Rhubarb	
Yeast	Skunk cabbage	
	Tobacco	
	Tulip bulb	
	Wild mushroom	
	Yew (Japanese-especially the berries)	
	Amaryllis and bulb	
	English Ivy	

For Dummies: Bestselling Book Series for Beginners

Puppies
FOR
DUMMIES®
2ND EDITION

by Sarah Hodgson

WILEY

Wiley Publishing, Inc.

Puppies For Dummies®, 2nd Edition

Published by
Wiley Publishing, Inc.
111 River St.
Hoboken, NJ 07030-5774
www.wiley.com

About the Author

Sarah Hodgson has been a trainer of dogs and their people for over 20 years. She has had many famous clients, including TV personality Katie Couric, actors/actresses Richard Gere, Glenn Close, Chazz Palminteri, Chevy Chase, and Lucie Arnez, business moguls George Soros, Tommy Hilfiger, Tommy Mottola, and Michael Fuchs, and sports greats Bobby Valentine and Alan Houston.

Sarah is the author of eight dog training books, including *Teach Yourself Visually, Dog Training; Dog Tricks For Dummies; DogPerfect;* and *PuppyPerfect.* Soon to be released: *Miss Sarah's Book of Etiquette for Dogs.*

Sarah lives in Katonah, New York, with her daughter, Lindsay, and her black lab, Whoopsie Daisy. For more information, you can visit her Web site: www.dogperfect.com.

Dedication

To Lindsay and all the paws to follow: You are my joy. I am grateful for every day we spend together.

Author's Acknowledgments

By the time I write the acknowledgements for a book, the book writing is practically over. My excitement at being at the end of a project is so palpable that I feel like running out and hugging all the people who have been there for me, in numerous ways, throughout its writing. From my friends and family who are there to keep me sane and smiling to my helpers who keep the wheels of my life turning, I could not enjoy my existence as much without you.

And to my editorial staff, some of whom I only know by initials, I am eternally grateful. Your insightful tweaks and comments raise the quality and comprehension of this book to a height I could never reach alone. Thanks!

Of course, none of my knowledge would have been formed without the lessons I've learned at the side of each and every dog. Your spirits have been my guide. What a life it's been! I'm grateful for the opportunity to know you and be your teacher.

Publisher's Acknowledgments

We're proud of this book; please send us your comments through our Dummies online registration form located at www.dummies.com/register/.

Some of the people who helped bring this book to market include the following:

Acquisitions, Editorial, and Media Development

Project Editor: Christina Guthrie

Acquisitions Editor: Mike Lewis

Copy Editor: Jessica Smith

Editorial Program Coordinator: Hanna K. Scott

Technical Editor: Patty Kovach, DVM

Editorial Manager: Christine Meloy Beck

Media Development Manager: Laura VanWinkle

Editorial Assistants: Erin Calligan, David Lutton

Cover Photos: © Legacy Photography, © DAJ, © Karl Weatherly/Photodisc Green, © Image Source

Cartoons: Rich Tennant (www.the5thwave.com)

Composition Services

Project Coordinator: Tera Knapp

Layout and Graphics: Carl Byers, Denny Hager, Joyce Haughey, Clint Lahnen, Barry Offringa, Heather Ryan, Brent Savage

Special Art: Illustrations by Barbara Frake; Color section photos by Isabelle Francais

Proofreaders: Leeann Harney, Jessica Kramer, Joe Niesen, Techbooks

Indexer: Techbooks

Special Help

Elizabeth Rea, Danielle Voirol, Carrie Burchfield

Publishing and Editorial for Consumer Dummies

Diane Graves Steele, Vice President and Publisher, Consumer Dummies

Joyce Pepple, Acquisitions Director, Consumer Dummies

Kristin A. Cocks, Product Development Director, Consumer Dummies

Michael Spring, Vice President and Publisher, Travel

Kelly Regan, Editorial Director, Travel

Publishing for Technology Dummies

Andy Cummings, Vice President and Publisher, Dummies Technology/General User

Composition Services

Gerry Fahey, Vice President of Production Services

Debbie Stailey, Director of Composition Services

Contents at a Glance

Table of Contents

Introduction

*T*o say that I love puppies would be an understatement. They make me absolutely giddy. Their paws and silky ears, their little bellies, their infamous puppy breath, and each individual reaction to my "happy voice" all awaken the child in me. Even though I spend countless hours doing grown-up things such as driving, cleaning, cooking, and nurturing my human family, when I have my arms around a puppy or when I'm curled up with my own dogs, my daily responsibilities seem to drift away.

Even though raising a puppy is also a daily responsibility (and a huge one at that), it's like many other projects in life: After you understand how your puppy is thinking, how you can communicate with him effectively, and how you can structure your environment to limit your frustrations, the day-to-day things immediately become simpler. The comment I get most often from clients after our initial visit is: "You are a miracle worker!" But I know that the real miracle is the puppy — I just facilitate the communication between the two species.

In this book, you find a common-sense approach to selecting your puppy, loving hints to help you through those first critical months, and support in problem solving and training. You find straightforward info on what to do and just how to do it — in plain English. Nothing more and nothing less — I promise.

About This Book

As with raising children, how you manage your puppy's day-to-day needs, optimize his successes, and deal with daily frustrations will be directly reflected in your puppy's demeanor. Behind every happy puppy is a supportive, understanding, and nurturing family cheering him on. If you're feeling overwhelmed with this project now, don't despair: *Puppies For Dummies,* 2nd Edition, will give you a whole new outlook, provide easy steps to resolve every frustration, and help you civilize your puppy in no time flat!

This book is all-inclusive, providing all you need to know to raise a puppy. From choosing the right breed and identifying a puppy's temperament to managing your first day and training your puppy through the first year — you'll find it all here.

Conventions Used in This Book

While writing this book, I used a few conventions that I want you to be aware of:

- ✔ To avoid any "puppy gender bias," I refer to puppies as both males and females throughout the text. Except for anything that's strictly related to females or males, you can be sure that the info applies to your puppy regardless of gender.

- ✔ Anytime I introduce a new term, I *italicize* it.

- ✔ Keywords in lists appear in **boldface.** Also, when I present a list of steps to perform, the action you need to take is **boldface** as well.

- ✔ Web sites and e-mail addresses appear in `monofont` to help them stand out in the text.

What You're Not to Read

Though I'd be honored if you read every word of this book, I'm realistic. Who has the luxury or time to read a nearly 400-page book on any subject these days? Don't be stressed out by the size of this book, though. I've written it to be enjoyed one chapter at a time and further used as a reference guide.

In addition, there are bits that you can skip if you're pressed for time or if you're simply not interested in anything other than the bare facts. If you fall into this camp, know that you can skip the sidebars, which are gray boxes of text that contain interesting but nonessential information. As well, you can skip any paragraphs that have the Technical Stuff or Just for Fun icons attached to them.

Foolish Assumptions

Here's what I assumed about you, dear reader, when writing this book:

- ✔ You know that puppies have four paws and a tail — or at least a stump of a tail.

- ✔ You either have a puppy right now or are considering getting one, but you don't know much about raising a puppy.

- ✔ You don't want to obtain a PhD in training techniques and dog physiology or psychology. You just want the basics on things such as what supplies to buy, how to train your puppy to perform basic commands, the best dog food to use, how much exercise to provide, and how to keep your pup healthy in general.

If you fit into any or all of these categories, this book is for you.

How This Book Is Organized

This book is divided into parts, each one having its own colorful theme. Here's a quick rundown.

Part I: A Match Made in Heaven

Here you find the scoop on choosing a puppy — from the right breed to the perfect personality. You may have questions: Are dog breeds all that different? What's with the new designer mixed breeds? Can a pup's personality be predetermined? Where's the best place to find a puppy? You can find all the answers and more in this part.

Part II: Nurturing Your Puppy Day to Day

Those first few days with your new puppy can be a real challenge. What do I do? What do I need to buy? What should I expect? You find all the answers in this part. Plus you find out how to think with your puppy, socialize him to all of life's nuances, and communicate to him so you can condition the right habits from the start. By 12 weeks, your puppy's brain is fully developed — and you can definitely tell. He sleeps less and plays more. His true personality emerges, and it may not always jive with yours. But, take a deep breath. This part is here to help. It helps you understand your puppy's needs and developmental phases, and it shows you how to work with your children and all the other people in your life to shape good behavior from the start. In addition, I provide tips on travel and on life changes that you and your puppy are likely to go through together.

Part III: Training Your Puppy

Let the training begin. In this section, I cover training stages by tailoring what you teach and how you teach it to the age and personality of your prize pupil. In this part, you discover basic lessons, hints on housetraining, and ideas on how to inspire family cooperation. In addition, I give you an up-close look at the workings of some cool tools and techniques that are available to you — from clickers to target training. Then, after you've mastered the basics, delve into off-leash lessons and take a look at all the different events and activities available to a well-trained puppy — from agility to Flyball and pet therapy.

Part IV: Overcoming Behavioral Problems

In this part, I target the array of frustrations most everyone experiences with their puppies. Instead of looking at the issues as problems, I examine them from your puppy's perspective. Soon you'll realize that all of your puppy's behaviors communicate something to you. This mindful approach helps you shape a fair response and develop an appropriate displacement activity to even the most frustrating difficulties. You'll feel proactive and empathetic when dealing with specific issues, such as separation anxiety, chewing, jumping, nipping, and even aggression. The best part is that your relationship with your puppy will grow stronger from working together to resolve your issues.

Part V: In Sickness and in Health

If you want a happy dog, you have to take care of more than just training. You have to take care of your dog's health, too. This part gives you the information you need to know about good nutrition and exercise, about taking care of your dog when he's feeling fine, and about what to do if he gets sick.

Part VI: The Part of Tens

Last but not least, in this part, I give you ten of my favorite games and ten crowd-pleasing tricks. Enjoy!

Icons Used in This Book

Throughout this book you'll find icons that appear on the left-hand side of the page and that point out different types of info. Following is a list of the various icons you may encounter:

This icon highlights useful tidbits and helpful advice — such as how to snap the leash just right to avoid hurting your pup while still getting the response you want.

These friendly reminders won't let you forget the main points — such as leaving a full bowl of water for your pup on a hot summer day.

"Warning, Warning!" Need I say more? Be sure not to skip this one.

This icon alerts you to factoids and technical information that isn't necessary to know but is quite interesting.

When you see this icon, you can be sure that you're about to read some fun information that's good to know (but not necessary to the task at hand).

Where to Go from Here

The coolest thing about this book is that you can jump in anywhere. It's a no-rules reference for anyone who has a puppy or anyone who has ever thought of getting one. Just look in the table of contents or index for the topic you want to know about. Then flip right to that chapter to get the scoop.

You can also read this book straight through from front to back if you want, starting with Chapter 1 and digging right in.

Regardless of where you begin, remember this: Puppies are a lot like babies. They need to be nurtured but not spoiled. They need to be loved but not overindulged. They need guidelines — not unlimited freedom. They need to play, but they also need limits. Your ability to reason and understand gives you the responsibility to make the necessary adaptations. You must be your puppy's leader, safe keeper, friend, and voice. Your efforts will forever be your reward.

Thank you for picking up my book and adding it to your library. Everyone feels inept sometimes, unable to figure out how to simplify or master a project, hobby, or sport. But, with time and information, things do get easier — even enjoyable. Whether you read this book chapter by chapter or reference it one section at a time, the information teaches you how to successfully communicate to your puppy and raise him to be a wonderful pet and member of your family.

Part I
A Match Made in Heaven

In this part . . .

Choosing a dog to bring home may be the only chance you have to pick a relative, so choose wisely! If you're still undecided about what breed of dog would mesh well with your lifestyle, you have an exciting project ahead. With closer examination, you'll be able to pair the needs and demands of your lifestyle with a dog's breed and personality. Are you a mover and a shaker? Do you have a fast-paced lifestyle that cries for canine involvement? Or are you more comfortable with a puppy that can stay home and relax while you're out? What type of dog are you looking for: big or small, shaggy or furless, energetic or mellow, bright-minded or relaxed? Believe it or not, there's a breed to suit each specification. And just think, when breeds are mixed, a whole new range of options presents itself.

Farther on in your journey, you'll get to decide on a personality to best reflect your own. You can find a wide range of puppies: bossy puppies, mellow puppies, silly puppies, and shy puppies. Before settling on your match, consider what personality would be most welcome under your roof. If you're a pushover, a bossy, dominant type may not be in the cards for you: He'll have you trained before he's done cutting his puppy teeth. On the other hand, if you're structured and stern, a mellow or shy puppy may drive you to insanity with his never-a-care personality.

In this part, I clue you in on how to decide what kind of puppy best suits your lifestyle, and then I show you how to choose your puppy after you've narrowed your options.

Chapter 1

Raising a Puppy: Making Heads and Tails of It

In This Chapter

▶ Understanding the differences between puppies

▶ Helping your pup settle in with the family

▶ Training with your pup's age in mind

▶ Dealing with the infamous puppy behavior

▶ Taking care of your puppy

*I*f you parallel your puppy's first year with the first 18 years of a child's life, you'll have a good sense of what's in front of you for the next 360 days. Civilizing a puppy is a lot like civilizing a child — fortunately, though, it only takes a year. And, your puppy won't ever wreck the car, max out your credit cards, or leave for college!

This first chapter lays the groundwork for what lies ahead. With these guidelines in hand, you'll have no trouble getting through the first year.

A Puppy Is a Puppy — Right?

Wrong! Just as no two people are exactly alike, no two puppies are alike either. Even though you may see two puppies of the same breed and think "Wow! They look exactly the same" or see a litter and not be able to tell one from the other, remember that each puppy has his own unique take on life, which is shaped as much by the people who surround him as his breed's specific impulses.

If all this talk of breeds is sounding a little foreign to you, you're not alone. Until now, you may not have given dog breeds much thought. Instead, you may have thought that the only thing separating one pup from the other was coat color and size. Unless your plan is to choose a dog that compliments your couch cushions, you have to know a little bit about the types available.

And you're in luck because this section helps you with just that — it focuses on the difference between breeds and how those influences impact your life on a daily basis.

In addition to breed, a puppy's personality and temperament should influence selection. Like kids, each puppy has a personality that's markedly defined by the time he's 8 weeks old. However, unlike kids, you can pick your puppy's personality.

A word on breeds

Before starting out, it's a good idea to get a handle on the word "breed." A *breed,* as defined by *Webster's New World College Dictionary,* 4th Edition, is more or less a group of animals descended from common ancestors. If you look to the *American Kennel Club* (AKC), they define a breed as "a line of dogs with similar ancestry." Ancestry, then, is the keyword here: By belonging to a certain breed, a puppy's lineage can be traced along a family tree. If you invest in a purebred dog (versus say, a mixed breed), you can decipher just where his great-grandfather lived and what made him so special, whether it be championship ribbons or obedience titles.

Most breeds can be traced back in history to the time of their conception. Generally a breed is created when a person or a group of like-minded advocates mindfully pair two dogs that have similar instincts or looks. For example, the conception of the Parsons Russell Terrier (also known as the Jack Russell Terrier) was the project of Rev. Jack Russell, who lived in the mid-1880s. Until that time, hunters carried a short-legged terrier on horseback to rush a fox from its hole after the hounds had cornered it. Russell sought to breed a dog with legs long enough to keep up with the hounds but with enough agility and drive to follow through with its task of rushing a fox from its hole. Russell's first breeding female, the queen bee so to speak, was a cross-bred terrier named "Trump," whom he bought from a milkman.

Your dog's ingrained need for a job

A puppy's instinctual skills, with a few exceptions, are no longer necessary to human survival. But, please don't let your puppy in on this secret. His skills are his life's talent and employing them will give his life a sense of purpose. No sheep to herd? The neighborhood kids will do.

No snow in Savannah? Pulling a skateboarder will satisfy a Siberian Husky. No ducks to retrieve? A tennis ball will do just fine. Dogs love to work, and they can't quell their passions just because you have a late meeting.

Over time more than 420 known breeds have been developed worldwide. Each of these breeds has specific characteristics that allow the dogs to withstand the environment of the lands of their original decent. Each breed has a defined look, temperament, and interest that continues to get passed down from generation to generation.

Deciding what breed (if any) is right for you

In Chapter 3, I discuss the difference between breeds, and I group them into seven categories as I explore the ideal home environment, as well as the necessary exercise, training, and socialization commitments of each. In addition, I look at the allure of mixed-breed dogs, which are made up of the latest designer breeds as well as the generic mixes who cost considerably less. A quick peek at the concept of *hybrid vigor* will help you to appreciate a dog who looks and acts unique.

You find nifty tables and personality charts to help you keep track of the ones best-suited to your lifestyle. Your heart's pick may be a high-energy breed from the sporting group, but if you're out most of the day and you prefer vegging to jogging, this puppy will lose his appeal when you find him climbing your walls.

After you've narrowed your breed choice, you're ready to begin the adventure of finding your puppy. First impressions count — make sure your puppy's first home, whether it's a breeder, shelter, store, or private home, is a safe, positive, and relaxed environment where you feel comfortable asking any pertinent questions and voicing your concerns. Many good breeders will question you because they want to find good homes for the puppies they love like infants.

As I said earlier in this chapter, puppies, like children, have distinct personalities. In Chapter 4, you find a temperament test that you can take with you when checking out a particular puppy. Visualize the ideal characteristics you value in a dog and list them in the margin. For example, do you want a dog who's devoted to making you happy and who's needy for attention and delighted to do your bidding? Or, are you more comfortable with a puppy who's affectionate, but independent? Maybe your heart's set on a timid puppy who needs patience, coaxing, and love to come out of his shell. Believe it or not, you can make accurate behavioral predictions such as these when puppies are just eight weeks old.

Helping Your Puppy Jump into the Family Groove

You've been excited for days, weeks, and perhaps even years to bring your puppy home! Few things in life are as exciting as adopting a puppy.

Regardless of your mood, this initial trip can be scary and overwhelming for your puppy, who may be separating from his first family for the very first time. Plan ahead by organizing both the trip home and your arrival. Make your puppy-supply purchases, which are listed in Chapter 5, well in advance. Also, before your pup comes home, be sure to set up his first room, and explain your itinerary to family and friends. Having a plan puts your mind at ease, which will help your puppy get through this transition stage. Your puppy will bond to you and his new life in no time.

Understanding your puppy's point of view

Your puppy will thrive on consistency and predictability, and so will you. In Chapter 6, I focus on your puppy's daily needs and how to structure a schedule around them. Knowing how your puppy likes to organize his day takes the guesswork out of this experience and humanizes many of his communication skills and dependency issues. In fact, Chapter 6 points out just how much a human toddler and a puppy have in common — from a routine bathroom and sleeping schedule to predictable stages of development. I offer several example schedules and charts to help you structure a realistic day and bring some regularity back into your life.

Further along in Chapter 6, I help you explore Doglish, which is, of course, your dog's language. Puppies need a lot of direction and feel most comfortable when it's given in a language they understand and by someone who's clear-minded and calm. Even though you may think your bossy, hyper puppy is having a ball, he's likely not. All puppies want someone to admire and please; otherwise, they feel lost.

Teaching your puppy is a lot like teaching a foreigner English — you have to translate your teachings into the person's native language. For example, as you know, your puppy doesn't understand English. So, to help your puppy understand your thoughts, you have to translate them first into Doglish, your puppy's native language.

Positively overdoing socialization

If you want a well-rounded, gently mannered dog, there's one secret you must know: Overdo socialization in puppyhood! Overdo socialization even more so than training. Expose you puppy to everything — objects, surfaces, sounds (inside and out), places, and people of all ages, races, sexes, and sizes. Expose your pup to other animals and pets too. Even changes in weather patterns must be handled mindfully. If your puppy is startled or concerned, a soothing reaction from you may actually be misinterpreted as mutual fear. To teach him how to manage himself, reassure your puppy with your confidence and direction. Knowing how to calm him when he's stressed can make the difference between a pet who rolls with the changes and one who emotionally locks up or reacts defensively. (Chapter 7 gives the lowdown on socializing your pup.)

Until your puppy is fully inoculated *do not* take him out in public to socialize. Various life-threatening viruses are airborne and can be picked up by simply sniffing about. In addition, I've heard reports of young, playful puppies who have not had their rabies inoculation forcibly euthanized after nipping a stranger. Take precaution.

Raising a pup with children and within a neighborhood

Bringing home a puppy to raise with your family or to entertain the grandchildren when they come to visit adds another dimension to your months ahead. Kids are often pigeonholed as other puppies and can be perceived as rivals for toys, food, and attention.

Chapter 8 offers a proactive (rather than reactive) approach to raising a puppy with children — from phrases to use to groovy games and activities to play. By organizing fun activities, you're giving the child license to both control and enjoy the puppy, while the puppy is learning respect for everyone who walks on two legs. If you already suspect sibling rivalry, the signs, symptoms, and solutions can be found in Chapter 8, too.

If you're raising your puppy in a neighborhood or urban environment, Chapter 9 gives you clever ways to stay on everyone's good side and shows you how to make a few extra friends to boot. Nobody likes to step in puppy poop on their way to work, so be a good neighbor and check out Chapter 9 to find out the best way to scoop a poop.

Enduring life changes

Puppyhood is a time for many changes, both physical and emotional. During their first months, puppies go through different cycles: One day they'll love your neighbor and the next day they'll hide. One day they'll be bold and assured when entering your car and the next they'll put on the brakes and refuse to follow you. Don't worry, this behavior is nothing out of the ordinary — puppies have a lot of nuances to contend with. These periods are scary for any puppy, but they give you the perfect opportunity to strengthen your connection to him by managing his anxiety with concern and confidence. You become the Great Oz as you increase his trust and reliability in your judgment.

You also need to examine your own life and think about any anticipated changes that may affect your puppy in the near or distant future. Ask yourself: Are you single now but anticipate having children? Is this puppy your first pet, but you're hoping to introduce a cat or rabbit in the months or years ahead? Make the transition simple: Condition and socialize your puppy when he's young.

Tackling Training through Your Puppy's Growth Phases

Think of this year as your golden opportunity to influence and civilize your puppy. The chapters in Part III introduce you to directions and problem-solving techniques that are age-appropriate and are designed to build your puppy's confidence, both in you and in the world surrounding him. Each chapter is broken into easily understandable exercises that are fun to do and easily repeated by others.

Knowing what you're in for

Here's just some of what you have to look forward to as your puppy grows through his first year:

- **Infancy:** Infancy is a magical time for your puppy! Delightfully self-centered and curious, he's experiencing his world — and all the people in it — for the first time. This phase isn't the time to interject your opinion too strongly. Let him explore while encouraging positive behaviors and structuring your schedule and affections around his needs. Shouting "No" repeatedly is a turnoff: Like an infant, your puppy doesn't have the capacity to comprehend right from wrong.

✔ **Terrible Twos:** Before the terrible twos start, you may be convinced that you've adopted an angel. During his infancy, your puppy will follow you everywhere, sleep for hours, and run to you when you call. Then it will happen almost overnight: Your puppy will fall from grace. Suddenly you'll be under slipper assault, the nipping will be relentless, and racing away from you will be your pup's new game. During the terrible twos phase, you may dream about the day you adopted him and may fantasize about leaving him on your neighbor's doorstep. If it's any consolation, all his mischief is a wonderful sign of normal development. Your puppy is growing up. Knowing how to handle his behavior and how to control your own frustration is critical in getting through this trying time. Help is on its way.

✔ **Budding Adolescent:** Okay, by now you're getting a good glimpse of your puppy's personality. Is he needy, confrontational, strong willed, dependent, focused, obstinate? You get to the point: Your puppy is maturing faster than you can keep up with. This is the time to start fun, positive training routines and to increase games that encourage interaction. Bear in mind that cooperation at this age is not part of his emotional repertoire. Adolescents naturally test the limits of their guardians — no matter the species. Exploration and curiosity also come into bloom during this stage. Matched with a puppy's spiking hormonal and energy level, it's a wonder they behave at all!

Though you may dream of a puppy who comes consistently, don't put too much pressure on him now. Mindful obedience isn't a realistic goal for one so young. Your demands and rising frustration will not win you any brownie points either, although patience is noted and calm interactions are mirrored. The best approach for this age: prevention and playful lessons that highlight his focus and successes!

✔ **Puberty:** Experiencing puberty with your puppy may prompt a quick midnight phone call to your parents to apologize for your quirky behaviors during puberty. Random defiance, running off for hours, ignoring direction: Don't take any of your pup's frustrating behavior personally. Your puppy must challenge you in order to grow up. Through this age-appropriate behavior, he's testing your authority to ensure that he can trust your judgment. It's simply a part of nature.

Managing yourself is the most important concentration during this stage. Anger and frustration will spell your ruin — your puppy will view your loss of control as a weakness, and he'll either assert his control or become unsure and manic. Keep your puppy safe from his own impulses by keeping him leashed or in a contained space, and follow the exercises in Chapter 14. Lesson by lesson you'll shape his worldview, raising him into doghood with a tremendous respect for your confident attitude and levelheadedness.

✔ **Trying Teen:** During this phase, you have the perfect puppy — devoted, responsive, and mindful. Well, that's to say, most of the time. Sometimes your almost-adult puppy still tests his independence; sometimes that incorrigible three-month-old puppy reemerges and he's up to his old tricks. But, for the most part, you can see the light at the end of the dark tunnel.

If you're like many people, you'll experience a strong desire for off-leash control, and you may have a wanderlust for extracurricular activities, such as agility or pet therapy activities. This is an ideal stage to work on off-leash exercises, which are discussed in Chapter 15. Remember, though, you must practice patience with these exercises. Removing the leash is often as scary for your puppy as it is for you, and managing this experience well is the key to ensuring the invisible, human-puppy bond that lasts a lifetime.

No puppy, no matter what the extent of his training is, should be allowed to run free near a crowd or near roadway traffic. Too many unpredictable variables are present in these areas to risk the chance.

Does committing the next year to training your puppy sound like a project? Well, you're right — it is! Once you commit to the role of your puppy's teacher, he can learn all he needs to know throughout his first year — from where to potty and what to chew to polite greeting manners and how to conduct himself in a crowd. He won't learn these things overnight, however — like human school, puppy training is a stage-by-stage process.

Words your puppy should learn and love

Familiar words make your dog or puppy feel directed, connected, and safe. Just think of being in a foreign country — you'd be most comfortable with those who spoke your language. Teach your puppy the words in Table 1-1 to better communicate your expectations and help your puppy feel most secure in your relationship.

Table 1-1	Basic Instructions for Your Puppy	
Word	*What It Does*	*When and Where to Use It*
\<Name\>	Your puppy's name should have a positive, magnetic association. Connect with food in 8- to 10-week-old puppies.	Use to encourage your puppy's attention for positive interaction and motion directions like "Come" and "Heel."
Let's go	"Let's go" is a loose walking direction encouraging your puppy to follow you.	Around the house, on loose lead walks, and in a field.

Word	What It Does	When and Where to Use It
Wait and Okay	"Wait" is about impulse control. It encourages your puppy to stop and look to you for permission before moving ahead. "Okay!" releases him.	Use this combo when going in or out of doors and cars, crossing curbs, or on stairways. Also use with food and toys to encourage gentle mouth habits.
Excuse me	"Excuse me" encourages spatial respect and reminds your puppy of his manners.	When your puppy blocks your path, leans against you uninvited, steps on you, or ignores a direction.
Stand	A level 1 containment position.	Great for grooming, bathing, or steadying your puppy in a crowd or at the doctor's office.
Sit	A level 2 containment position.	This is the 'Say please' position. Use it before offering your puppy something positive — a toy, treat, pat, dinner, and so on.
Down	A level-3 containment position — lying down on the ground or floor.	Use "Down" when sitting quietly or when at a cafe, friend's house, and so on.
Settle down	Use "Settle down" to direct your puppy to a certain area (preferably on a mat/bed).	For repetitive quiet times, such as dinner, homework time, or TV.
No	This direction discourages inappropriate behavior.	Best used when catching a thought in process. Should be said in the same tone as any other direction.
Ep, Ep	"Ep Ep" works best for puppies under 4 months. It discourages inappropriate behaviors.	Use to discourage interest in garbage, objects, rooms, or counters.

Chapter 14 provides detailed advice on how and when to teach your puppy these words and instructions.

Different strokes for different folks

There are many approaches to training and as many gadgets to help you convey and emphasize your directions, from clickers and target sticks to training collars and leashes. If you randomly try these objects or mix and match your approaches simultaneously, you're likely to confuse your puppy.

Read through Chapters 5 and 11 to discover all the equipment and gadgets available to you before analyzing which make the most sense for you and your puppy. Before heading out to the pet store and setting an educational plan for your puppy's first year, consider the following:

- To treat or not to treat?
- What's a clicker and how do you use it?
- How do you use treat cups, target sticks, and snack packs?
- Should your puppy's breed or temperament influence your training approach?
- What about all these different collars and leashes?

The ideal application and the benefits and drawbacks of each object or approach are found in Chapters 5 and 11. If you have family members involved in your pup's training, have a group discussion to ensure that you're all on the same page. Consistency is oh-so-reassuring to your puppy.

Day-to-Day Frustrations — and More Serious Problems

Your puppy's naughty behaviors — the ones that frustrate you to tears — aren't such big issues to him. In fact, he sees many of the routines as games and will repeat them whenever he's bored. Habits are formed at these most aggravating moments, leaving you stranded and in a vicious cycle. Ironically, this cycle is your own creation. Sure it feels like you must do something when your puppy tears off with your napkin, but screaming and isolating him just don't impede repetition. And, think about it: If cruising the counters brings you back into the room, your puppy will repeat this tactic no matter the consequences.

There are of course more serious issues: what I call "red flag" issues that warrant concern and reaction. Aggression comes to mind, as does separation anxiety and destructive chewing. Bear in mind a puppy who exhibits this behavior isn't happy; your corrections won't lighten his intensity. Find a more cheerful approach, modify your behavior, and help your puppy develop a more cheerful, go-with-the-flow attitude. You'll all be a lot more relaxed.

You and your puppy are two different species with two very different views on morality. Take the time to understand your puppy's mindset and try a whole new approach to resolving your differences. In Chapters 16 and 17, I show you this new approach by reconstructing several frustrating behavioral situations so that you can teach your puppy the concept of "No" when appropriate and refocus him on more appropriate activities. You never know — this new approach just might work!

Your puppy can't understand the concept of "No" until he's more than 4 months old. Even though a young puppy may look like he knows what you're talking about when you shout "No," his reaction is really only fear and confusion. Nobody wants to scare their puppy. In Chapter 14, I discuss how to teach your puppy the concept of "No." Until your pup is ready for the "No" direction, follow the techniques in Chapter 14 to convey your disapproval effectively, and tidy up your home until he's truly old enough to contain his impulses.

In the chapters in Part IV, I dissect all areas of frustration from nipping and jumping to the more serious infractions, such as aggression. Even though this book doesn't take the place of a professional when your situation is dire, use it to shed light on everything puppy — from a wagging tail and puppy breath to adolescent defiance. Here are two aggravated reactions explained:

- During infancy your puppy may nip when exhausted. If you physically reprimand him for this behavior, you'll confuse your puppy, and he'll view you less as a nurturing parent and more as a challenging puppy.

- If you hear a slight rumble in your puppy's throat when your neighbor pays a visit, this is a clear signal that he simply doesn't know how to handle this situation and doesn't know who's in charge. This behavior is your cue. Yelling at him will only escalate his tension, so don't do it. Instead, follow the instructions (in Chapter 17) to teach Back and Stay, and your pup will feel assured in the strength of your direction.

There is a sensible reason for every puppy behavior, whether it's counter sniffing or jumping on guests. Investigate and understand why your puppy is reacting in a certain way. Then, juggle the variables to meet his needs as you redirect him to more appropriate activities.

A Clean Bill of Health

If you take care of the inside of your puppy, the outside can better take care of itself. Chapters 19 and 20 help you make pertinent health care decisions, balance your puppy's diet, stay on top of his daily hygiene, and understand his healthy vital signs so you can react calmly in an emergency.

A sick puppy is like a toddler: When he's ill or troubled, your puppy is unable to articulate it in words. He will, however, respond in ways that would be obvious to another dog. So, in Chapters 20 and 21, I help you decipher your puppy's signals so that you know how to both keep him healthy and happy and how to respond to him when he's ill.

These chapters don't take the place of regular checkups or consultations with a veterinarian. Your veterinarian has a medical degree and may recommend tests or blood work to determine a specific ailment. Use these chapters to educate yourself on what signs and symptoms to watch for and how to read what your puppy is saying to you when he's unwell. Sharing this information with your veterinarian is more than invaluable — it could save your puppy's life.

Spaying and neutering your puppy is crucial. I have yet to share my life with a dog who has not been altered before their first year: It's a responsible action and our duty to stem the growing overpopulation and hence widespread euthanasia that seems to be the only other solution. Even though controversy abounds on subjects that include age, surgical choice, and aftereffects, knowing the facts will give you the ability to choose your course of action wisely.

Chapter 2

Pre-Puppy Considerations

· ·

In This Chapter

▶ Asking yourself why you want a puppy

▶ Considering how a dog fits with your current and future family arrangements

▶ Figuring out what you want in a dog

▶ Fitting a puppy into your daily routine

· ·

*Y*our puppy may be the only family member you get to handpick. You choose based on anything from looks to personality type. Make the most of it!

In this chapter, I walk you through five questions to ask yourself when choosing a breed, or mix of breeds, to suit your lifestyle.

Why Do You Want a Puppy?

Raising a puppy is a project, a fun project mind you, but a project just the same. From the onset, your puppy needs to be housetrained, which requires repetitive trips to his area throughout the day, and initially, the night too. And the excitement doesn't stop there. Depending on the breed, your puppy may need constant attention. Between grooming, exercise, and meals, the only activity more energy-consuming is raising a child. Fortunately, puppyhood only lasts about a year!

I don't want to turn you off of the idea of purchasing a puppy — you can find few things as rewarding as raising a puppy successfully. Through the nurturing phases, you'll get to know your puppy and will exalt his humanly qualities (devotion, love, and attentiveness) to anyone who will listen. But puppies are not all love, fun, and games — they're a lot of responsibility too. You'll need to be as mindful of their needs as you would any other baby, from feeding them on time to providing water and places to sleep. Housetraining is another project in itself and it will take time and patience.

Travel considerations

We can't leave out the question of travel. Do you enjoy the flexibility of flying out on a moment's notice? Does your career pull you away for days at a time? If you're nodding your head yes, think this through. Do you have a friend or family member lined up who welcomes the responsibility of a puppy? Do they tolerate the adolescent mischief that strikes puppies from the ages of 7 to 11 months? Or, can you afford to pay someone to kennel your puppy or dog or to stay in your home while you're away? Kenneling a dog can cost between $15 to $100 each day, depending on where you live and what extra bonuses you purchase to embellish your dog's stay, such as extra walks, training lessons, or a deluxe suite.

Of course, if you're committed and willing to make the effort of raising a puppy, you're in for a real treat: Truly no other species can offer you the same level of devotion as a dog. You'll note moments between you and your puppy, or between your puppy and your children, that you'll remember for a lifetime. You'll take photos of your puppy and then reminisce when he gets his first gray hair. Raising a puppy is one of life's great rewards. The question is, are you up for the adventures in between?

If the thought of midnight potty runs leaves you feeling cool to the idea of raising a puppy, perhaps you'd be better suited to adopt an older dog. Shelters are filled with them, and rescue clubs for specific breeds can be found easily by calling or visiting the American Kennel Club (www.akc.org). Even puppies older than 6 months are beginning to have better bladder control.

What's Your Day Like?

Take a moment to think through your typical day, from morning to night (as it is now without a puppy). In Table 2-1, I use a typical schedule created by one of my clients, Joe, who outlines a typical day with his family. Create your own table showing your typical routine in one column and how you will change it to fit puppy care into your schedule in the other column.

Table 2-1	Making Room for a New Puppy
Joe's Typical Day	*Changes Joe Makes to His Schedule*
My alarm rings at 7 a.m. I often hit the snooze button a couple of times before getting up. I have to leave for work by 8:30 a.m. I'm usually rushing.	I'll set the alarm for 6:30 a.m. (and not hit the snooze button!) and will walk, feed, and play with the puppy for 30 minutes.

Joe's Typical Day	*Changes Joe Makes to His Schedule*
I usually come home on my lunch break for 30 minutes. I read the paper during this time and if it's a nice day, I sit outside.	I will come home on my lunch break and make the puppy a higher priority than reading the paper. On the days I can't come home, I have contacted a local dog walking professional to come for the puppy's midday outing and feeding.
My mother comes over at 3 p.m. to watch the kids, who get off the bus at 3:30 p.m.	My mother is willing to help out provided that we find a breed she can manage. The kids have committed to playing with the puppy for 30 minutes before settling down to do homework and play computer games.
My wife gets home at 5:30 p.m. She usually goes out for a walk with the kids or a run on her own. I get home 6:30 p.m. and we start dinner.	My wife is reorganizing her schedule to get home at 5:15 p.m. to take care of the puppy. She'll start dinner earlier, postponing her run until I get home at 6:30 p.m. I will get dinner on the table.
Dinner is on the table between 7:00 p.m. and 7:30 p.m. After dinner we either come together in the family room, or everyone goes off to play, work on the computer, or do homework.	Family time will be moved into the kitchen until the puppy is trained and won't pee on the rugs in the rest of the house. The kids can do their homework on the table and hang out with the puppy.
The kids go to bed at 8:30 p.m. My wife and I go into the bedroom by 9 p.m. and watch TV until 10 p.m. or 11 p.m.	I will be in charge of the last puppy outing at 11 p.m.

I asked my client Joe to summarize his life story. Here's what he wrote:

> *My children have wanted a puppy since they could talk. Now they're 7 and 9 years old and we feel ready for this challenge. We have a house and ½ acre of land in a busy neighborhood. Neither my wife nor I know anything about dogs, but we like them and want to make raising this puppy our family project. Even my mom, who is elderly and planning to move in with us in a few years, is excited. Her one condition is that we pick a breed that she can handle. We plan to fence the yard, and we're all looking forward to taking the new puppy with us on family walks and to the kids' activities.*

So what's your story? How are you planning to care for this new addition to your family? A dog is like no other species in the world. As a puppy, he'll bond with you as he would another dog, and between his emotional affection and his potty schedule, you'll quickly feel as though your puppy is your newly adopted child. With this relationship comes the responsibility of integrating your puppy's schedule into your life and civilizing his manners. (Flip to Chapter 13 to find out how to better your puppy's manners.) With this next year planned, organized, and behind you (I will get you through the year, I promise!), you'll be delighted by the relationship that enhances the next decade and a half of your life. Anchors away!

Who's under Your Roof?

The following sections help you decide on a breed that will be best suited for your lifestyle, now and in the future. For example, if you're single now but are considering the "marriage and children" route, you want to get a breed or a mixed breed that will groove with the chaos and taunting of young children. When deciding on a breed, consider the following: Are you single, retired, expecting to have children, or planning to invite your parents to live under your roof as they age?

Children add a lot of dynamics to anyone's life: Your furry, four-legged child is no exception! If you're a newly married couple eager to title your puppy as "our first child," you'll have to socialize your puppy extensively with babies so that he doesn't feel displaced when you bring in your second, human child. Map out your life now, and then look five or ten years into the future to determine what breed will enjoy living with you over the long haul.

Just me

You're single, free, and have few responsibilities to tie you down! Even though the constant companionship of a puppy may sound dreamy, it's a major responsibility. When bringing a puppy into the home, you very suddenly become a parent of sorts. With that responsibility comes all the commitments and demands that properly raising a puppy requires. If you dig sleeping until noon, forget it. Your puppy will have you up before dawn and often in the middle of the night for several weeks. If the joy of sitting at the cafe for hours at a time tops your list, cross it off or forget about getting a puppy. Most cafes frown upon inviting in anything but the human species. Walking, grooming, and feeding your puppy all require a mindfulness that leaves your carefree days in the dust.

If you're truly up for the challenge, remember that your puppy will be your responsibility for well over a decade. If you plan to fall in love and eventually share a household with someone of the opposite sex, socialize your puppy with that group so that he won't get his hackles up when that special someone sweeps you off your feet. Also, think about whether you might have a family of your own some day. Choose a breed that enjoys children and start socializing that puppy with kids from the get-go! (Flip to Chapter 7 for more on puppy socialization.)

Just us

Just you and your honey — and now puppy makes three. Ah, owning a puppy together is your first true test of cooperation. Raising a puppy is a lot easier with two to share the responsibilities, but consistency is a key factor. If the two of you join forces, following similar guidelines for structure and training, your puppy will mature quickly and thrive in the consistency. If one of you wants the puppy on the furniture and eating from a dish at the table, whereas the other prefers a more civilized approach, your puppy's worldview will be skewed and he won't know which rules apply and when.

Have a heartfelt talk with your honey, ideally before bringing your puppy home. Your topics of discussion should include:

- ✔ Where will the puppy sleep?
- ✔ What are your separate visions and hopes for adding a dog to your life?
- ✔ How will you share responsibilities, from feeding and walking to exercise and training?
- ✔ What are your feeding philosophies, from kibbles in the bowl to handouts from the table?
- ✔ How much money will you apportion to health maintenance, training, and grooming?

To avoid arguments, you should discuss ahead of time how you will raise this puppy and what rules make the most sense for your lifestyle and future situation. Here's your first opportunity to try out the roles of parenting. Your puppy will live and love most serenely in a household where you can both agree.

Planning a family? Avoid protective, guard, or fighting breeds unless you're committed to early socialization and training — and lots of it! I discuss these breeds in Chapter 3.

Maybe you're retired empty nesters. That's terrific because you're probably home more often, which means you can be attentive to your puppy's schedule. However, remember that a young puppy's needs can be very demanding. If you already did the 4 a.m. diaper-changing thing, and you'd rather skip these experiences than relive them, consider an older puppy. Also pay close attention to the exercise requirements when choosing your puppy. You need to ensure that you and your soon-to-be-adult dog will be a solid match.

And baby makes four! (children under age 5)

Raising a puppy with children under the age of 5 is a tremendous undertaking, and it's one that often creates more stress than it's worth.

Until the ages of 5 to 7, a child can't grasp another's feelings — whether the other is a person or pet. Though a tight squeeze may signal love from your three-year-old to you, it could instill panic or pain in a young pup. A squeezed puppy may bite defensively even if under normal circumstances he wouldn't react this way. If you don't control this situation, the puppy could mature into a dog with an innate fear of young children or into a dog who's immediately tensed in their presence.

Are you ready to take the plunge? If you're getting a puppy to raise with your young children, you may suddenly feel like you have twins (only one may be slightly furrier than the other). Flip to Chapter 8 for tips on raising kids and puppies together.

If you have a needy toddler, postpone getting a puppy for at least a couple of years. Your child needs all your attention to develop a strong sense of self. A puppy not only will pull you away from your parental duties but will challenge and rival the toddler for your attention. This situation is a nightmare in the making. Introduce the puppy only when your child is more emotionally steady and is also excited and ready for the addition.

If you're convinced this is the right time to add a puppy to your family, always consider the option of an older puppy. Find a 6- to 10-month-old puppy who has been given up for reasons such as human allergies to the puppy or a move. After they're past the intense nipping phase, puppies are less likely to think of the kids as younger siblings. Also helpful is the fact that an older puppy may be more capable of controlling his bladder, if he's not already completely housetrained.

Us and a few more (families with children over age 5)

Got kids over 5 years old? I'd guess that at some point they've begun lobbying for a dog as a holiday or birthday gift with the promise "We'll take care of him ourselves . . . Pllleease?!"

If you feel yourself about to cave, realize one thing: No matter how much your children promise to take part, the puppy will always be your responsibility. Kids can't be expected to remember everything. Many still have to be reminded to tie their shoe or flush the toilet. Even though they take part in the daily responsibilities, you won't be sidelined. You'll be the coach, the cook, and the social director for your children and your new puppy.

This isn't to say that your kids won't help out. But, if you head into the project thinking they'll do all the work, you'll be sorely disappointed. Your best bet is making the puppy a fun family project from the start. Involve the whole family in all the early decisions, from what breed and personality to choose, to where the puppy should eat and sleep. Other activities may fall into your hands, but if you make those activities look like fun, you may have them clamoring to take part. The greatest joy is seeing your children parent the puppy. Only yesterday they were the ones in diapers!

With all the chaos and comings and goings of a family with children, I caution you against protective or territorial breeds. These breeds may suffer from career stress when trying to keep track of all the activity in your home, and they may subsequently lash out at the unsuspecting children. Unless you can dedicate your family to a consistent and extensive training program, stick to rough-and-tumble, ready-for-play breeds who accept everyone as long-lost friends.

A whole menagerie (other pets)

Is your house a zoo? Are you trying to replicate a dog pack in your living space? Sharing your life with many animals can be a harmonious existence — or a complete nightmare. How you plan, introduce, and treat each pet is the dominant factor here. Choosing a breed or mixed breed with the right temperament also influences how well he will be accepted into your existing group.

A variety of pets

If you're adding a dog to a household of other critters, spend a long time searching out a breed that isn't genetically programmed to corral, maim, or kill those other critters. Even though your Siberian husky may accept your bunny rabbit in his hutch, when Hopper races across the floor, your growing puppy may not be able to curb his impulses.

Search out a breeder who has exposed his puppies to other animals at a young age. If the breeder had cats and you also have cats, your puppy may actually think he's a cat! Provided he's not terrorizing your kitty, allow the strong friendship to develop. For more tips on handling initial introductions, see Chapter 5.

Other dogs

Do you have an older dog or a multitude of other paws parading through your kitchen? What do you hope the dogs' relationship will be like with a new puppy? Even though most dogs play well with other dogs when introduced properly, few relish the relentless chaos and interaction of a young pup. As your puppy matures, a strong relationship may develop. However, some dogs would prefer remaining your only pet. Imagine if your spouse brought in a new, younger spouse to keep you company. If your dog can't get enough of you, adding a puppy may not be his first choice. For more tips on introducing a puppy to your resident pets, flip to Chapter 5.

If you're trying to decide what breed is compatible with your dog, put yourself in his paws. Two Jack Russell Terriers have a lot in common and could spend the whole day digging in the garden or listening to creaks under the floor boards. A Jack Russell Terrier and a Rottweiler, on the other hand, is a combination similar to oil and water. Though I'm sure some exceptions exist, bringing these two under the same roof will be anything but relaxing for the dog, the pup, or the members of the household. By nature, Rottweilers are stoic, serious-minded, self-contained dogs who are mindful of their surroundings. Jack Russell Terriers, however, are the poster dogs for chaos and impulsivity. Think about both the breed you have and the one you're thinking of adding, and make sure, at the end of the day, they'll have enough in common to coexist.

Picking from the same breed groups, as described in Chapter 3, is a good way to go: Two herding breeds can get along well, as can two hounds or two terriers. You can mix from the different groups, but avoid the extremes!

Personality is also a factor. If you coexist with a sweet, gentle dog and then bring home a dominant, bossy puppy, be aware that the new pup will have your resident dog whipped in no time. This is sad to see. After all, you know who came home first. A bossy puppy may rule your roost in the end, regardless of house order or your personal wishes. However, you can simplify your life by choosing dogs whose personalities mesh.

What Are You Looking For in a Dog?

When searching for your perfectly suited companion, don't ask yourself what sort of a *puppy* you want. Instead, ask what sort of *dog* you want. All pups traverse their first year through the typical phases, from curiosity nipping to their defiant adolescence, but how they mature is largely predictable based on breed-specific characteristics.

Because it's the adult dog that you'll be living with, choosing a breed that, when mature, is compatible with your vision should be priority number one. Most people find an 8-week-old Golden Retriever puppy irresistible, and many melt at the sight of a Shar-Pei puppy, but fast-forward ten months: Will your likes and dislikes line up with the adult versions of these puppies?

In this section, you first take a look at yourself. Take this opportunity to examine your lifestyle and decide how a dog may mesh with it. After you've chosen a breed to match your ideals, you can then focus on a specific personality type that will match your temperament. Just think — this may be your only chance to handpick a new best friend.

Looking at yourself

Before you venture into Chapters 3 and 4, which deal with choosing your puppy, take a good look in the mirror. Use the following questions to outline who you are and what you hope to get out of the experience of raising a dog. If other people are involved, factor them into the equation as well. With this knowledge, you're more prepared for the puppy selection process.

- **How much free time do you have?** Since you only have 24 hours in a day, consider how much extra time you have left over. Are you craving something to fill that space, or do you end each day wishing for extra hours to get everything done?

- **What do you enjoy?** TV, gardening, reading a book, hiking, work, coffee breaks, socializing, and shopping are a few examples. Take a moment to list five things you enjoy. If more than one person needs to be considered, place your lists side by side.

- **Can your adult dog join you in these activities?** Sure puppies are cute, but until they're vaccinated and housetrained, they need a structured routine and limited exposure to outdoor environments. Additionally, a young puppy may not want to leave the "den" (your home) and may need time to develop physically before joining you in any strenuous activities, such as running long distances or hiking. This question targets the adult dog your puppy will grow into and outlines your chief activity for the next ten months: namely, raising your puppy.

- **What's your personality like?** Are you controlling, relaxed, permissive, structured, intense? Be honest with yourself. In choosing a breed, it's better for all involved to choose one who will understand and flow with you. If you're getting your dog so that he can bond with a specific family member, make matching their personality traits the highest priority.

- **What personality traits make you feel uncomfortable?** Think of this question in terms of other human beings. Does someone who is too relaxed cause your fingers to strum? Can you feel your buttons being pressed when you're dealing with a person who needs a lot of direction? Does someone's intensity overwhelm you? If these human traits bug you, more than likely the dog versions will too.

No matter how much you may like their looks, don't pick a breed with qualities that may add stress to your life. Stress affects everyone badly — from you and your family to, most of all, your puppy. Too much stress will force you to take a quick review of your lifestyle, and, unfortunately, the newest addition is usually the first to go. For example, Border Collies are stunning, but if their intelligence and intensity aren't directed, they can make a cup of coffee nervous.

Creating your dream dog

Now, remember you get to pick this relative! Before you analyze the different breeds, make a quick study of your dream dog by circling your ideals, from their energy level to intelligence and demand for attention.

> I want my dog to have *a lot of energy/moderate energy/a little energy* on a daily basis.
>
> I want a dog who's *super bright/is smart/doesn't think too much.*
>
> I *love/am interested in/am not that committed to* training my puppy.
>
> I *am eager to/am willing to/don't want to* groom my dog.

Again, be honest with yourself. You may not find the thought of training your dog appealing. Though I can argue the merits, at the end of the day you'll be happiest with a dog who is simple-minded and eager to go with the flow. Personally, I'm not committed to grooming. Though I adore many long-coated breeds, if I were to bring one home, it would quickly become a tangled mess, which wouldn't be fair to the puppy!

Though an intelligent dog sounds like the right choice, smart dogs sleep less and need a lot of direction, which places high demands on your time and energy. If your schedule is full or chaos is a part of your day, choose a relaxed dog with average smarts. And yes, you can predict this in an 8-week-old puppy. Chapter 4 tells you how.

Take some time to consider yourself, and then move on to choosing your puppy. You can use this book to shoot for the stars or to simply ensure your puppy potties in the right place.

Chapter 3

Picking the Right Kind of Puppy for You

. . . .

In This Chapter

▶ Pinpointing your ideal breed or mixed breed

▶ Understanding what makes a breed (or mix of breeds) unique

▶ Getting the scoop on the terms "breed groups," "designer breeds," and "hybrid vigor"

. . . .

Sure, almost all puppies love dog biscuits and a scratch behind the ears, but the similarities pretty much end there. All dogs face the world in different ways. Some thrive on human interaction; others prefer an independent lifestyle. Some love the general mayhem created by small children, while others find it less than thrilling. Some see houseguests as long-lost friends, and others see them as potential enemies. Some dogs cherish quiet, solitary times; others eat your house if you come home too late. What sounds good to you?

In this chapter, you find out all about dog breeds and what happens when the breeds are mixed. Each puppy is a genetic splendor, and although a purebred puppy offers some predictability, a mixed-breed puppy contains what we professionals call "hybrid vigor." Starting off the chapter is a questionnaire to help you discover both your desires and your expectations. Getting a breed that's predisposed to a trait or look you admire, or figuring out what breeds are in your mixed-breed puppy, takes much of the guesswork out of the puppy's developing look, behaviors, and needs.

Assembling Your Needs and Wants: A Breed Questionnaire

Does the thought of choosing the right breed or finding out what mix of breeds is most appropriate for you leave your head spinning with excitement? Are you feeling overwhelmed with the choices that lie in front of you? Whether your wish list includes a Miniature Poodle, a Weimaraner, or a Beagle, you can use this chapter to get an idea of the differences between breeds and to determine just how their traits will impact your life. (The only thing similar about these three breeds is the number of teeth they have! Their energy levels, coat requirements, and trainability run the gamut.)

Getting a puppy is no short-term thrill. In fact, the thrill is relatively short-lived. As your puppy grows, you'll be responsible for all the care, love, and training of a developing dog who will share the next decade and a half with you and (hopefully) enrich your life.

The following questionnaire should encourage deep consideration of your life now and your hopes for the future. Sure a 6 a.m. run with your well-trained companion sounds great, but if you're addicted to the snooze button, you'll quickly grow to resent your puppy who just can't be shut down. This is the time to be honest with yourself and your family so that you give your puppy the best chance of living up to your expectations.

This questionnaire has been split into three subsections to better help you gain perspective on each consideration. If you're committed to the effort required to care for a puppy, devoted to meeting his needs, possess the patience to deal with typical puppy phases, and are mindful to choose a breed and temperament closely suited to your lifestyle and family situation, you're certainly on your way to a lovely, lifelong bond with your puppy. Good luck!

The questions

Before jumping into the breed descriptions, take a look at yourself. And be honest! Though you may like the idea of an active lifestyle or a giant breed, adopting a puppy is a big commitment. Think about who you are first, and then match this information to a breed description that's most suitable.

Interpreting your answers

Now what? Look back over your chart and note whether you're getting some ideas of the type of dog that will suit your lifestyle in the long run. As I help you analyze the questionnaire, make a mental sketch of your ideal dog. Would it be small, medium, or large? Would it have a high energy level or be comfortable taking walks every couple of days? Keep the questionnaire in mind (make a copy if you need to) as I walk you through the description of the various breeds or mixed-breeds available to you.

The Look

1. What size dog do you want?
   - ☐ Extra Large
   - ☐ Large-Bulky
   - ☐ Large-Agile
   - ☐ Medium-Bulky
   - ☐ Medium-Agile
   - ☐ Small-Bulky
   - ☐ Small-Agile
   - ☐ Tiny

2. Do you have a coat preference?
   - ☐ Short-coated
   - ☐ Long-coated
   - ☐ Feathers
   - ☐ Hair (non-shedding)
   - ☐ Shaggy (needs regular professional grooming)
   - ☐ Shaggy (hand brushing at home)
   - ☐ Curly-coated

3. I prefer a dog whose ears are
   - ☐ Folded
   - ☐ Tipped on the end
   - ☐ Always standing straight up
   - ☐ Cropped
   - ☐ Cut close to the head

4. I like a tail that:
   - ☐ Curls
   - ☐ Is cut short or is naturally short
   - ☐ Is slightly curved
   - ☐ Is straight

5. As far as facial definition, you admire a
   - ☐ Long snout
   - ☐ Square snout
   - ☐ Rectangular snout
   - ☐ Pushed in face

Day-to-Day Behavior

6. Which personality do you prefer in a dog?
   - ☐ Interactive
   - ☐ Needy
   - ☐ Independent

7. How much attention are you able or willing to give your dog?
   - ☐ Constant
   - ☐ Occasional
   - ☐ Little

8. How much exercise will you give your dog?
   - ☐ A lot of rigorous exercise
   - ☐ Some, including daily walks
   - ☐ A couple of outings a week
   - ☐ Playtime with other dogs
   - ☐ Yard freedom
   - ☐ Little exercise

9. You want to take your dog along with you whenever possible.
   - ☐ Yes
   - ☐ No

10. My dog will sleep in or near a bedroom at night.
    - ☐ Yes
    - ☐ No

11. You want your dog to sleep on the bed.
    - ☐ Yes
    - ☐ No

12. You're planning to limit your dog's house freedom to a specific area.
    - ☐ Yes
    - ☐ No

13. How do you want your dog to act toward newcomers?
    - ☐ Welcoming
    - ☐ Accepting
    - ☐ On guard

14. With regard to children, you want a dog who is
    - ☐ Trustworthy
    - ☐ Playful
    - ☐ Accepting, but aloof

15. How often do you want your dog to bark?
    ☐ Little to none   ☐ When hearing a noise
    ☐ Loud and protectively when hearing a noise

16. When considering training, how much time can you devote?
    ☐ A lot and it will be a hobby ☐ As much as necessary and no more and no less
    ☐ Very little and I want a dog who doesn't need a lot

17. How much time can you devote to grooming?
    ☐ Every day   ☐ Couple of times a week   ☐ Occasional   ☐ None

18. Please check some favorite pastimes you hope to share with your dog.
    ☐ Jogging   ☐ Hiking   ☐ Walking   ☐ Gardening
    ☐ Water activities ☐ Outdoor   ☐ Sporting events ☐ Watching television
    ☐ Computer games   ☐ Reading   ☐ Knitting   ☐ Sitting at the cafe
    ☐ Cooking   ☐ Elderly care   ☐ Volunteer work   ☐ Visiting with friends

19. What other pets do you have?
    ☐ Dogs   ☐ Horses   ☐ Cats   ☐ Rodents
    ☐ Amphibians   ☐ Bird/birds

20. Any other considerations? Circle or list others.
    ☐ Special-needs home arrangements   ☐ Child on the way ☐ Other

What About You?

21. Have you owned a dog before?
    ☐ Yes   ☐ No   ☐ What kind?

22. Have you trained a dog before?
    ☐ Yes   ☐ No   Were you successful?   ☐ Yes   ☐ No

23. What size home do you live in?
    ☐ Large   ☐ Medium   ☐ Small

24. Do you have a yard?
    ☐ Yes   ☐ No   Is the yard fenced in?   ☐ Yes   ☐ No

25. How committed are you to reorganizing your life around the needs of a puppy?
    ☐ Very   ☐ Somewhat   ☐ I don't want to change my schedule

26. Which adjective best describes your personality and home life?
    ☐ Organized/scheduled   ☐ Laid back   ☐ Chaotic

27. When you're around a child you feel
    ☐ Unsettled   ☐ Uncomfortable   ☐ Relaxed   ☐ In control

28. The thought of being with a group of children is
    ☐ Scary   ☐ Unappealing   ☐ Tolerable   ☐ Fun

29. When your house is out of order you feel
    ☐ Out of control   ☐ Stressed   ☐ Like cleaning ☐ No concern

30. When in charge of some task or game you are
    ☐ Rigid   ☐ Structured   ☐ Democratic   ☐ Placating

Questions 1–5

Even though your dog's appearance shouldn't be a chief motivating factor in your breed selection, it's still important. These questions are meant to guide you along and help you narrow your decision.

You'll find high costs associated with healthcare and maintenance of many breeds. For example, long-, thick-, or curly-coated dogs need regular professional grooming. Professional groomers charge between $35 and $100 and are needed every three to six weeks. Also, short-snouted dogs are prone to respiratory problems that may warrant medical attention. Developmental complications, such as joint dysplasia, chronic skin and ear conditions, heart murmurs, and eyelid malformations, are also found in some breeds. All this healthcare and maintenance costs money — are you prepared to pay?

Questions 6–20

Now we get into the meat of the questionnaire with personalities, behaviors, and exercise. I prompt you to think seriously about your long-term commitment. Sure, the idea of choosing an active dog that will encourage you to run five miles a day has exercise appeal, but if jogging becomes just another one of your passing phases, will you be able to keep up with your dog's activity level?

✔ **Questions 6 and 7:** These questions target the essence of your dog's personality. Some breeds are spirited and fiercely independent. Others watch you closely and can't seem to make a decision without weighing your opinion. And then you'll also find the in-between breeds who would choose to follow but won't destroy the furnishings if you go out to do errands. What appeals to you: A dog who needs you desperately (for example, a Shetland Sheepdog or a Cavalier King Charles Spaniel) or a dog who's content with time apart (such as a Cairn Terrier or an Airedale)?

✔ **Question 8:** The amount of exercise you're able to give your new pooch should be a key factor in choosing a dog breed. If you're honest here, this question will help you discover what breed's energy level you can match. Even though an active breed may sound dreamy, if you can't provide constant attention and exercise for the next decade, cross it off your list.

A Golden Retriever is an acclaimed family dog, but he'll need a lot of attention, reassurance, and exercise — pent-up energy or isolation can cause the retriever to destroy the house or to become clingy and impulsive. These behaviors will no doubt be frustrating for your family.

✔ **Questions 9–11:** How involved in your life would you like your dog to be? If socializing is high on your priority list, choose a breed that was bred to take direction and follow humans around (Retrievers and herding breeds, for example). Though all dogs will enjoy being near you 24/7, breeds that were designed to work independently of man (such as Siberian Huskies, Terriers, and guarding dogs) are more mentally equipped to handle periods of isolation.

✔ **Questions 12–14:** These questions pinpoint why you're getting a dog. Does the thought of a dog's protection appeal to you? If so, you may want a Rottweiler or a Mastiff. Do you like being alerted to outside noises, or do you want a companion who just rolls with the comings and goings of the outside world? If you're interested in a playmate for your children, a retrieving breed or spaniel may be an ideal choice.

✔ **Questions 15–16:** These questions dive deep into the time-commitment issue. Training a dog to bark at the "right" things is a key consideration for all breeds throughout their first year. The amount of time you need to commit is determined by both the breed and the personality of each individual puppy. Strong, independent, and dominant puppies, such as boxers or bull terriers, need more structure and stern reinforcement than passive, dependent, and sweet-natured puppies.

✔ **Question 17:** Grooming is another time consideration. All dogs need a good brushing from time to time, but long-, thick-, curly-, or feathery-coated breeds (such as Golden Retrievers, Shepherds, or Shih Tzus) need a commitment (daily brushings) and periodic professional groomings, which may become costly!

✔ **Question 18:** Sharing time with your puppy is a healthy way to establish trust and friendship. Consider your favorite pastime and find a breed that is in the same groove as you. For example, if you've got a fetish for Frisbees, you'll have to decide whether you want a dog who fetches them relentlessly or one who shows no interest (so that you can actually play a civilized game with friends or family).

✔ **Question 19:** Introducing a new puppy to other pets in your household can be tricky, so take this question seriously. If you breed prize-winning rabbits, avoid breeds genetically programmed to kill them (such as Terriers). If you have another dog, choose a breed that will mesh with his traits and personality.

✔ **Question 20:** If you have other considerations write them down and think through them in terms of the future. For example, say you were planning to have a child in a couple of years. Does that mean you want a protective dog to stand guard, or a cheerful spirit to welcome your child at the door?

Questions 21–30

These questions target *you* and your lifestyle. Getting a puppy is like falling in love: The lines between your commitment and your own needs aren't always clear. Sure, now you may say you'll groom your 10-week-old Shih Tzu every day, but what happens when you miss a day and notice he has become a knotted mess? Can you afford a groomer? Are you really willing to commit to this daily task? You should also consider how well you handle stress. Puppies can be annoyingly impulsive and scattered. Are you going to need medication to get through the early years, or can you roll with it? If you're a neat freak, pick a dependent, composed breed that will (hopefully) have greater respect for your wishes.

Do You Want a Pure or Mixed Breed?

All dogs you see, no matter what country they're from, have a *genetic inscription* — or a small bundle of codes — that determines each of their traits from the color of their coat and the shape of their tail to the sound of their bark and their reactions to strangers. Just as humans are random pairings of their parents' traits, so are dogs. Each set of dogs having these same traits, or genetic inscriptions, is classified into groups called *breeds.* The first decision you'll need to make is whether you're a purebred type or a mixed-breed variety. Here's the difference:

- ✔ **Pure breeds:** There are over 420 identified purebred dog breeds around the world. Each has been fine-tuned by humans to perform a specific function in society. Although most breeds don't "work" anymore, fanciers continually devote themselves to breeding and selling puppies that reflect their traditions. Choosing a specific breed will enable you to predict the size, weight, and interest of your puppy.

- ✔ **Mixed breeds:** Dogs are blind to these specifics. An unorchestrated meeting can result in a mixed variety of puppies. Since these puppies are often produced "by accident," many of them end up being given to the shelter or given away. No love is lost, however — a mixed-breed dog is often healthier due to the increased gene pool, and these dogs are just as capable of loving their owners.

Predictability reigns: Discovering purebred dogs

When you purchase a purebred dog, you're buying into a generational lineage: Over time each breed was created by breeding dogs who had specific looks or traits or who were happiest doing certain jobs (such as herding, pulling, retrieving, or cuddling) with dogs who had other admired traits. Breeding created predictability in both appearance and interests.

Currently, more than 420 breeds are registered worldwide. Being a purebred dog is like belonging to an exclusive club: Only dogs with similar looks and interests get in. Once they're in the club, they're only allowed to breed with other dogs who have membership. Even though it's a big club, few variations are available to the next generation.

Of course if a member of the team breaks code and mates with another breed, you've got what people in America call a "mutt" or mixed breed. Equally capable of love and devotion and often more healthy due to the increased variation potentials, these puppies are considered mistakes and are often given away or relinquished to an animal shelter.

What are some other differences between a pure and mixed breed? Purebred dogs cost more — between $300 and $3,000 (although rare, some purebred dogs with parents who are renowned in the show ring can fetch this price).

Mixing the breeds: Discovering hybrid vigor

A mixed-breed dog is every bit as delightful as a purebred dog, and as some argue, healthier mentally and physically by virtue of *hybrid vigor*. Hybrid vigor is a term that refers to a mixed-breed dog's gene pool: By matching two completely different breeds, you get an ever expansive possibility of traits. Hybrid vigor advocates attest to healthier dogs because of the greater number of available genetic bundles. When mixed breeds are mated, it's assumed that the healthy traits will be dominant, and because there are more options, the genetic make up of the dog is better. Do I believe in this theory? Absolutely!

Because purebred dogs have a limited number of genetic bundles available to them, their appearance may not vary much from generation to generation. A soft-coated Wheaten Terrier, for example, is always wheaten in color — with little variation. If this breed mated with a chocolate-colored Labrador Retriever, however, you'd see varying coat colors. Since the coat types are also different, it's likely each puppy would come out with its own unique look.

Designer mixed breeds are the latest craze to hit the dog world. To create a designer mixed breed, breeders mindfully mate two purebred dogs to create a new, unique breed. The practice has become rampant enough to warrant attention. Since they're now coined designer breeds, these puppies come at a price at or higher than a purebred puppy.

This idea began with an attempt to create hypoallergenic seeing eye dogs by mating Standard Poodles with Labrador Retrievers. The resulting dogs were coined "Labradoodles," and though they didn't catch on as seeing eye dogs, the craze caught on in the public sector. Now breeders have created designer mixes of every shape and size — the list of designer breeds is nearing 100. Here are just a few of these fun new breeds:

Designer breed name	What they're made of
Chiweenie	Chihuahua/Dachshund
Doodleman Pinscher	Doberman Pinscher/Poodle
Jack-A-Bee	Jack Russell Terrier/Beagle mix
Labernese	Labrador Retriever/Bernese Mountain Dog
Pomimo	American Eskimo/Pomeranian

Designer breed name	What they're made of
Puggle	Pug/Beagle
Shorgi	Corgi/Shih Tzu
Torkie	Toy Fox Terrier/Yorkshire Terrier
Zuchon	Shih Tzu/Bichon Frisé

Are you wondering how a breeder can get away with selling these mixed breeds at such high prices? The answer is that the people breeding these mixes have bought into the hybrid vigor argument hook, line, and sinker. If breeders are reputable in their passions, they're taking two healthy specimens of each breed and trying to design a line of puppies who have the healthy traits of each breed.

For example, the Puggle (Pug and Beagle cross) has a longer snout than the Pug, which is genetically healthier, hands down! Personality-wise, most owners hope that with this cross the Beagle's scent-chasing obsessions will be toned down and that the marginally higher trainability of the Pug will seep in.

One catch to choosing a designer breed is that you can't exactly be sure of what you're going to get. A purebred dog can be predicted down to the size, weight, and interests. A mixed-breed dog, designer or not, will have a random mix of either traits in no particular order. If you're thinking of buying one of these fun and fancifully named breeds, make sure you like both mixes — you could end up with the look of one and the personality of the other.

Beware of buying a "designer mix" from a pet store. Commonly bred in puppy mills in deplorable conditions, they're separated from their moms far too young and then sold at exorbitant prices. It's a travesty — buyer beware — the puppy suffers!

Picking Your Pup among Seven Standard Breed Groups

In this section, I discuss some of the most common and/or popular breeds recognized by the *American Kennel Club* (AKC). Even though the AKC is by no means the only kennel club to recognize dog breeds, it's the one most recognized in the United States.

Each year the AKC hosts the Westminster Dog Show in New York City, where dogs who have received their championship title compete for Best in Show. Winning Best in Show is considered the highest honor for dogs and their breeders. The AKC breaks down the breeds into seven groups, each of which

---

I discuss in detail in this section. Each group contains breeds that share a similar instinct or life purpose. Though each breed within a group varies, certain commonalities thread each breed to its group.

The first Westminster Dog Show was held in 1877, making this annual event the second oldest sporting event in the United States. Only the Kentucky Derby, which began in 1875, has been around longer.

Team players: The Sporting Group

A proactive lot, dogs in the Sporting Group (see Figure 3-1) were bred to help man sustain himself by flushing (scare out of hiding) birds and retrieving those that were shot. In this day and age, you're unlikely to shoot your supper from the sky, but don't tell that to your dog. Born with a fetching fetish, they thrive on an active and involved lifestyle and won't retire just because you're well fed. No ducks to claim or birds to point out? Your slippers will do, and so will the pigeon perched on the windowsill.

Figure 3-1: The American Spaniel is a fun-loving, high-spirited breed that needs lots of exercise and activity.

Following are the four types of dogs that comprise the Sporting Group, along with specific breeds within those types:

- **Pointers:**
  - German Shorthaired Pointer
  - German Wirehaired Pointer
  - PointerVizsla
  - Weimaraner
  - Wirehaired Pointing Griffon

✔ **Retrievers:**

- Chesapeake Bay Retriever
- Curly-Coated Retriever
- Flat-Coated Retriever
- Golden Retriever
- Labrador Retriever

✔ **Spaniels:**

- American Cocker Spaniel
- American Water Spaniel
- Clumber Spaniel
- English Cocker Spaniel
- English Springer Spaniel
- Field Spaniel
- Irish Water Spaniel
- Sussex Spaniel
- Welsh Springer Spaniel

✔ **Setters:**

- Brittany
- English Setter
- Gordon Setter
- Irish Setter

Even though these loyal and cheerful dogs have well-earned reputations as patient family pets, they need both mental and physical stimulation. They can't cope with long hours of isolation, because it, along with lack of exercise, will only fuel anxiety. An unhappy Sporting Dog is destructive, hyper, and impulsive. This isn't a good mix — especially for your couch and end table.

When these puppies are exercised, directed, and included, there isn't a group that's more happy-go-lucky and accepting of life's random chaos.

Which way did he go? The Hound Group

The dogs in the Hound Group (see Figure 3-2) are a happy lot with a one-track mind; their fascination with hunting propels them through life and allows them plenty of opportunity for employment. Though you may have no interest in hunting a fox, chasing deer, or treeing a coon, your hound puppy probably will.

Originally teamed in pairs or packs, each was prized for its instinct to follow game without depending on human direction. As a result, a hound's affable manner and pack mentality results in a dog who enjoys family life and yet is independent enough to entertain himself.

Figure 3-2:
The Beagle, one of the scent hounds, will happily sniff for hours but may not prioritize direction without a lot of positive reinforcement.

Following are the types of dogs that fall under the Hound Group, along with specific breeds within those types:

✔ **Sight hounds:**

- Afghan Hound
- Basenji
- Borzoi
- Greyhound
- Ibizan Hound

- Irish Wolfhound
- Pharaoh Hound
- Saluki
- Scottish Deerhound
- Whippet

Sight hounds must be kept on a lead when outdoors because you can't outrun them, and their instinct to chase hasn't been bred out of them. In addition, you need to socialize sight hounds to common household pets (like cats, birds, and rabbits) at an early age; otherwise, they may confuse them for lunch as they race across your floor.

✔ **Scent hounds:**

- Basset Hound
- Beagle
- Black and Tan Coonhound
- Bloodhound
- Dachshund

- American Foxhound
- English Foxhound
- Harrier
- Otterhound
- Petit Basset Griffon Vendén

✔ **Large game hounds:**

- Norwegian Elkhound

- Rhodesian Ridgeback

Leave it to me: The Working Group

The breeds in the Working Group (see Figure 3-3) vary in chosen occupation, but their work passion unites them. Whether participating in guarding, pulling a cart or sled, water retrieval, protection, or police work, they're a task-oriented group.

Figure 3-3:
The Bernese Mountain Dog is one of the draft dogs in the Working Group.

Choose a dog from this group only if you can use and appreciate his skills. For example, Great Pyrenees and Kuvasz were originally bred to guard flocks. Because their work ethic is still intact, they make ideal watchdogs when trained. If left to their own devices, however, they often take their instincts to the extreme, assuming you and those in your circle are sheep that need to be protected. Dinner guests won't be welcome, and the postman best beware!

The breeds in the Working Group may be large, but if their schedule is maintained, training is approached mindfully, and exercise is provided, they can adapt to any lifestyle with ease. Although these dogs must be contained when living in the country, they can adapt to apartment dwelling when given daily walks and an occasional romp in the dog park.

Following are the types of dogs that fall under the Working Group, along with the breeds within these types:

> **✔ Sled dogs:**
>
> - Alaskan Malamute
> - Samoyed
> - Siberian Husky

With their double coat, sledding breeds aren't much for really hot weather. If you live in a hot climate, consider another breed. These dogs would be miserable.

✔ **Draft dogs:**

- Bernese Mountain Dog
- Greater Swiss Mountain Dog

✔ **Guard dogs:**

- Akita
- Anatolian Shepherd
- Bullmastiff
- Great Dane
- Great Pyrenees
- Komondor
- Kuvasz
- Mastiff
- Rottweiler

Raising children and dogs is challenge enough. Territorial breeds can overstate their job as guardian, protecting your home and children against all intruders — including friends, extended family members, daily workers, and even other children. These dogs quickly suffer career stress in busy houses. If your heart's set on a territorial breed, structured training is a must.

✔ **Personal protection dogs:**

- Boxer
- Doberman Pinscher
- Giant Schnauzer
- Standard Schnauzer

✔ **Rescue/water dogs:**

- Newfoundland
- Portuguese Water Dog
- Saint Bernard

Shepherd or sheep? The Herding Group

The Herding Group breeds (see Figure 3-4 for an example) were developed during the agricultural age when their herding skills were prized by sheep and cattle herders across the globe. Man put great effort into fine-tuning these herding instincts when developing the breeds in this group. Even though these skills are no longer a priority, each dog's behavior in the home is reflective of them. For example, a dog bred to herd sheep is often seen herding children.

JUST FOR FUN

So how big is large?

Dogs come in all shapes and sizes. Unfortunately, the sizes aren't as simple as big and little. The following table can help you figure out how big large is and how little small is — just in case you ever need to know.

Category	Height	Weight
Small	Up to 10 inches	2–20 pounds
Medium	10–20 inches	20–50 pounds
Large	20–27 inches	50–90 pounds
Giant	27+ inches	90+ pounds

Following are the types of dogs that make up the Herding Group, along with the breeds that fall under each type:

✔ **Sheep herders:**

- Australian Shepherd
- Bearded Collie
- Belgian Malinois
- Belgian Sheepdog
- Belgian Tervuren
- Border Collie
- Collie
- German Shepherd Dog
- Old English Sheepdog
- Puli
- Shetland Sheepdog

✔ **Cattle/sheep driving dogs:**

- Australian Cattle Dog
- Briard
- Bouvier des Flandres
- Canaan Dog
- Cardigan Welsh Corgi
- Pembroke Welsh Corgi

WARNING!

If the herding breeds aren't given an outlet for their impulses, they can develop obsessive, patterned behaviors like circling a table or chasing fast-moving targets such as automobiles or joggers. For drovers that are under-stimulated, their pacing creates a well-trodden path in a yard or field. Guarders must be trained, lest they adopt their people or children as sheep to protect. Cattle dogs are serious-minded, strong, and stocky dogs who can develop repetitive behaviors such as nipping your (or your children's) moving ankles.

If properly trained and exercised, you'll find these dogs to be deeply loyal. Also, when the males are neutered, they aren't prone to roaming.

Figure 3-4: Lassie has ensured that everyone recognizes a Collie. This lovely breed is warm, yet persistent, keeping track of the family as though they were a herd of sheep.

Hot diggity! The Terrier Group

The breeds in this group (see Figure 3-5 for an example) were designed either to track down vermin in barns or fight other animals for sport. Determined and tenacious by design, they work independently and don't prioritize human direction. Because they're spirited and spunky, and not easily impressed or persuaded, terriers aren't a great match for control freaks. Even though they thoroughly enjoy human companionship and a good romp, they must be confined or leashed to prevent roaming or hunting.

Figure 3-5: The Border Terrier is one of the plucky vermin hunters from the Terrier Group.

Following are the two types of dogs in the Terrier Group, along with specific breeds that make up each type:

✔ **Vermin hunters:**

- Airedale Terrier
- Australian Terrier
- Bedlington Terrier
- Border Terrier
- Cairn Terrier
- Dandie Dinmont Terrier
- Fox Terrier (Smooth and Wirehaired)
- Irish Terrier
- Jack Russell Terrier
- Kerry Blue Terrier
- Lakeland Terrier
- Manchester Terrier
- Miniature Schnauzer
- Norfolk Terrier
- Norwich Terrier
- Scottish Terrier
- Sealyham Terrier
- Skye Terrier
- Soft Coated Wheaten Terrier
- Welsh Terrier
- West Highland White Terrier

Don't be surprised if your terrier breed lifts his lip as you (or anyone else) reach for his bone or food bowl. It's a natural reaction called *spatial aggression,* and it's similar to what a young child who doesn't want to share a favorite toy does. Other dogs known for this behavior include some working breeds, hounds, and certain toy breeds. For suggestions in overcoming this dilemma, refer to Chapter 18.

✔ **Fighters:**

- American Staffordshire Terrier
- Bull Terrier
- Miniature Bull Terrier
- Staffordshire Bull Terrier

Although the fighting breeds have a combative history, most of the breeding lines have all but extinguished this impulse. Extensive socialization can ensure a friendly attitude toward other dogs and pets.

Though rare, some owners still use some of the fighting breeds for sport. These owners usually won't neuter the dog (as doing so would diminish their fighting tenacity) and often neglect them. Because of this mistreatment, these dogs' genes can seep into the domesticated gene pool, possibly causing the breed to be more aggressive. When choosing a dog from this group, trace its history or talk openly with the breeder or previous owner about their breeding philosophy and the temperaments of the dog's parents.

All mixed up: The Non-Sporting Group

The Non-Sporting Group is the catchall group (see Figure 3-6 for an example). When a dog's orientation is too varied to fit anywhere else, it ends up here. Dalmatians, for example, were bred to follow horse carriages over great distances and, when parked, to lie under the carriage and guard both the contents and the horses from vagabonds. Keeshonds, a Norwegian breed, were bred to accompany man on sea travels, cheerfully alerting him to any commotion. Though each dog's ancestry is varied, they're threaded together by their devoted participation in human affairs.

Figure 3-6:
The Bichon Frisé is a happy clown from the Non-Sporting Group.

Following are the dogs that make up the Non-Sporting Group:

- American Eskimo Dog
- Bichon Frisé
- Boston Terrier
- Bulldog
- Chinese Shar-Pei
- Shiba Inu
- Chow Chow
- Dalmatian
- Finnish Spitz
- French Bulldog
- Keeshond
- Lhasa Apso
- Löwchen
- Poodle (Standard and Miniature)
- Schipperke
- Tibetan Spaniel
- Tibetan Terrier

Snuggle puppy: The Toy Group

The lovable little miniatures in this group (see Figure 3-7 for an example) have been bred down from larger dogs. Even though they can be cuddle companions, many still have their original breed characteristics firmly set in. Take the Miniature Pinscher for example. A distant relative of the Doberman Pincher, the "Min Pin" is an astute watch dog who sounds a visitor's arrival before they've even knocked at the door.

Figure 3-7: Pugs are a plucky, solid breed from the Toy Group, but don't tell the Pugs — they've got a big-dog mentality in a small package.

Following are the breeds that make up the Toy Group:

- Affenpinscher
- Brussels Griffon
- Cavalier King Charles Spaniel
- Chihuahua
- Chinese Crested
- English Toy Spaniel
- Havanese
- Italian Greyhound
- Japanese Chin
- Maltese
- Miniature Pinscher
- Papillon
- Pekingese
- Pomeranian
- Pug
- Shih Tzu
- Silky Terrier
- Toy Manchester Terrier
- Toy Poodle
- Yorkshire Terrier

When assessing specific breeds, research their ancestry. Even though their size is clearly different, their genetic impulses may be undeniably similar. Don't pass on training them simply because of their stuffed-animal-like appearance. Constant affection without direction results in a Napoleon-like complex, which is reflected in behaviors from chronic barking to marking and often aggression. You'd be surprised how much damage a 5-pound dog can inflict!

Toy breeds are fragile by design. Even though certain breeds are stockier (the Pug and the Cavalier King Charles Spaniel, for example), they're all tiny — especially as puppies. Be mindful of this puppy around larger dogs and young children. Toddlers can easily hurt or overwhelm the puppies because they may mistakenly confuse them for stuffed animals.

Chapter 4

Finding and Choosing Your Puppy

· ·

· ·

*L*et the search begin! You can find a puppy in so many places, from serious breeders of purebred dogs to ads in the newspaper. To ease the stress of finding your perfect puppy companion, consider all your options, noting pros and cons of each, and then scout out and test as many puppies as you need to until you find the one whose breed impulses and personality best match your own. Nothing is more disappointing (for you and the pup) than bringing a puppy home and it not working out. That pitfall can be avoided with many of the tips found in this very chapter.

Your ideal puppy can be found anywhere, but deciding where to concentrate your focus can help eliminate confusion. Whether you choose to look at a breeder, shelter, private home, or pet store, knowing the right questions to ask and the possible drawbacks of each location can help you anticipate what your search will bring.

Unfortunately, the search isn't over after you've found a puppy. Every puppy has a unique personality — one that you can assess when he's 8 weeks old. Test each puppy you meet with your dream dog in mind, and don't be afraid to go home empty-handed. The temperament test in this chapter can be a useful tool when assessing your prospective pups. I tested more than 20 puppies before finding my Labrador, Whoopsie Daisy. Three years later, I can assure you she was worth the wait. Although, at the time, it was hard to leave those other puppies behind!

Where's the Puppy Coming From?

Sure, where a puppy comes from biologically is important, but the type of environment he comes from also impacts his behavior in your home. A puppy from an environment that isn't stressful, such as a home or reputable breeding kennel, is generally calmer than a puppy who has been abruptly severed from his litter or who has been neglected, transported, or kenneled with many other puppies at a young age. The reason is simple: Until your puppy reaches 12 weeks of age, his brain is still developing and life stress can have a much greater impact at this time.

When considering the various options open to you, be mindful of what you're getting into. Some puppies who are stressed at an early age mellow out and develop a high tolerance for chaos — making them ideal for chaotic, unstructured homes. Other dogs, however, can't handle the stress and flip out when things don't follow their routine.

Breeder

A dog breeder raises, sells, and often shows dogs of a specific breed. As is true in all professions, you'll come across good breeders and not-so-good ones. Top breeders conscientiously raise dogs with good genetic lines, and they temperament test every puppy before pairing them with an ideal home. Also, before breeding, and when possible, a reputable breeder will test each parent to ensure it's free of any congenital defects.

If some of this talk is sounding rather foreign to you, don't worry. Here are some explanations of key terms to keep in mind when searching for and dealing with breeders:

- **Genetic defects:** These defects are passed down from parent to pup and can result in a host of maladies from hip dysplasia to heart murmurs. A conscientious breeder tests each parent before breeding them to ensure they're clear of these congenital defects. As you research each prospective breed, list possible defects and question the breeder's awareness before looking at his puppies.

- **Line breeding/breeding for show:** Breeders of show dogs mindfully try to "create" puppies who, when grown, adhere to the breed standard. This becomes an issue when a breeder breeds relatives who may look beautiful but are closely related to one another. The puppies are often a neurological mess or totally spacey, or in other words, aggressive or dumb.

If you're interested in a puppy for show, you could overlook temperament for beauty, but if personality matters to you, skip a breeder whose pedigrees show the name of a dog repeated again and again. The rule of thumb is that five generations should separate one relative from another.

In the United States, a breed standard is documented by the American Kennel Club. Pages are written listing each breed's specific ideal characteristics from coat color and personality to the skeletal carriage and direction of each toe. Each detail is very precise, and perfection is the golden chalice every show-oriented breeder reaches for. However, if you're getting your puppy just to be the ideal family pet or companion, a maligned freckle or slightly offset toenail won't matter at all!

✔ **Breeding for temperament:** When a breeder says he's breeding for temperament, you know you've found a reputable one. Breeding for temperament means he's just as interested in delightfully-acting puppies as ones that look good. If you're getting your puppy to be a pet, this attribute in a breeder trumps all others.

Finding a breeder who breeds for temperament is also important when choosing a breed whose skills won't be in high demand. Unless you want to wake at the crack of dawn to go hunting with your retriever or sledding with your Siberian Husky, finding a breeder who's more mindful of temperament than skills is step number one.

✔ **Temperament testing:** A temperament test is a series of handling exercises performed on a puppy who's 7 weeks of age or older. These handling exercises are designed to enable you to predict the future temperament of your chosen puppy. They also provide a fairly accurate assessment of a puppy's personality and eventual adult demeanor, from dominant and bossy to shy and withdrawn. Later in the chapter, I include a temperament test that you can use on all your prospective puppies. However, you'll find that many breeders perform these tests on their puppies before placement.

Finding breeders to help you understand both the positives and negatives of the breed they work with is worth their weight in gold. If they're serious about the placement of their puppies, they'll ask you a whole list of questions. You may feel more scrutinized than if you were adopting a child, but don't be put off by their questions because in the end, you'll end up with a puppy who has been loved and well cared for since its very first breath.

Go with your gut. If you drive up to a breeder's kennel and get a bad vibe for any reason, such as dirty facilities, odd mannerisms, or not being allowed to see your puppy's mother (or father, if he's on the premises), leave. The urge to save a puppy from this environment will be overpowering, but go with your gut because ending up with a sickly or poorly socialized puppy is an emotionally wrenching experience that may not end well for you or your puppy. In addition, you can call the local chapter of the American Society for the Prevention of Cruelty to Animals (ASPCA) to report them, which helps put people who are breeding purely for financial gains out of business.

Home breeder

Puppies who are bred in someone's home may be purebred or mixed. These homebred puppies usually come from dogs who have mistakenly escaped their owners' yards and have mated with unknown sires. However, sometimes these pups come from dogs who live with people who thought breeding two purebred dogs would be fun, educational for the kids, or lucrative. If you see a sign highlighting puppies for sale, here are some good things to keep in mind.

- ✔ If they're purebred puppies, ask whether the pup's parents were tested for genetic defects known to the breed and whether you can meet the parents.

- ✔ If they're mixed breed puppies, ask whether the mix of breeds is known or has been speculated.

- ✔ Ask how old the puppies will be when they're sold or given to a good home.

Don't adopt a puppy younger than 8 weeks old. Seven weeks is the exception, and that's only if you're a seasoned dog owner. You don't want to adopt before 8 weeks old because a pup's mother would normally spend weeks 6 through 8 socializing and teaching her puppies. The result of this socialization is good for you because the puppies will have more organized elimination habits, respect, and bite inhibition.

Puppies taken home early are often coddled by well-meaning, adoring humans. During a developmental stage when their mother would be teaching respect and impulse control, a person is often categorized as another puppy. In this case, everyone becomes a target for nipping and bullying behavior. When a puppy is brought home in advance of or during this critical stage, the people must act like dogs!

Shelter

Going to a shelter to look for your puppy is a noble deed. Prepare yourself, however, because you'll see some faces that'll show up in your soup for a while. Even though you'll feel the temptation to take them all home, you can't. You've come for one puppy — your ideal puppy — and if you don't find him that first day, plan to come back.

Shelter puppies come from all walks of life. Some of the pups' situations are known, although others aren't. Some arrive in baskets only to watch their moms ride away with forlorn heads hanging out of backseat windows, and others are found alone by the roadside.

When looking for your pup, talk to the staff. These well-meaning volunteers all have one thing in common: They love dogs! Here are some questions you can ask them:

- Do you have any history on the puppies?
- Have you spent time with the puppies? What do you think of their different personalities?
- Have the puppies been introduced to children or cats? If so, what was their reaction?

If you have other pets or kids, I recommend examining a potential puppy's reaction to them. Nothing is more disappointing than having to bring a puppy back.

Most of the puppies found at a shelter are mixed breeds. A staff member can give you his opinion of the breed, but if you have a friend who knows his breeds, you may want to bring him along for a second opinion.

Consider how each breed in the mix will fit into your lifestyle. For instance, if you're looking for a low-shedding, small- to medium-size dog who will sally up to anyone, pass on the Chow-Akita mix, no matter how cute he looks sitting there in the cage. As an adult, he'll be large and aloof to strangers and will have heavy shedding seasons — and those characteristics don't match your initial description at all!

Pet store

Pet stores get a very bad rap. But, whether you believe it is up to you. A pet store is in the business to sell pets. When a store is licensed to purchase puppies for resale, it has to find breeders who are willing to sell them puppies. A reputable breeder is unlikely to sell puppies to a pet store. So, the pet store then contacts *resale breeders* who often breed many dogs, or a variety of breeds, simultaneously to meet the demands of the pet store. The resale breeders stretch both themselves and their breeding dogs to the limit, and their facilities (referred to as *puppy mills*) are usually understaffed, resulting in puppies who don't get proper care or socialization with the human world. Messes aren't cleaned up immediately, water is not changed regularly, and bacteria isn't checked and can quickly spread from puppy to puppy.

More mindful breeders who choose to send their puppies out for resale don't usually send the pet stores the cream of their litter. The puppies they send are usually undersized or of poor conformation, from an ankle joint that's out of place to an undershot jaw. Resale breeders aren't likely to spend money to ensure their breeding dogs are free from genetic defects.

If you find yourself with a really young pup

If you find yourself with a puppy younger than 8 weeks old, do your best to mimic both the consistency and structure of a mother dog, and socialize your puppy with a healthy, inoculated, patient dog who will aid you in those early life lessons.

If you have a young puppy, use some of the many soft handling techniques that mirror his mother's nurturing. These techniques, which will bring him to near nirvana, can be practiced at any age throughout his life.

✔ **Bracing:** Anytime a mother handles a puppy, she braces the puppy with her body or mouth. To mimic this sensation for your pup, either kneel on the floor, tucking your puppy between your legs, or use the thumb of your right hand over his collar as you gently brace his waist with the index finger and thumb of your left hand. Use this technique when presenting something unfamiliar such as replacing his collar or medicating him.

✔ **Soothing effects of mother tongue:** During the early socialization period, a pup's mother will use her tongue to clean or calm a puppy. Simulate this ritual by tucking your puppy between your legs (as described above), and create a "tongue" out of your flat palm. Then, with constant, soothing pressure, "lick" (with your hand) your puppy from head to toe. This technique provides a wonderful reminder of your nurturing authority and is a handy calming tool if your puppy gets out of control.

✔ **Pin hold:** Some puppies are incorrigible and must be reprimanded immediately to learn self-control. Again, this lesson should be taught, at least initially, by the pup's mom. But, to replicate it, hold your out-of-control puppy between your legs or cradled in your arms. If your puppy grows more aggravated, discontinue this technique immediately. He may be over-tired and need some quiet time to regroup. If he shows outright aggression, seek professional help.

So here you have a puppy coming from a less-than-ideal environment who is abruptly shipped, bused, or trucked to various locations around the country. This is no dream trip home to be snug on someone's lap. Instead, it's hardcore transportation with people who have little regard for the emotional welfare of their cargo. These little 8-week-old creatures are ripped from their moms' teats and severed from their littermates and are suddenly shipped around like boxes of doughnuts.

Upon arrival at the pet store, the puppy is either welcomed, if it's a friendly shop, or simply plopped into a cage for display. After they're in their cages, the pups then endure the hundreds of touches from people milling in and out. Some people handle the puppies sweetly and with care but others are unconscionably rough. Occasionally a puppy is adopted immediately. However, others may sit there in that small, indoor kennel for months.

Many of the puppies buckle under the strain and get so sick that they must be destroyed. Others become manic and unpredictable and suffer from Early Stress Syndrome (ESS), which can cause them to become sporadically aggressive. Luckily, others pull through with remarkable temperaments. It's as though the stress somehow mellowed them for life.

In addition, pet store puppies often suffer from untreated parasitic disease and many times develop respiratory illness two days to two weeks after coming home. Even though these conditions are usually treatable, they can also be costly. Get a good history of vaccination and deworming and find out what the pet store health guarantee is.

Even though I'm not a big fan of purchasing a puppy at a pet store, I also know the lure of a puppy's eyes. I have purchased my puppies and dogs from many different places — yes, even one from a pet store. I'm not ashamed, nor did I love her less than any of my other dogs.

 If you're considering the pet store option, spend a little extra time finding a reputable pet store. A pet store's reputation can be measured by the friendliness of the staff toward their puppies, their knowledge of individual breeds, their interest in your situation, and their willingness to let you communicate with the puppy's original breeder.

Observing a Pup with His Littermates

You can tell a lot about an 8-week-old puppy by watching him with his littermates. These littermates are his first friends, as well as his siblings. Each puppy has a distinct character within the group. A bossy pup will dominate other puppies to show his position as top puppy. A tender puppy may be bullied by the other puppies and as a result may choose to stay close to Mom or people. In addition, within the litter, ongoing, universal communication skills are at work — you can replicate some of them at home. When choosing your new puppy, watch how he relates to his group: Pick one whose style will mesh with your family — this is how he'll act when you bring him home!

Bite inhibition

Puppies play with their mouths. Nipping is considered normal interaction, but each individual puppy has his limits. If one puppy is trying to engage in play with another, he must respect that puppy's tolerance level — or he just won't play. And running to Mom for protection isn't restricted to children! When one puppy bites another too hard, the other puppy runs to Mom and yelps loudly to convey his sensitivity level.

You can replicate this littermate communication by yelping "Ouch" when your puppy bites too hard. If your puppy doesn't pull back, take his collar or leash and pull him away from your body. Don't push or shove your puppy because physical reactions are interpreted as confrontational play. For more help with a nipping pooch, refer to Chapter 16.

Who makes the rules?

More dominant puppies eat first and set down the rules of play and interaction. When choosing a pup, study the litter to see who's making his claim when food or toys are passed out. Do you notice how some puppies do what they want, while others stand back and are submissive? Now think of this puppy in your kitchen: Do you want a puppy who challenges your authority or who follows your lead? The puppy you select will use these same tactics to determine who heads your household.

One early means of determining rank within a litter can be seen in relationship to *spatial definition*. For example, whoever moves around the other is conveying respect and special deference for the Top Dog's position.

To be Top Dog in your house, get started at home immediately. By using the command "Excuse me" (see Chapter 14), you communicate loads in terms of your overall leadership.

The Art of Selecting Your Puppy

The day has finally come to select your puppy! Regardless of where you're going to look for your furry companion, I want you to prepare yourself for the obvious: If you're choosing from many puppies, they're all going to be unbelievably cute. To stop yourself from taking home every puppy you lay eyes on, repeat this mantra: Only one puppy, only one puppy, only one puppy.

In this section, I show you how to evaluate a pup's personality based on how he acts with his littermates, and I also share an easy but essential temperament test that you can take along when picking out your pooch.

If you're testing an 8-week-old puppy, remember that his brain won't be fully aroused or awake until he's 12 weeks old. Try to schedule your visit just before feeding or stay for a few hours to watch him during various activities. Test your puppy when he's active, not when he's tired or sleepy.

Two puppies: Twice the fun or double the trouble?

The answer to that question depends on how much time and patience you have. If you're short on either, don't overextend yourself. Two puppies, unless coddled and trained separately within your home, will bond to each other more than they will with you. Mischief peaks to a whole new level when puppies plot trouble together. Housetraining two puppies simultaneously is also quite a chore.

If you want to have two dogs, I suggest raising one, and after a year, bringing home your "second child."

If you really feel up for the challenge of two puppies, though, you'll have the best chance for success with a male and a female or with two males (as long as they don't share strong, dominant temperaments). Two females can become hormonal and difficult. Also, when selecting the personalities, don't pick the extremes. You'll get polar opposites — one who'll bully and overshadow, while the other shakes in the corner.

Getting into the testing mindset

Where you go to choose your puppy isn't a predominant factor. You can find lovely puppies anywhere. The key is getting into the right mindset and knowing ahead of time what to watch out for and what to ask:

- **With the breeder/home breeder:** Often a breeder will tell you when to come by. If not, ask about the puppy's schedule and how long you can stay. Ideally, you want to visit when the puppies are awake and playful. Avoid nap times or late-night visits. When possible, ask to stay for a couple of hours so that you can watch and interact with the litter over an extended period of time.

- **At a shelter:** When you speak with the staff members, ask them how many puppies are available for adoption and if they know the breeds or mix of breeds. Ask whether the shelter has a litter of puppies or just individual pups. Also ask the staff whether they know when the puppies were separated from their mother and where the puppies came from. Early stress can backfire, sadly making a pup nervous or impulsive.

  Find out whether the puppies are allowed to interact with each other and at what time. Ideally, you want to see your candidate interacting with littermates or other puppies to determine his sociability within a group.

- **At a pet shop:** Pet shop puppies are often shipped alone or with one or two siblings. After they arrive, they're either crated alone or with a puppy of another breed. This is a very confusing situation for a young puppy to be in, and because of this stress, many of the puppies may seem dulled by the experience. When isolated in a greeting room, however, you'll be better able to test his personality.

If you're serious about one puppy in particular, spend at least 30 minutes with him. You should interact, hold, and play to get an overall view of his personality. In addition, bring other puppies into the room to discern his sociability with peers.

An outsider looking in: Personality profiling

Selecting a puppy from a litter? Each puppy has a discernable personality that can be judged at 7 weeks of age. Here are six personality types to watch for:

- **Bully:** On first glance, the bully may seem overtly social and interactive. You may think "Good, that one has spirit." However, keep watching. Does he steal the toys from the other puppies, or does he play too rough? Does he scale the enclosure or climb on the backs of his littermates as though they don't exist?

  These are sure signs of determination, smarts, and will power, but you have to decide how those characteristics will mesh into your home life. If you have the time to channel (and challenge) this puppy, take him home! However, if you have other demands on your time and you're hoping for a puppy to reduce your stress, pass on the bully.

- **Rebel Rouser:** Puppies in this group are quick-thinking, fun-loving, and engaging puppies. They hold an equal fascination with toys and play as their bullying brethren, but they're clearly more sensitive. In fact, the bully and the rebel rouser may be seen playing together with the rebel rouser taking the submissive roll when the bully flexes his muscles (in "Doglish" this may be seen by a belly roll or head pinning).

  Rebel rousers are engaging without being too headstrong. This is an ideal temperament for an active person or family with older children.

- **Independent Thinkers:** These puppies tolerate and interact in playful encounters some of the time but are also happy sitting or playing with a toy on their own. Stoic and contained, these independent thinkers seem to have been born with an old soul.

  These pups are ideal in a structured home where owners fully respect their sense of self and make a commitment to teach them. Because they're mindful and alert, these puppies are ideally placed in calm homes, with older or no children.

- **Eager to Please:** This lot is eager to please and is always interested in your opinion. This attitude can lead them to the head of the class or into the doghouse depending on how you play it. If you direct and reinforce good manners, you'll have more than 100 percent cooperation. On the other hand, if you try to correct your puppy's naughty behavior, he'll see your interaction as a reason to replay it over and over and over.

Because of their trainability, these puppies are wonderful companions, but they can end up on the B list if they don't receive direction.

✔ **Just Chillin':** This relaxed lot beautifully balances play, interaction, and sleep — doing all three on their own time. Perhaps less intelligent than their more active siblings, pups with this personality type simply do what they want, when they want.

These puppies may sound dreamy, but remember, motivating them takes some creativity. They're not ideal for controlling owners, but they complement a relaxed household and fit beautifully into a home environment with young children, provided the breed is suitable (see Chapter 2 if you need help selecting a breed).

✔ **Sweetie Pie:** Soft-natured and gentle, these puppies are most often seen under the other puppies who are taking advantage of their docile nature. These pups are also passive and eager to please, so their sweetness will be palpable. Within their litter, these puppies stay close to their mother and use her protection as a shield.

This personality is for those owners who prefer doting attention over rigorous training. Puppies with this personality are less likely to roam because staying close to home will be a top priority.

✔ **Timid:** These puppies, who are clearly not born with a strong sense of self, may appear to have been abused, even though it's more symbolic of their dislocated character than misguided nurturing. When approached, they often creep on their bellies or arch their back in total submission.

Your heart may go out to pups with this personality, but only select this type of puppy if you have the time and patience to devote to fostering their self-esteem.

Regardless of your effort, timid puppies may always be overwhelmed and in need of direction, so they aren't a suitable choice for families with children.

Temperament test: Take it along!

Here are ten quick temperament tests that you can administer as you're deciding whether you and a puppy will be compatible. It's as important for your puppy to match your personality as it is for you to match his.

Cut out or copy the test and then use the questionnaire in Chapter 3 to decide ahead of time what breed of dog you want. I ran through these exercises with more than 20 dogs before I found Whoopsie, our Labrador Retriever. Truth be told, I wasn't looking for her when I found her. I had scanned the shelters in the area, testing puppy after puppy. Then I was called to select a puppy from a litter for a client. That's when it happened: I temperament tested a puppy who hit the score I was waiting for. I practically cried. Now it's your turn!

Using the score card

Figure 4-1 is the form you should bring with you when you're testing puppies. Using the key notes written below, score each puppy with the following scale:

A = Active Response   N = Neutral   P = Passive

Active puppies are smart and interactive, which means a lot of work but also a lot of fun. Spirited and intelligent, active pups are well appreciated by those owners who have the time and determination needed to train them. Neutral puppies are relaxed and undemanding — sort of the regular guys of the dog world. Passive and shy puppies appreciate love and support but are fearful of change, so they do best in consistent environments.

Puppy Assessment Form

Name / Number of Pup	1. Observe	2. Play	3. Cradle	4. Call Back	5. Tuck & Pat	6. Bend Over	7. Nose Kiss	8. Toe Squeeze	9. Startle Sound	10. Crash Test	11. Uplift

Figure 4-1: Use this assessment form whenever testing puppies.

Performing the tests

If possible, temperament test each of your prospective puppies to assess their personalities and how they will mesh with your lifestyle. Ask whether a quiet area is available to handle puppies individually, or use an isolated corner of their resting area.

1. Observe.

You can tell a lot about your puppy before you've even said hello. Watch your puppy if he's playing with other puppies. What is his personality? Is he bullying or being bullied? Does he prefer jumping into group activities (A), hanging in the midst of the activity (N), or staying on the sidelines (P)? Is he stealing the bones (A) or submitting when approached (N or P)? After you've observed the pup for a few minutes, assign him a score in the first column.

2. **Play.**

When you first take a puppy aside, play with him. Is he hyper (A), easy-going (N), or does he just want to be petted (P)? Bring out some toys. Does he show interest in them? Does he show you what he has (N), insti-gate tug of war (A), or covet the object immediately? Coveting is an early sign of possessiveness, which may lead to aggression.

I brought a Frisbee when I was searching for a dog who would catch and retrieve. Ask yourself what's important to you.

3. **Cradle (see Figure 4-2).**

Cradle your puppy in your arms. Does he relax (P), wiggle a bit and then relax (N), or kick like crazy (A)? Which action matches your expectations?

Figure 4-2:
Cradle test.

Don't choose an A type if you have children.

4. **Call back.**

Using a treat or a squeak toy, call to your puppy as you back away from him. Does he race after you while jumping or nipping your ankles (A), follow happily (N), or hesitate and need coaxing (P)?

5. **Tuck and pat (see Figure 4-3).**

Kneeling on the floor or sitting in a chair, settle the puppy between your legs. Pet him in long gentle strokes as you praise him softly. Does he wriggle free as he nips (A), wriggle and then relax (N), or simply melt in your embrace (P)?

Figure 4-3:
Tuck and
pat test.

6. Bend over.

Stand up, stretch, and relax. Now go to your puppy and lean over to pet him. Your doing this may seem overwhelming to the pup because you're so large and he's so small. Does he jump up to your face (A), cower in confusion (P), or just relax and let it happen (N)?

7. Nose kiss.

Cradle your puppy's face in your hands and kiss him on the nose. Does he bite you back (A), accept the smooch calmly or return the interaction with a soft bite or kiss (N), or pull back in confusion (P)?

8. Toe squeeze.

In this exercise, you're testing your puppy's reaction and sensitivity to discomfort. While petting the puppy, gently squeeze the skin between his toes. Does he attack your hand? If so, he's definitely an A type with high sensitivity. A neutral puppy may lick or mouth gently, whereas a passive puppy will cringe fearfully.

9. Startle sound.

Take a bunch of keys, and when your prospective puppy least expects it, rattle them above his head. Gauge his reaction: Attacking the keys gets an A; a nonchalant glance, an N; and a fear reaction noted by cowering or withdrawal, a P.

10. Crash test (see Figure 4-4).

Stand and wait until your puppy is no longer interested in you. Suddenly fall to the ground as if you've tripped and exclaim "Ouch!" Does the puppy race over and pounce (A), come to sniff or lick your face (N), or cower and run in fear (P)?

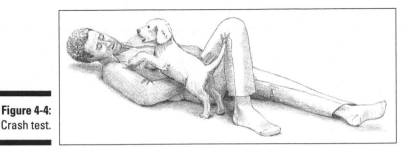

Figure 4-4:
Crash test.

11. Uplift (see Figure 4-5).

Lift your puppy 4 inches off the floor by cradling his midsection. Hold him there for at least 5 seconds. Does he wriggle and bite furiously (A)? Does he relax and look around (N)? Does he look fearful and constrict his body posture (P)?

Figure 4-5:
Uplift test.

Rating the results

After you've completed the ten tests, tally your score. Don't be surprised if you get mixed results. Following are some tips for interpreting the tallied score:

- **All A's:** This dominant puppy is bright and interactive. Raising him will take concentration, consistency, and time. His favorite expression: "What's Next?"

- **All N's:** Easygoing and contained, this puppy will be pleasant and self-assured, though perhaps not terribly motivated to follow your agenda when it conflicts with his own. His favorite expression: "Is this absolutely necessary?"

Involve the kids and other pets in the puppy selection process

If you have children or other pets, and you can involve them, do so. Some facility staff or breeders may balk, but try to persuade them. You want your puppy to succeed in your home environment, and that means getting along with your sometimes disgruntled resident Schnauzer or your shy 6-year-old son. Finding a puppy that best suits their temperaments can be a plus because not every puppy personality will jive with them. Children over 5 years old can take part in the exercises, and other pets can be introduced after you've narrowed your choice.

- ✔ **All P's:** This puppy has a weak self-esteem and needs your reassurance to feel safe. Without proper lessons and socialization, he'll be shy. His favorite expression: "It's been three minutes, do you still love me?"

- ✔ **Mix of A and N:** This active puppy will want to be in the middle of everything but will show slightly more impulse control when stimulated. His favorite expression: "Let's do it again!"

- ✔ **Mix of N and P:** This self-assured puppy will be easygoing and gentle yet with a stronger sense of self than a completely passive pup. Because he's more composed, he'll be an ideal puppy for a calm house with or without older children. Favorite expression: "Another backscratching please!"

If you've found a puppy whose score matches what you're looking for, great! If not, you're going to need to keep looking. Don't get discouraged, and don't settle for a puppy who doesn't quite suit you just because you've been looking for a long time. I've been there — finding the right puppy is worth the wait!

Going for an Older Puppy?

If you've decided to adopt an older puppy, you may be hoping to skip the tasks involved with the younger set, from nipping to housetraining. With the right pup, you may be able to avoid some of these situations. However, no situation is perfect, and very few puppies can glide into a new life without a few setbacks. If you're getting an older dog or puppy from the pound, try to find out why he was left there — you may be adopting an older dog who couldn't be housetrained or who shows aggression when chewing a bone.

Considering the source

Depending on where you're going to look for your older puppy, following are some things to ask before taking your little guy or gal home.

- ✔ **Breeder:** A breeder often keeps a puppy for showing purposes. If the puppy doesn't grow into "show dog" potential, he'll be placed in a home. Sometimes it's like hitting the jackpot, provided the puppy has had individual attention and has been well socialized. Other times, it's a disappointment, especially if the puppy has lived in a kennel for the last six months.

   Because a breeder's older puppy may be unfamiliar with the routines of home life, he may not know what stairs are or may not have spent time in a yard. And, no matter what they try to tell you, a puppy who has spent the majority of his time in a kennel isn't housebroken! Find out where this puppy spent his early months before racing into this venture. A puppy who can't emotionally acclimate to your home life isn't a reasonable candidate for you.

- ✔ **Pet store:** These puppies usually sell for a discounted price after they've grown out of their cute phase. Though your heart (and mine) goes out to each of them, consider their reality before you adopt. A virtual lifetime spent behind bars can take an emotional toll, and housebreaking will be a project because they've not been introduced to the concept of "holding it." It's also likely that this puppy has had little, if any, exposure to home living, from everyday sounds to stairs, grass, and cars.

   Once a puppy is beyond that peak socialization period, you risk raising a pup who won't warm to everyday stimulations. Some older puppies who get adopted may turn out fine, but you're always going to run a risk.

   A puppy who was stressed during infancy chews more often than other pups. Nervous energy needs to be displaced, and because running to the refrigerator is off limits and nail biting isn't an option, they chew on whatever is available. Provide plenty of satisfying options or you may see your sofa disappear, one cushion at a time.

- ✔ **Shelter:** If you find an older puppy at a shelter, ask about his history. Was he found on the side of the street, or has he grown up in the system? Was he tied to a post or brought in by a good Samaritan? Has the puppy in question been returned more than once? Ask what the reasons were and what the staff thinks of the puppy's personality.

Guidelines for testing older pups

The temperament test I provide earlier in this chapter is targeted at younger puppies, but you can also apply it to older pups.

Following are some additional guidelines and tests I suggest you use to see whether the older pup you're considering is a good match for your lifestyle. You have to be strong enough to let your head lead your heart. Nothing is sadder than rescuing a dog only to have to return him because the dog couldn't cope with your lifestyle. Be strong — find out ahead of time whether you and the puppy are suited by performing the following tasks:

- **If you have kids, make sure you introduce them to the puppy before you bring him home.**

- **Startle the puppy.** Toss your keys on the floor. Does the puppy fall to pieces or attack them? Neither is a good reaction. A startled reaction to the noise, followed by an investigative sniff, is an ideal response.

- **If you have an animal menagerie at home, make sure the puppy can cope with the creature chaos.** Ask whether other animals are in the owner's current home, or whether anyone has conditioned this puppy to other creatures.

- **Ask one of the staff members (or the previous owner) to lift the puppy.** What happens? Intense fear or frustration isn't a good sign. The ideal puppy may squirm but is still accepting.

- **Bring a soft brush and try to groom the pup while feeding him treats.**

Bear in mind that older puppies are less accepting of strangers and strange situations than infant pups, so allow some room for edginess. But, if you see anything more extreme, back off, especially if what you see is aggression. Unless you want a major training project, look for a puppy who's accepting of you and each of the exercises or conditions mentioned in the previous list.

Part II
Nurturing Your Puppy Day to Day

The 5th Wave   By Rich Tennant

"I got him a bowl, a collar, and since he's a dalmatian puppy, a small fire extinguisher to make him feel right at home."

In this part . . .

I'm going to tell you a little secret: Your puppy, from the moment he meets you, will think of you as another dog. Your friends and family will be thought of as dogs, too. Little children may be seen as other puppies perhaps — but as canines just the same. In his mind, you all share the same worldview. If you do a good job of raising him, your puppy will worship you as the leader, guardian, and protector of his world. The first step is to nurture him like his mother did — with equal love, structure, and nurturing day after day.

In this part, you discover how to nurture and care for your puppy on a daily basis from supplying him with all he needs to socializing him to helping him live with kids and life-changing events.

Chapter 5

Home Sweet Home

· ·

· ·

Mom's right again: First impressions really do count. To make your puppy's transition into your home as smooth as possible, you have some choices to make — from where to put the crate to what to buy at the pet store. In this chapter, I lead you through the days building up to the main event and show you how to get everyone on board and how to outfit your home in preparation.

Now is the time to have some heartfelt discussions with your friends and family. Each person will have her own vision and idea of how things should go and what should be done, but you don't want to confuse your puppy. A disjointed approach can overwhelm her. In this chapter, I shed light on the "how and why" of your first week together so that you're able to back up your rally call with puppy facts. By following my advice, you can welcome your puppy into a calm, consistent, and supportive new environment.

Shopping for Initial Supplies

When you first walk into a pet store, you won't see just one of anything. Today's market is flooded with as many dog toys and gadgets as there are for children. And like a toy store, everyone has different tales to tell — one puppy loved such and such a bone, while another stuck it up her nose; one loved this bed, while another preferred to sleep on the floor; one puppy needed a crate, but another housetrained just fine in a gated bathroom. So, what works for you? In this section, I run down the list of what you need to consider and buy before you bring your puppy home.

Shopping for your puppy can be a mind-boggling experience. In order to avoid blowing your budget (and your mind), remember that less is more, at least initially. Though you may have the temptation to buy everything you can for your pup — from the latest toy to a designer raincoat — I suggest you bring a list and stick to it.

Bowls

Your puppy needs two bowls to start: one for water and one for food. Stainless steel is ideal because it doesn't break and it's heavy, which reduces the chance of the bowl being knocked over. Ceramic is fine as well, although it will break and can chip. Plastic is another viable option. However, some puppies chew their bowls, and others can develop a reaction that causes nose discoloration.

Crate

All right, I agree with you: The sight of a crate looks like an oversized guinea pig cage. However, the truth is, your puppy will like it because the enclosure feels like a cozy den. Especially useful during the early stages of training, the crate helps your puppy feel safe when you're away. Crating a pup also encourages bladder control because puppies don't like to potty where they sleep.

Still not sold on crate training? Think about it this way: Having her own special place to play and rest is synonymous to giving a child his own bed and tucking him into it when it's time to rest. You wouldn't let a child sleep in the middle of a large, unprotected room, would you?

When you shop for a crate, you'll have more options than in buying coffee at your local coffee shop! You'll find all sorts of different sizes, materials, and colors. Should you get a divider or leave space for potty paper? Should the sides be covered or open for air flow? Whew! Here's the scoop:

- ✔ Plastic crates are standard for travel and can also be used as an everyday crate in a well-ventilated environment. If you plan to travel, buy this type — it will give your pup more security when you're away from home. It also will give your puppy more security when she's away from the home.

- ✔ Wire crates allow for better air flow and viewing and can be covered with a blanket at night to create a more denlike experience. Dividers are also available to size the crate according to your puppy.

- ✔ A wicker crate is less of an eyesore. However, you have to pray that after paying top dollar, the puppy won't decide to chew her way out!

Crates can be an invaluable training tool, but they can also be emotionally destructive to your puppy if overused. Crates are ideal in the following situations:

- ✔ If you're leaving your puppy alone for a duration of time not to exceed six hours.

- ✔ During sleeping hours for young, unhousebroken, or mischievous puppies.

- ✔ As a feeding station if your puppy is easily distracted.

- ✔ As a timeout for overly excitable pups. In this case, don't use the crate as a form of punishment; simply lead your puppy there with a toy and place her in calmly. Sometimes, you both need a timeout from each other!

A crate does have the following drawbacks, however:

- ✔ It doesn't communicate leadership.

- ✔ It separates you from your puppy when you're at home.

- ✔ It can't communicate how to behave in the house.

If the idea of a crate turns your stomach, or if you're home all day and you can get through the early stages without one, use a playpen or small, gated room. If your puppy is older, you can lead or station her to keep her close as described later in the chapter.

Gate

Gates come in handy to do the following:

- ✔ Close off a playroom when you're around to supervise your puppy or play with her

- ✔ Block stairways

- ✔ Control your puppy's access to a dangerous or off-limits room

Some people feel less guilty when leaving their puppies in large gated areas, rather than in small rooms or crates. Big mistake. Big rooms make a puppy feel displaced and lonely — she may potty or chew out of sheer anxiety. Dogs are den animals who feel safest in small, manageable spaces. If your goal is peaceful separations, enclose your puppy in a crate or small enclosure when you leave for more than a few minutes. If you're leaving for more than six hours, consider the playpen as a happy medium, and locate a dog walker to break up her day. See the next section for more info on playpens.

Playpen

A playpen, which is a fully functional enclosure, is quite the multifunctional little purchase. It can be used for the following purposes:

- Acclimating her to other pets
- Containing your puppy when you're out of sight
- Keeping her out of wide thoroughfares
- Paper training her
- Temporarily containing her outside

A folding playpen (see Figure 5-1) can be tucked away or transported easily.

Figure 5-1:
A playpen is a safe and portable place for your puppy to stay.

Toys, bones, and treats

Promise me one thing: You won't buy out the pet store when in the toy and bone aisle. Puppies, like children, have specific likes and dislikes, and over-whelming your pup with options is disruptive. She'll grow up thinking everything on the floor is fair game — even your beloved, oh-so-broken-in slippers.

Your puppy's first days will be spent nosing about — interactive play can take 2 to 4 weeks to emerge. Even older puppies have to get their bearings straight before they feel comfortable enough to play. Meanwhile, test your puppy's likes and dislikes by giving her one toy or bone at a time. When you discover one that strikes her fancy, you can then buy multiples.

Toys

Puppies like things that bounce and roll. You'll have plenty of selection, and for the record, your puppy won't mind if you choose a red ball or a blue one — it just needs to bounce. Toys come in as many different shapes as you'd find in a high school geometry book, so prepare yourself. The psychology behind an odd shaped toy? Animals of prey never run in a predictable pattern, thus why should your toy? Some squeak, others make noise, and many have holes in which you're encouraged to stuff a creamy spread or kibbles. Choose a couple, discover what capture's your puppy's heart, and you're set.

You'll also find stuffed toys at the pet store, most of them containing squeaks — again meant to stimulate the sound of prey animals. Many puppies love to toss and play with these. However, some insist on ripping them limb from limb to dismember the object until the squeaker is removed. This isn't an ideal toy for this crowd: For these pups, search for toys with the word "indestructible" on the packaging.

Bones

When you say the word "puppy" at the pet store, you're going to get tons of advice on which gadget or bone is best. Some people say one is great, while others may disagree. Generally, you can't go wrong with indestructible plastic, but the problem is that most puppies find them, well, boring. Rawhide is accepted by the masses, but it's problematic with dogs who chew obsessively because they gulp it as they go.

Personally, I've had the most luck with pressed rawhide, animal-part sticks, and vegetable-matter pulp bones. Test it out yourself — find a bone that satisfies your puppy's craving, make sure it passes the "systems" test (her digestive system, that is), and buy it in bulk!

Treats

To treat or not to treat? That used to be the question. Now the question is "What type of treat is best?" Honestly, if your puppy is gaga for her kibble, use it to reward her, borrowing against portions of her meal. If she's cool on her kibbles, test out some small or easily broken treats from the pet store. Remember that it's not the size of the treat but your enthusiasm when sharing that's the best reinforcement!

Avoid grocery store treats. Most are junky and fill your puppy up with additives that can cause stomach upset, gas, and behavioral frustrations.

Bedding

Even though you'll find some adorable and comfy dog beds on the market, resist the urge to buy a collection until your puppy is housebroken and past her chewing phase: Either habit can make waste of your cozy purchase!

Instead, fold up an old quilt or purchase flat mats that can be spread out to help your puppy identify with a place in her room. Toys can be contained to her mat, and her food and water dishes can be placed nearby.

If the puppy has a strong chewing tendency, skip the bedding. Ingested blankets and towels can cause serious intestinal problems in puppies.

Take your pup's mat with you wherever you go. It will help your puppy feel safe and at home whether you're going to the vet, for a stay at the kennel, or on a family trip. It's like having a security blanket!

Two leashes

I discuss training leashes in the section "As Puppy Grows Up: Training Leashes and Collars." For now, all you need to purchase is a lightweight nylon leash and a long line, which you use for outdoor playtime in open areas (away from streets) and, later, for advanced training.

A drag lead

Drag lead is a fancy term for a short (4 to 6 feet), lightweight nylon leash that stays on your puppy when you're together in the house. A drag lead is useful for quick corrections that distance you from the activity, whether the activity be jumping on the counters, chewing a plant, or nipping at the kids.

A long line

Long lines (30 feet and over) are great to let your puppy romp around the yard and to encourage distance control. Constructed from canvas or nylon mesh, a long line allows freedom to play, and yet it also gives you plenty of leash to grab onto to retrieve your puppy if she should wander off.

For young puppies, long lines are great for wandering in a yard or field — take along some favorite snacks and reward your puppy each time she checks in with you. You can also use long lines to encourage off-lead training.

Microchips: Built-in lifesavers

Your veterinarian and breeder are likely to suggest that you microchip your puppy. I strongly recommend this too! Your veterinarian will inject into your puppy's neck or shoulder (no more painful than a typical shot) a preregistered, computer-recognizable identification chip. If your puppy gets lost or ends up at a shelter, a simple wave of the wand allows your puppy to be returned to you immediately. Many breeders have a microchip inserted in each puppy's shoulder before sending them home. If your pup hasn't had a microchip inserted, make an appointment immediately.

ID tag

Even though you won't secure this tag on your puppy until she's conditioned to her collar, it's good to have one on hand. Some national-chain pet stores now have machines that create personalized tags in minutes. I find the best message to write is "Please Help Me Home [555-555-5555]." Use an ID tag in addition to the microchip, since lay people can't identify the information on the microchip without the appropriate machinery.

I suggest that you not add your puppy's name to her tag because it could endear her to wrongdoers. Also, you can add the word "Reward" if you're prepared to offer one.

A few other odds and ends

- **Treat cups:** To create a treat cup for your puppy, purchase an inexpensive plastic container (or use an emptied deli container), cut a small round hole in the lid, and fill it half full with dried kibbles or broken-up dog treats. By connecting the sound of the cup shaking with a food reward, you can use the treat cup to cheerfully condition your puppy's cooperation from game playing to name association to fetching.

  More on its uses in Chapters 8 and 11.

- **Snack packs:** Purchase or find a fanny pack. Stow snacks and poop bags in it and take it with you when you go outside with your pup. You'll have the snacks handy for rewarding your puppy for returning to you and for outdoor pottying. Check out Chapter 11 for more uses of snack packs.

- **Clicker:** A clicker is a small handheld toy that, when depressed, lets out a clear noise that is unmistakable. When this sound is paired with a treat, your puppy will go to great lengths to initiate the noise. You may use the clicker to teach basic skills or shape household manners like housebreaking and greeting rituals. Flip to Chapter 11 to find out more.

As Puppy Grows Up: Training Leashes and Collars

Later, after your puppy gets settled into her new home and starts growing up a bit, you'll need to make another trip to the store — for training leashes and collars. This section covers some of the different kinds of equipment you'll encounter at the store.

Training collars and leashes may make you and your puppy's lifestyle feel restricted, even overly structured. When used properly, however, they aid in helping your puppy to earn household freedom — besides, using them is a temporary thing!

Training leashes

Leads are a training essential. They also enable you to keep your puppy secured. The car comes to mind quickly. While you're driving, keep your puppy secured for her safety, as well as your own peace of mind. During romps, too. If you're not in a confined area, don't let your puppy run free.

Retractable leashes

Retractable leashes are fun when used in the right setting. The longer, the better. Initially, this leash is great for exercising. Your puppy can run like mad while you stand there reading the morning newspaper. When you progress to off-leash work (see Chapter 15), the retractable leash is a staple. Its design works like a fishing reel, letting length in and out. Although using it takes some coordination, once you've mastered it, you probably won't be able to live without it.

You do need to take a few precautions, however. Don't use a retractable leash near roads or heavily populated areas. Its high-tech design takes getting used to, and even a seasoned pro can lose hold of the slack. If you're out with other people, watch their legs. Most puppies get a little nutty when you give them some freedom to run. If a person gets sandwiched between you and your prancing puppy, he's in for a wicked rope burn. It's best to keep play-times private.

Teaching Lead or equivalent

As your puppy matures, she'll want to hang with you when you're home. The same puppy who curled up quietly in the kitchen while you showered will eventually protest the separation. Simply dismantling the gates won't be the answer. A young puppy gets overwhelmed with too much freedom, even inside the house, so you'll want to keep her on a lead. (Don't worry about keeping your puppy on a lead in the house; it's only temporary.)

To keep it simple and structured, you can use a technique called the Teaching Lead Method, which I explain in more detail in Chapter 13. The three aspects of this method — leading, anchoring, and stationing — are invaluable to condition your puppy to household freedom and civilized walking manners. Use this chapter to find out how the Teaching Lead Method can

  ✔ Take the place of the crate when you're home.

  ✔ Encourage good manners inside and out.

✔ Teach everyday commands, such as "Stay," "Heel," and "Come."

✔ Resolve housebreaking, jumping, nipping, and other annoying habits.

Seat Belt Safety Lead (SBSL)

Letting your puppy ride in your lap or hang her body halfway out the window when you drive may seem like a good idea, but it's really not. Maybe I've witnessed too many accidents, but to me, cars aren't toys, and your puppy is too precious to lose in a fender bender. Here's my safety rule: Confine your puppy while driving. If you're preoccupied with your puppy when you should be paying attention to the road, you're creating a safety hazard for both of you and other motorists.

Either use a crate to block your puppy in the back seat or cargo area of a station wagon or SUV, or secure your puppy with a system I call the *Seat Belt Safety Lead* (SBSL), which protects puppies in the same way a seat belt protects people.

You can reference my Web site (www.dogperfect.com) for photos specifying leash use and collar options.

Short lead

"Short" is relative to the size of your puppy. A short lead should not be more than 8 inches; for small dogs, 1 to 3 inches will do. You can use it for encouraging manners and for off-leash training. Here's the theory behind both:

✔ **Encouraging good manners.** A lot of clients complain that their puppies behave like a saint on leash, but when they take the leash off, the old derelict emerges. A short leash can serve as a nice transition from using a regular leash to full-fledged freedom. Wearing a short lead reminds the puppy that you're still watching her; it also gives you something to grasp for correction purposes if you need to.

✔ **Off-lead training.** When you progress into off-leash work (see Chapter 15), the short lead again serves as a reminder of your presence and authority. In addition, it gives you something to grab graciously if your puppy slips up.

Training collars

Adjustable collars made of cotton, nylon, or leather are called *buckle collars.* Buckle collars don't slide or choke. Their purpose is to carry your puppy's ID tags. On the flip side, the purpose of a training collar is to discourage lunging and leading you on the leash as you use positive reinforcement to encourage your puppy's focus. If you have a puppy who would rather chase a leaf than stay with you, you need to invest in a training collar. This section clues you in to the different types of training collars available.

You can't simply ask for a training collar. You need to be more specific. Many different types of collars are available, and finding the one for your situation is a must. An ineffective training collar can hurt your puppy, as well as hinder the training process.

You have quite a few collars to choose from. If you're confused about which one is most appropriate, ask someone who knows: Other trainers, veterinarians, pet store professionals, or groomers may be helpful. Keep in mind, though, that some dog people are one-collar oriented and tell you that only one type works. Stay away from that advice; every situation is different. What may work wonders for you could be someone else's nightmare. Choose a collar that works for you from those described in this section (try them all out if you have to).

Although head collars and no-pull harnesses (discussed later in this section) are safe options and will condition cooperative walking skills from the start, avoid using all other training collars on a puppy younger than 16 weeks. Remove the collar when you leave your pup unattended because it can be deadly if snagged. Put your puppy's tags on a buckle collar.

Head collar

Head collars are my favorite choice for puppies, and they can be used from the start — even with puppies as young as 8 weeks of age. They're also ideal when original training collars fail. All my dogs have used the head collar system in their first year: It's a nonconfrontational conditioning tool that encourages cooperation and good following skills from the start.

You may think this collar looks like a muzzle when you first see it. Trust me, though; it's not a muzzle. Puppies can eat, chew, and play happily while sporting their head collar. In fact, using this collar is probably the most humane way to walk a dog. It eliminates internal or external pressure around the neck. Using it is similar to handling a horse on a halter.

So how does this wonder collar work? It works on the "mommy" principle. When your puppy was very young, her mom would correct her by grasping her muzzle and shaking it. This communicated "Hey, wild one, settle down!" The head collar has the same effect. Left on during play, the pressure on the nose discourages rowdiness and mouthing. By placing a short lead on your puppy when you're expecting company, you can effectively curb jumping habits. Barking frenzies are drastically reduced, and training is made simple as you guide your puppy from one exercise to the next.

For those of you who can look beyond its muzzlelike appearance, the head collar is a safe, effective, humane training tool that gives you a leg up in correcting negative behavior patterns. Another plus is that leading by the chin demands minimal physical strength, so nearly everyone can use it — kids too. Here are a few more notes:

✔ **Wearing time.** How often you should leave the head collar on is a question best answered by your puppy. If yours is relatively well behaved, you can use it exclusively during walks and lessons. If she's the mouthing, jumping, or barking type, leave the collar on whenever you're around. Remove it at night or when you're out.

✔ **Sizing your head collar.** Head collars have a sizing scale. The head collar must fit properly around your puppy's neck. If it's too loose, your puppy can pull it off and perhaps chew it. You want the neck strap to fit watch-band tight around your puppy's neck about her ears, with enough room to fit two fingers under her neck. You may need to tie a knot with the remaining slack after you adjust it to prevent it from loosening.

✔ **Observe how your puppy reacts.** Initially, puppies don't love the idea of a head collar. Their reaction reminds me of the first day my mother dressed me in lace — I hated it. But after an hour or so, I hardly noticed it at all. I learned to tolerate it. So will your puppy. When you see her flopping about like a flounder, take a breath. After she realizes she can't get the collar off, she'll forget about it. Some puppies take an hour to adjust to the feel of the collar; some take a day or two. If you give this collar a try, you may have to tolerate some resistance. Be patient.

If a head collar irritates your puppy's nose, buy Dr. Scholl's moleskin at the drugstore and wrap it around the nose piece. It's softer and will feel more comfortable. If that treatment is ineffective, remove the head collar and contact your veterinarian for ointment.

Harnesses and other gadgets

On the market are several no-pull harness designs that I've found very effective in encouraging good following skills in puppies as young as 8 weeks. Further, a harness is an ideal system for small or giant-size breeds and can be used safely if a puppy's neck is simply too fragile to bear the resistance of a neck collar (noted by constant hacking when attached to a neck collar). It prevents pulling by humanely curbing your puppy's gait.

Some people use other generic harnesses. Although you can use a harness, with many puppies, harnesses may instigate a pull-back response, forcing your puppy in front of you, not beside you. A regular harness is best used to sport tags with smaller breeds or to be used in car travel.

The original correction collar

I call this collar the "original" because it has been around the longest. It has some other names too, like a *chain* or *choke collar,* even though when used properly, it should never choke your puppy. Choking and restraining only aggravate problems. It's the sound of the collar, *not* the restraint, that teaches. To be effective, you must put on the collar properly and master the zipper tug.

If put on backwards, this collar will catch in a vise hold around your puppy's neck and do what the collar is not supposed to do — choke.

Take these steps to ensure you put on the collar correctly:

1. **Decide which side you want your puppy to walk on.**

   You must be consistent; puppies are easily confused. Because left is traditional, I use *left* as my reference.

2. **Take one loop of the collar and slide the chain slack through it.**

3. **Create the letter *P* with the chain.**

4. **Holding the chain out, stand in front of your puppy. Show her the chain.**

5. **Give your puppy a treat as you praise her and slide the loop of the P over her head.**

In order to effectively train your puppy with this collar, you must master the "zipper tug." Your puppy should learn by the *sound* of the collar, not the restraint. When used properly, a quick tug, which sounds like a zipper, corrects your puppy's impulse to disobey or lead. Practice the zipper tug without your puppy:

1. **Stand up straight and relax your shoulders, letting your arms hang loosely at your sides.**

2. **Place your hand just behind your thigh and snap your triceps so that your elbow swings back freely.**

   If it helps, pretend that someone else's hand is there and you're trying to hit it.

After you have the hang of the movement, find your puppy. Place your hand over the leash and tug quickly as she starts to lead forward.

If you find yourself in a constant pull battle with your puppy that's only broken by occasional hacking, investigate other collar options, especially the self-correcting collar or head collar.

How many ways do you think you can hold the leash? Just one way when you're training your puppy. If you hold the lead improperly, pulling up instead of back, you'll pull your puppy off the ground, which chokes her. To hold the leash correctly, wrap your thumb around the bottom of the lead and your fingers over the top. Keep your arm straight as you walk your puppy and quickly tug straight back when necessary.

Nylon training collar

These collars work best on fine-haired dogs. Like the original choke, you slide it over the head in a P position. You can use this collar with more cooperative dogs. Count your blessings if your puppy falls into one of these categories.

Self-correcting collar

I admit that this collar is big and bulky, and the stainless steel version looks nothing short of torturous. Fortunately, though, this collar has been replicated in plastic, which is visibly more appealing and far less intense for your puppy. It's humane for hard to manage dogs — especially if you fall into the *I can't-stop-choking-my-puppy* category using an original training collar. This collar works wonders for puppies who are insensitive to pain or too powerful to be persuaded with simpler devices.

The plastic collar has been termed a "good dog collar," though the metal version is still referred to as a *prong collar;* I reference both throughout the book as *self-correcting* because the collar requires little strength on your part. A slight tug will alert even the rowdiest of puppies to slow down.

If you decide to try this collar, let me warn you: Occasionally, these collars pop off. To prevent a possible emergency, purchase an oversized training collar and attach your leash to both when walking in an unconfined area. Use this collar only when you're working with your puppy on a leash.

Prepping Your House for Your Puppy's Arrival

Prepping your home for a puppy is much like setting up a nursery. Like formal preparations for bringing home a baby, readying the house before you get your puppy will take a load off your mind when the day finally arrives. Lay out your purchases and read on to get started!

Puppy's room

Your puppy needs her own space to get away from the hubbub. Because a tired puppy can become ornery (just like you), designate a quiet area that can be darkened like a child's nursery. Whether you choose a crate or a gated room, make it cozy by laying down a flat mat and a couple of toys to occupy her when she's restless (think pacifier). Avoid fluffy beds or cushions because both can encourage chewing or accidents. A radio can be placed nearby to play calming music while you're out of the room.

An especially helpful product for puppies is called a SnugglePuppy, which mimics the warmth and comfort of a pup's mom. The substitute companion has a pocket for heating packs and has a motorized beating heart. These features make the SnugglePuppy ideal for easing your puppy's transition from her first family to her final one.

Free play zones

Designate a *free play zone,* which is an enclosed room for play and interaction. A carpet-free space is ideal — especially if your puppy isn't housebroken. Roll up area rugs too because the fringe and corners may tempt a pup to chew and the absorbent texture may prompt elimination. Tape wires down, remove low-sitting temptations, and place your shoes elsewhere. You can also create a play station in this room (see the next section).

If your free play zone will correspond with another pet's domain, reorganize their area well in advance of the puppy's arrival. For example, if your cat's bowls and litter box are within the puppy's area, relocate them ahead of time so that your cat won't feel displaced by the new arrival. For more tips on introducing your pup to the resident pets, flip to the section "Introducing other pets," later in this chapter.

Play stations

Help your puppy identify an area of the free play zone that is home base. This area will be your puppy's play station. Place a flat mat, folded quilt, or bed in a spot set off or portioned by walls. Put your puppy's toys and bones on the mat, and if possible, arrange her dishes nearby. Sit there with your puppy and treat her so she thinks that area is special. If you make this area the focal point of your interactions, your puppy will bond to it quickly (see Figure 5-2).

As you introduce new rooms in the house, either bring your play station or create a permanent one in this room. Your puppy should have a pre-established play station in each room you plan to share.

Figure 5-2:
Establish
play stations
throughout
your home.

If you're adopting an older puppy, create play stations in every room and she'll always feel welcomed.

Feeding areas

Feed your puppy by her play station in her free play zone or, if she's distractible, in her crate. Place one dish for water and one for food. Take up the bowls at appropriate times and wash the dishes after every feeding.

The route

Whether you're paper training or teaching your puppy to go potty outside, decide on a route through shared rooms to the door or papered location. (See Chapter 12 for a diagram.)

Place papers in the decided area or select a door and potty area no more than 10 to 20 feet from your home's entrance.

The Ride Home

The day has finally arrived. You've thought ahead, prepared family members and friends, and probably shared your excitement with a few strangers. Yes, this ride will be a literal thrill ride for you. Your puppy, however, may feel a little differently. Leaving her dog family for the first time and being separated from her birth mom can be stressful and scary.

Make every effort to plan as stress-free a trip home as possible. If you can, arrange the trip during her nap time. Also think through both the best- and worst-case scenarios, so that you'll be prepared for anything that may happen. For example, think of the following scenarios:

- **Best-case scenario:** Your puppy will sleep the entire way home. Keep your energy subdued and speak softly to your puppy if she wakes up. Calming music may also be effective.

- **Worst-case scenario:** Your puppy will throw up, howl, or have an extreme case of diarrhea. The worst-case scenario is a drag, I know, but it happened to me once and it may happen to you. Pack three rolls of paper towel, plastic bags, your favorite carpet or upholstery cleaner, and towels. No matter how disappointed, disgusted, or frustrated you become, don't stress or correct your puppy.

Here's your checklist for the trip:

- Paper towels

- A towel to spread under the crate to prevent slipping or to clean up accidents

- Light collar with an identifying phone number in case of emergency or accident

- A few chewies or a soft toy

- A SnugglePuppy, if you've purchased one — batteries and heat packs included

You're good to go!

If you're traveling in a car or by plane, crate your puppy in an appropriately sized plastic kennel. Plastic kennels can be purchased at a local pet store in advance. Ask the breeder or caretaker what size is most appropriate for your pup. In the car, secure the kennel by bracing it with pillows or literally tie it down on a leveled surface and play calming music as you navigate home. If you've purchased a SnugglePuppy, use it now and for the next few days to help ease your puppy's sense of isolation. If others are riding with you, ask that they sit near the opening of the kennel and speak softly to the puppy when she wakes up.

Don't sit the puppy in your lap while driving. Driving is enough of a chore, and to make matters worse, a slight fender bender may release the air bag. Like infants, your puppy won't survive the blow.

Making the First Introductions

When planning your first day with your new pup, remember to keep it simple. If you have kids or other dogs, tire them out and use bribes to ensure their cooperation. Don't tolerate fighting and commotion — your puppy will have enough on her mind. Keep all stress at bay for the next 24 hours. One simple way to relieve some stress is to reschedule home-repair appointments. Let this be your puppy's day.

If you're welcoming home a young puppy, between 8 to 12 weeks, introduce her to one main room, such as the kitchen, for the first week. An older puppy can be gradually exposed to new areas of the house, but make sure you use a leash because unleashed she's likely to explore or chew or soil areas you rather she not. You'll be forced to interfere, which can cycle into a pattern of behavior because your attention is the strongest reinforcement. On leash a gentle tug can guide her to areas or toys and help her to format acceptable behaviors from the start. If you're planning to let your new pup sleep near you at night, use a large, open box or crate as a bed and carry her there after her last potty run.

Rolling out your welcome mat

The day that your puppy first comes home may be on a future "fondest memories of childhood" list — talk about excitement. However, it's your job to keep the kids calm because too much squealing and loving in the first five minutes can be somewhat overwhelming for a pup.

Explain the situation ahead of time and ask your children to help you make the puppy feel comfortable. The rule is that they can follow quietly and speak gently, but roughhousing, shouting, and fighting is forbidden. This may be your last peaceful moment for a while, so enjoy it!

Forming a welcome circle

Gather everyone and create a large circle by spreading your legs so your feet touch. Give everyone a handful of the puppy's kibble and place her in the center of the circle. Let her approach everyone on her own and show everyone in advance how to pet and hold her to make her feel safe and welcome.

Calming the kids

If you have more than one child, chances are likely that they'll compete with each other for the puppy's attention. Here are a few tricks I've found useful in dispelling early tension, frustrations, and physical fights:

- **Model, model, model:** The saying "Monkey see, monkey do" applies to children, too! Because your children pick up on habits by watching you, show them how to act with actions instead of words. I can assure you that something is bound to not go as planned (your child will have a tantrum, your partner will not be as excited or interested as you), but if you stay calm and ignore the impulse to badger or boss, you'll have a calmer home on your hands. Kids, and even some spouses, react poorly to negative reprimands. Stay cheerful and model the right behavior as your children are watching. Like monkeys, they see — and then they do.

- **Assign tasks:** Assign everyone a task ahead of time by using the chart in Chapter 8. Make raising the puppy a fun family affair where everyone plays the role of the parent.

- **Advanced discussions:** Talk to your children ahead of time. Get them involved in your plans and warn them of all the possible situations that may arise. Tell them that the puppy may be sad and withdrawn and may not want to interact with anyone. Though this may be a letdown, you must respect the puppy. The transition is rough, but she'll snap out of it in a few days and will be delighted to have such a respectful, loving group to bond to. On the other hand, the puppy may be nippy and rough. So that the children don't go running from the room, make sure they're aware and help them interact with the puppy when she's calm.

- **Watch, listen, and share:** Have a talking toy to pass around the table at mealtimes. Whoever has the toy gets to share a story or a thought about the puppy. We have a sharing shell at our house and whoever has the shell gets to talk (uninterrupted) for as long as they want.

- **Take the puppy away:** Your puppy will get easily riled by your children and may express herself through nipping, jumping, and tugging. To prevent this behavior, tell your children in advance that if they get too riled up, you'll take the puppy aside. The key to this technique is to follow through.

Talk to your kids about the different phases of puppyhood — comparing it to different-age children they know. Using the section "The Five Stages of Puppy Development" in Chapter 6, help your kids understand exactly what's going on with your puppy at each age.

For example, an 8- to 12-week-old puppy needs a lot of sleep because her brain is still developing. Thus, yelling should be avoided because it only creates fear or (worse) confrontation. Older puppies may nip a lot and want to engage in tug of war, which shows they're determining where they fit into the group and just who they can boss around.

Introducing other pets

Though it may come as a letdown to you and your family, you have to realize that your resident pets will not be wearing party hats when you walk through the door with a new companion in your arms. Young puppies in particular are annoying — and the oodles of attention she'll garner from everyone will be totally off-putting to the resident pet. It may take some time for the two to get used to each other.

Here are some tips to help ease the tension:

- **Keep your new puppy in a confined area.** If you choose an area (the kitchen, for example) that has been the feeding area for your other pet, think ahead. A week before your puppy comes home, change the feeding area to a quieter environment. Do this for litter boxes and caged pets, as well. Move them well ahead of time to ensure a positive association.

- **After your puppy is in the home, introduce the smell of the resident pet to your puppy first.** Then take a blanket from the pup and place it near your resident pet.

- **If the resident pet is caged, bring your puppy into its room after a meal and playtime.** This restful state calms the scenario. Bring in your puppy's favorite mat and chew toy and sit near the cage, petting your puppy calmly. Repeat this exercise often.

Royalties to the resident pets

All royalties go to your resident pets — especially in the initial stages. Here's some advice regarding your resident pets:

- Feed them first (dividing their meals into three parts if necessary).

- Treat, greet, and play with them first and foremost.

- If the resident is a dog, let her pass first (on stairs or through doorways).

- If your resident pet approaches you while you or anyone is interacting with the puppy, turn away from the puppy and address her immediately.

If you follow these tips, I assure you that your puppy's feelings will not be hurt. She'll grow respectful of your other pet and act accordingly. Aside from conditioning your resident to the idea that the new addition guarantees more food and attention for her, you're reinforcing respect for those pets who came first.

Other dogs

It's unlikely that your older dog will be keen on the idea of sharing his space with a new puppy. If you're bringing home an older puppy, introduce the two in a neutral area. Otherwise, bring your resident dog out of the main living space to meet the new addition. Whatever his reaction, stay calm as you focus your affections on your resident pet. Follow these tips:

- ✔ Organize the introduction, preferably at a time your resident pet is most calm.

- ✔ If you're introducing a young puppy, have a friend hold her (if she's not inoculated, don't let her frolic in an open environment) as you approach with your dog on a loose leash.

- ✔ Feed your dog treats as you focus your attention on him.

- ✔ Once he's accepting, invite your friend to carry the puppy into your home.

- ✔ If you're concerned about your dog's reaction, buy a playpen or crate ahead of time and place the puppy in it as you continue to react with your dog as though the puppy were not there.

- ✔ Stay calm as they interact and keep your attention focused on your dog. If any altercations happen, side with your resident. It's normal for him to "put the puppy in her place," using seemingly dramatic postures. Stay calm and let them work it out.

- ✔ If you're introducing an older puppy, bring the two to an enclosed space and let them greet each other on their own terms. If you're nervous, you can muzzle both dogs, although I don't recommend it. Let them figure each other out, and then let your resident lead the new puppy into the home.

Growling, teeth snarls, and pinning are actually very good signs of normal acceptance. The big dog is showing the little dog who is boss. Your puppy may actually shriek, roll over, and pee. Again, don't interfere. If you comfort the new puppy, you may alienate your resident dog and make the relationship between them rocky. The puppy shrieks communicate volumes and let the big dog know just how submissive and defenseless the little dog is. It is all good. Let them work it out in their own way.

If you're earnestly concerned that your resident dog might harm the puppy, muzzle him or leave a leash dragging to enable easy interference.

Some older dogs completely withdraw, going so far as to act as if they've never met you. Don't be put off. Instead, just shower them with love and attention. If your youngster badgers or bullies your resident dog for sport, discourage it immediately by using a drag lead or a spray away.

Cats

Most cats could live without a puppy in the house. Some are fearful of puppies, while others are outright annoyed. Sometimes you'll see them head for the highest cabinet, only to stare at you reproachfully. If you have a confident cat, he'll probably wait stoically for the puppy to approach close enough for him to give the pup a solid bat on the nose. In any case, keep your responses lowkey. Overreacting can put all species on edge.

Following are some suggestions to make the introductions go as smoothly as possible:

- ✔ **If you're introducing a cat, place the puppy in an enclosed room or crate (with a special chewy for diversion) and let your cat wander around the room at his own will.** Don't try to influence or interfere in your cat's reaction. If your puppy starts acting wildly, however, step in to calm her.

- ✔ **When your cat is accustomed to the puppy's presence (it may take awhile, perhaps a week), place your puppy on a light drag lead and bring the two together in a small room.** Hold your puppy's lead if she acts up and divert her with a toy.

  Don't be too surprised if your cat growls or bats at the puppy. Corrections only make matters worse. Your cat is defining her space, which is a necessary boundary for coexistence.

If your cat can't come to grips with the idea, keep the two separated until your puppy is acclimated to a leash and collar and can understand the concept of "No."

Other animals

If you have other pets in the house, such as ferrets, birds, or rodents, give the puppy a few days to acclimate to you before introducing the rest of the menagerie. If your pup's reaction concerns you, attach a leash to curb her reaction.

Also try the following suggestions:

- ✔ If you have a free-roaming animal, introduce him as you would a cat.

- ✔ If this animal generally lives in a cage, bring the cage out when your puppy is calm and her needs (eat, bathroom, play) have been satisfied.

- ✔ If your puppy is impulsive, sniffing intently, place her on a head collar before you proceed.

- ✔ Use treat cups and/or a clicker to keep her focus on you while you simply hang out as if there were no cage in the room. If she looks at the animal calmly, fine; if she gets overstimulated, tug her leash and say "No." Redirect with a familiar cue. Work at short 10- to 20-minute intervals until your puppy is calm around your other pet.

When I was a kid, I got a French lop-eared bunny. Shadow, the bunny, grew to be a whopping 24 pounds. Unfortunately, another favorite pet of mine, Shawbee, my Siberian Husky-Shepherd mix, decided that 24 pounds was big enough. The inevitable happened: Shawbee ate Shadow. It was a horrible sight to see. The moral of this story is that if your puppy won't give up her snack-hunting vigil, you may have to reconsider keeping both under the same roof.

Saving your friends for another day

Everyone gets excited when they hear the word "puppy." Friends and neighbors crawl out of the woodwork and want to welcome you home. Don't be persuaded! Limit early introductions to only the closest friends and family. Resist extracurricular visits and drive-by welcomes until the next week, when your puppy has fully transitioned into your home and has bonded with you and the people closest to you.

Sometimes your friends can be the hardest to control. Many will have opinions and will, without provocation, share their views on everything from housetraining to how to discipline your puppy when she misbehaves. Promise me one thing: You won't listen to them. Even though they may speak the gospel about what worked for their puppy, you're not raising their puppy — you're raising your own. Like children, what works for one pup may not work for another. If you follow everyone's advice, you risk confusing your puppy. If you need more help than this book offers, skip your friends' advice and sign up for a class or call a respected professional.

When the time has finally come for you to introduce your new pup to your friends, here are some tips for the formal introductions: Ask your guest to come in calmly and sit on the floor. If your puppy is jumpy and excited, show your guest how to "close shop" by folding his arms in front of his face. Brace your puppy by clipping your thumb over her collar and resting your other hand on her back (Chapter 7). If she's still too excited or nervous, offer her a toy to dispel her anxiety. By ignoring her when she's excited and petting her when she's calm, you're getting a head start on encouraging good manners.

What to Expect the First Week

Well, you've made it home! All the anticipation has come to this very moment. Even though you want to rush in and give your newest member the full tour, hold your huskies! Simplify the day by showing her the main area that you've already customized, and share in her curiosity as she checks out the room.

Speak to her softly and don't correct her or respond if she has an accident or chews on something she shouldn't. Right now, she's too disoriented to retain anything, so you'll only succeed in frightening her. Relax. You'll do fine. This is just the beginning.

Surviving the first 24 hours

Prepare yourself and your family for the fact that the first day home with your puppy can be a little odd. After all the anticipation and preparation, your puppy is home. She may jump right into the mix, or she may pass out for days. You may get one who sleeps straight through the night, or she may be up all night whining. Your puppy may be rough, sweet, or completely aloof. Don't take anything personally. This adventure is all very new and she's just trying to get a handle on what's going on.

Initially, enclose her in a room and just observe. If she seems interested in your presence, follow her about, preferably on all fours. If she sniffs, sniff back. If she's interested in looking out the window, join her. Reflect her interests calmly. If your puppy wants to rest, be a quiet presence. When she wakes up, take her to her designated potty place and give her water. Try not to overwhelm her with your interests or affections. She needs time to adjust.

Days 2–7

The first week is very progressive. By day 2 or 3, you'll notice your puppy taking you in — watching you and getting excited when you walk through the door. You may be surprised to note the different reactions, but remember, her emerging personality is a sure sign that she feels safe and welcomed. Use the "Needs Chart" in Chapter 6 to organize the day, and remain patient with accidents or exploratory chewing, especially if she's young. If you notice your puppy chewing furniture or wires, use a distasteful spray like Bitter Apple to discourage her. Avoid loud or physical interference because it will only overwhelm your puppy and discourage bonding.

Right now, the most important lessons are

- ✔ Helping your puppy learn her name as outlined in Chapter 13.
- ✔ Teaching her where to potty as described in Chapter 12.

Make these lessons the focus of your first week and you'll be well on your way to a wonderful life together!

Bonding moments

When puppies are very young and are experiencing stress, they're not thinking about you too much. Absorbed in their own confusion, they just want to feel safe and calm. The best way to establish your first loving bond is to create an environment that satisfies both of these needs. Be present for your puppy, but remember silence is more calming than mindless chatter or yelling. If your puppy is small, she'll feel more nurtured if you're on the floor next to her than towering above. Puppies like to nestle, and they feel cozy when they find a little cubbyhole — your puppy may even curl into your lap if you let her.

The best approach is to follow your puppy's rhythm for the first week as she is getting acclimated to her new home and all the others in it. If your puppy wants to sleep, let her — put her in her crate or on her play mat. At feeding time, put her food on or near her mat and leave her alone for 15 minutes. Don't worry if she doesn't eat. She's probably just nervous. Give her some water and take her to her potty spot often.

Ideally, your puppy should sleep near someone at night. She may whine initially, so if possible, keep her at your bedside and lay your hand in the crate or over the side of a large open box.

Chapter 6

Life from His Paws: Understanding Your Puppy's View of the World

*I*n my opinion, the greatest gift you can give your puppy is a stress-free existence. Structure your puppy's world so that he feels safe. Provide for his needs, anticipating them before he does, and incorporate as much play-time into your daily routine as you can. A young puppy won't understand the word "no" or develop impulse control before 6 to 8 months, so put your expectations and frustrations on the back burner until you can channel both into useful communication. Puppyhood, like childhood, is short — let your puppy enjoy his to the fullest.

You have to understand the world from his perspective. He's brand-new to the planet, and curiosity is his guide. Though his curiosity may result in behaviors that you find aggravating, don't take any of his antics personally: After all, he's just a baby. Getting angry at a puppy is as silly and ineffective as yelling at a 6-month-old child. Not only will you not get through to him, you'll also frighten him. You, the very person he should feel most safe turning to, will be scaring and confusing him. This routine is neither educational nor good for long-term bonding. There is a better way to navigate through this time — a much better way.

In this chapter, I show you how to put yourself in your puppy's paws and understand just how your puppy views your world and life together. Consider learning about your puppy's worldview an adventure — let the fun begin!

Understanding Your Puppy's Basic Needs

Your puppy is a lot like a human baby. Okay, sure, your pup may have a curly tail and a full set of teeth, but many of the differences stop there. Like a child, your puppy has basic needs and an instinct to satisfy them. A baby communicates her helpless neediness through crying. It's a guardian's role to interpret the cry and satisfy the need. In essence, a cry indicates that the baby lacks the ability to associate a specific need with a bodily sensation. When she's hungry, her belly hurts. When she's tired, her brain shuts down. When she's thirsty, her throat constricts. If these needs aren't satisfied, she gets anxious. When the needs are routinely satisfied by a loving caregiver, without stress, discipline, or confusion, she'll develop a strong bond with that person.

The same holds true for puppies. Like babies, they have five basic needs: eat, drink, sleep, potty, and play. Unlike babies, puppies don't cry when their needs aren't met. Instead, they start nipping and, if directed, may bark and become frantic and fidgety. The behaviors are different, but the concept is the same. Both are easily overwhelmed when their bodies make demands. If initial nips are met with harsh discipline, the puppy may develop defense reactions, such as aggression or barking back.

You can help your puppy identify his needs by pairing directions with routines. Whereas a child will develop language and a more civilized approach to communicating her requests, your puppy will develop his own system of communicating by prompting the routine. Read about puppy needs in the upcoming sections, and use Table 6-1 to create your own routines — your puppy will be ringing the bell to go outside in no time!

Whoever satisfies a need is held in high regard. Though it may take some time for your puppy to "pay you back" with his love and devotion, each passing day brings you closer to that ultimate connection. Need by need, your bond will grow.

Table 6-1	Needs Chart	
Your Pup's Need	*The Word or Phrase You Say*	*The Routine You Follow*
Eating	Hungry or eat	Schedule feeding times. Place the bowl in the same spot and encourage your puppy to sit before feeding.
Drinking	Water	Keep the bowl in the same spot. Encourage him to sit before drinking.

Your Pup's Need	The Word or Phrase You Say	The Routine You Follow
Going potty	Outside, papers, go potty, or get busy	Encourage your puppy to nose/paw a bell to signal this need. Follow the same route to the same potty spot. Restrict attention until your puppy goes.
Sleeping	On your mat, in your crate, or time for bed	Designate one spot in each shared room. Take your pup to his mat or bed, provide a chew toy, and secure if necessary.
Playing	Bone, ball, toy, or go play!	Establish a play area inside and outside the house. Make sure all four paws are on the floor before you toss a toy or give a bone.

Eating

Puppies are happiest when a predictable routine has been set. A hungry puppy is understandably upset and may show you by eating anything — even the difficult-to-digest things such as tissues or walls! Schedule feeding times and stick to them as closely as possible. If you notice your puppy getting nippy or difficult, check your watch. The behavior could be a result of hunger tension. See Table 6-2 for guidance when setting up feeding times.

Table 6-2	Your Puppy's Feeding Schedule			
Age	Morning Meal (7 a.m.)	Midday Meal (11:30 a.m.)	Afternoon Meal (4 p.m.)	Late Evening Meal
8 to 10 weeks	*	*	*	*
10 weeks to 4 months	*	*	*	
4 to 6 months	*		*	

A young puppy has a high metabolism and should have more frequent meals. Schedule three to four meals throughout the day, slowly phasing out meals as your puppy matures. At some point after your puppy reaches 4 to 6 months, he'll naturally drop one meal.

Whoever feeds your puppy should follow the same organized routine that you do. Puppies (like kids) are happiest when they know exactly what will happen next. For example, in my house, whoever feeds our dog, Whoopsie, says "Kibbles," lifts her bowl, fills it up, and waits for her to sit before returning it to her eating station.

Drinking

Puppies need a lot of water, especially when the weather is hot or when chewing and playing. Even though it's important to allow them access to water when their system demands it, it's equally important to monitor their drinking habits. Bladder muscles are the last to develop, so what goes in, comes out quickly!

Establish a drinking station for your puppy and keep his dish there whether it's empty or full. Give your puppy water with his meals; after playing, chewing, or napping; or as you're on your way to his potty area.

If you're forgetful, it's better to fill his dish and leave it out for him throughout the day. Though it may delay your housetraining, it's better than having him go thirsty.

Restrict water after 7:30 p.m., unless you want to be up all night taking your puppy outside. If your puppy clearly needs a drink, either give him a small amount (no more than a cup for a large dog or ¼ cup for a small fry) or offer a couple of ice cubes.

Sleeping

We all love a good sleep, and you'll find that your puppy is no exception. Create a quiet space where your puppy can escape the daily hubbub and catch up on his z's whenever he needs too. Make it clear to friends and family that this area — perhaps a crate, bed, room, or pen — is off-limits to people when your puppy needs to nap. An overtired puppy is impossible to deal with. Like a child, a puppy will simply melt down. In fact, when pushed, his mouthy, testy behavior may turn into snappy aggression. Don't correct, worry, or admonish him. Have pity instead — he's exhausted.

Like kids, some puppies have a hard time putting themselves to sleep, especially when excitement levels are high. If you have kids, ask them to baby him by staying quiet until he's sleeping. Each time he seems tired, escort him to his resting area while saying a cue word like "bed." Eventually he'll go to this area on his own when he's tired.

Going potty

I don't think housetraining can be summed up any better than with the wonderful maxim "Whatever goes in must come out." Your puppy's biological clock will have him eliminating on demand. When his bladder or bowels are pressed, he'll let loose whether he's outside or on the papers — or on the rug, if you're not watching.

If your puppy is coming straight from Mom, she may have paved the way for you by urging her puppy to leave the "nest" when eliminating. This stage occurs between 7 and 8 weeks. If Mom was too relaxed or you picked up your puppy before this stage, the puppy will rely on you to clean up after him, a message of total care and devotion.

Your goals are to teach your puppy where to go and how to let you know if an obstacle (such as a door) is stopping him from getting there. Fortunately, you'll find this to be an easy task after you commit to a routine and are able to relax your expectations. Tension or expressed frustration is confusing; your puppy won't learn quickly and may grow increasingly more afraid of you. Your puppy needs a schedule, a routine, and a consistent pattern — all of which are within your grasp.

If you're having housetraining difficulties, refer to Chapter 12.

Playing

The urge to play and express himself energetically is one of the most natural responses in your puppy's repertoire. As with children, play and lighthearted interactions can be fabulous instructional tools and can be used exclusively during your first few months together.

How you play with your young puppy determines your long-term relationship. Rough, confrontational games, such as wrestling or tug of war, communicate confrontation, which can be detrimental to your relationship. A confronted puppy will be more likely to challenge you and ignore your direction. Games, such as the two-ball toss, soccer, and name games, instill cooperation and a fun-loving attitude — this puppy won't ever want to leave your side!

Speaking Doglish and Conveying Yourself as Top Dog to Your Puppy

Dogs have a lot of team spirit. Many people refer to this as their pack instinct, but I like to think of it in team terms instead. Team consciousness and the canine psyche have a lot in common. Teams focus on winning, with each player working for it, wanting it, thinking about it, and striving for it. Dogs live their entire lives, every waking moment, by this same team structure. Instead of winning, however, their mantra is bonding and survival. To your dog, you and your family are his team.

Some other, less obvious factors also determine a team's success: cooperation, structure, and mutual respect. Without these factors, even a group of phenomenal players would produce only chaos. A good team is organized so that all members know who's in charge and what's expected of them. And if one of them gets in trouble or gets hurt, he can trust that another teammate will help out.

For your dog to feel secure and safe, he needs to know who's in charge, and it's your job to teach him what you expect. In dog land, teams are organized in a hierarchy, so you must teach your four-legged friend that two-legged team members are the ones in charge. If you have more than one person in your household, teaching this concept requires some cooperation on everyone's part, but it's important if you want your puppy to mature into a dog who respects everybody.

If you don't organize the team hierarchy, your dog will, and that can be a real nightmare. If your dog has the personality to lead, you'll find yourself living in a very expensive doghouse under dog rule. If your dog doesn't have the personality to lead, but feels like he has to because no one else is, you'll end up with one big headache because dogs in this state are very hyper and confused.

So how do you organize your team and teach your dog the rules? You have to understand what motivates your dog's behavior, and you have to master his communication skills.

Your puppy doesn't understand English. Like a human plopped into a foreign country where no one speaks his language, your puppy will feel lost in translation. To be the best teacher, you need to be fluent in *Doglish,* the language of your puppy. Give your family or friends a lesson, too, and encourage consistency.

Doglish consists of three elements:

- ✔ Eye contact
- ✔ Body language
- ✔ Tone

In Doglish, words, feelings, and lengthy explanations don't count. Complex reasoning is impossible for your puppy to follow. In the following sections, I break down the three elements of Doglish so that you can put them into practice ASAP.

Figuring out Doglish may seem like hard work, but watching the techniques in action is quite fascinating. Your dog will respond to you more willingly if you make the effort to understand and use his language. With an ounce of effort, a little time, and some structure, you can earn your dog's respect, cooperation, and trust. Plus, you'll have a teammate who will be at your side when the cards are down. You can't beat that bargain.

Eye contact: Attention = affirmation

Are you constantly making eye contact with your puppy in stressful situations (someone's at the door and he's barking like a madman, or maybe he's stealing the dishrag)? Are you having trouble encouraging your pup to pay attention to you? Well, guess what? By making constant eye contact, your puppy thinks you're depending on him to be the leader. He thinks you want him to make all the judgment calls. Before you can figure out how to handle these situations (which I explain in Chapter 13), you have to understand that to train your puppy, you must encourage him to look to you for direction.

When you make eye contact with your puppy, you reinforce whatever behavior he's actively engaged in. Look your well-behaved pup in the eye and guess what you get? You got it: A well-behaved pup. However, if you make eye contact with your pup while he's running around the house with a wet wash rag flopping from his mouth, you'll reinforce that behavior because you're giving him the attention he so desperately wants.

Think of your puppy's energy on a scale from 1 to 10 with 1 being sleep and 10 being hyperexcited play. Between 1 and 8 is the focused, civil, happy zone, which includes all the endearing behaviors you love, such as relaxing during a heartfelt pat, bringing a toy to you for play, and chewing on a bone while you're busy. Between 8 and 10 is the impulsive, unfocused zone, which contains all the behaviors that drive you crazy. Some of these behaviors include jumping, stealing, nipping, and running out of control.

By realizing that dogs repeat behaviors that result in attention, you can see that you get what you interact with. By redirecting wild energy and focusing on the good stuff, you know what you get? A perfect little angel (well, almost).

The bottom line is this: Only make eye contact when your puppy is calm (in the 1 to 8 zone).

Believe it or not, the 8 to 10 zone is no picnic for your puppy. Even though he's rowdy and unfocused, this manic behavior is only a simple reaction to his misunderstanding of what you expect. Unfortunately, discipline doesn't help this situation because your puppy may interpret it as confrontational play. Structure, positive reinforcement, and training help the most. (See Part IV for more on resolving behavior problems.)

Body language: Stand up and stay calm

Body language is a funny thing. Imagine this: Your puppy becomes excited and hyper when company arrives at the front door. Desperate to save face, you start shouting and pushing your puppy as the company fends the both of you off with their coats. You try every possible command — Sit, Boomer! Down! Off! Bad dog! — but to no avail. The whole arrival scene is one big fiasco.

Body language is an integral part of Doglish. Play, tension, relaxation — they all have different postures. Your puppy thinks you're a dog, and he doesn't quite grasp the "I'm pushing you frantically because I'm unhappy with your greeting manners" concept. By dealing with the situation in this way, you're communicating differently than you think you are. In fact, by pushing and shouting you're actually copying his body language, which reinforces his behavior.

As you blaze the training trail, remember these guidelines:

- ✔ Stand upright and relax when directing your puppy. I call this the *Peacock Position.* (Imagine a peacock — beautiful and proud, chest out, confident, and in control.) When giving your puppy direction or a command, throw your shoulders back and stand tall like a peacock. Tell your family and friends about this position, and start strutting your stuff.

- ✔ Don't face off or chase your puppy when you're mad. He'll only think you're playing.

- ✔ When you're trying to quiet or direct your puppy, stay calm.

- ✔ Always remember that you set the example.

I hear your pleading already: Can I ever get down and play or cuddle with my puppy? Of course you can. Just don't play with your puppy when he's in a mischievous mood, or you're asking for trouble.

Tone: Using the three D's

If your puppy thinks of you as another dog and you start yelling, he hears barking. Barking (yelling) interrupts behavior; it doesn't instruct. It also increases excitement. Some of you may have a puppy who backs off from a situation when you yell (although he'll probably repeat the same behavior later). The reason he backs off is because your yelling frightens him. It's not because he understands what you're yelling about. Yelling is just no good.

Here are three tones you should commit to memory. I call them the three D's:

- **Delighted tone:** Use this tone when you want to praise your puppy. It should soothe him, not excite him. Find a tone that makes your pup feel warm and proud inside.

- **Directive tone:** Use this tone for your commands. It should be clear and authoritative, not harsh or sweet. Give your commands once from the Peacock Position.

    If you bend over when giving your puppy a command, don't be surprised if your puppy doesn't listen. You're doing the doggy equivalent of a *play bow,* which is a posture that invites a game. Think of it in human terms: If you ask me to have a seat while you're hunched over and looking at the floor, I'd be less interested in where to sit and more interested in what you're looking at. When giving your puppy directions, stand tall and proud like a peacock.

- **Discipline tone:** I'm not much of a disciplinarian. My approach encourages more structure than strictness, but you should have a few tones that tell your dog to back off or move on. The word you use doesn't matter as much as the tone. The tone should be shaming or disapproving, such as "How could you?" or "You better not touch that." Discipline has more to do with timing and tone than your puppy's transgressions.

Teaching kids how to use the proper tone

If you have kids, you've probably noticed that sometimes they call out to the puppy in a very high-pitched tone, and sometimes they don't pronounce commands properly, either.

Until kids are 12 years old, you're better off focusing on what they're doing right instead of homing in on their imperfections. My advice is simply to overenunciate all your commands so that the kids figure out how to pronounce them properly and in an appropriate tone. If you overenunciate each command, your kids will notice the effects and start mimicking you. And when your kids copy your intonations, they transfer the control from you to them.

Don't repeat your commands. Dogs don't understand words. Instead, they become used to sounds. Saying "Sit, sit, sit, Boomer, sit!" sounds different from "Sit" — which is what Boomer is used to. If you want your dog to listen when you give the first command, make sure you give it only once; then reinforce your expectations by positioning your dog. (When positioning, remember to gently squeeze the waist muscles and lift up on your puppy's collar.)

Gimme, Gimme, Gimme: Puppies Want All the Attention

Imagine being a puppy where humans are just big dogs milling all about, jabbering away in some nonsensical language, and providing virtually no instruction on what to do. When you lay a head in their lap or paw at them inquisitively, the human may shoo you off or lay a warm hand on your head, while often continuing to ignore your request for direction. The talking box on the wall and handheld objects hold more interest for the humans than your interaction. You hear noise and more noise. You catch sniffs that can't be explored or trailed. And you see sights that you're expected to ignore. Being a puppy in a human's world can be tough sometimes.

The power of positive attention

When I ask my clients what they do when they catch their puppy resting or chewing a bone quietly, most say, "Nothing. It's a moment of peace." I appreciate such honesty. However, it's those times when they ought to be showering their puppy with attention. Not wild, twist-and-shout, hoot-and-holler attention, but instead calm, soothing, loving attention that makes the puppy smile inside. A soft whispering praise is best mixed with a massagelike pat. My mantra is that your dog will repeat whatever action you pay attention to.

So you decide. What would you rather have: A puppy who stays by your side with a chew bone or a frantic sock stealer who races around the house like a maniac? If you prefer the sock stealer, close this book. But, if the quiet bone-chewer image appeals to you, stick with me — you're going places.

Dogs are drawn to positive energy fields. Think of yourself as his teacher and mentor. If you keep up the cheer, your puppy won't want to be anywhere else.

Why negative attention doesn't work

Picture a very excited, jumping puppy. You're trying to read the newspaper calmly, but he wants your attention. What do you think would happen if you tried to correct the dog by pushing him down and screaming "Off!"? In all likelihood, the puppy would jump again. Do you know why? Because you just gave him attention. Attention, in a dog's mind, includes anything from dramatic body contact to a simple glance. Yes, even looking at your dog reinforces his behavior.

Though this phenomenon may sound far-fetched at first, it's actually pretty elementary. Puppies think of you as another dog. If they get excited and then you get excited, they think you're following their lead. By mimicking their energy level, you communicate that they must interpret new situations. The fact that you're upset with their behavior just doesn't register. Being upset is a human emotion. Excitement and body contact, however, is the dog way. Even if you push your puppy so hard that he stops and slinks away, your only accomplishment is scaring him. And who wants to train a pup through fear? Trust me, there's a better way.

Let me give you another example. What happens if your puppy grabs a sock and everyone in the household stops to chase him? Think you have a dog party? You bet. Because the puppy views all humans as dogs, he's thinking "What fun!" as he dives behind the couch and under the table. Chasing doesn't come across as discipline; it comes across as *prize envy* — "Whatever I have must be really good because everyone wants it!"

Dogs often interpret negative attention as confrontational play: "You're animated, you're loud, and you're fierce. Let's play rough!" Out-of-control negative attention reinforces the very behavior you're trying to change. To resolve these problems, be patient and read on.

Teacher Be Taught: Showing Your Pup How to Live in a Human World

If this training isn't coming naturally to you, don't be discouraged. To be a school teacher for children, you'd have to enroll in 4 to 6 years of college education. However, to teach your puppy, you only need to understand the concepts and exercises outlined in this book.

A lot goes into being a good dog trainer, and most of it's mental. Puppies, like humans, have spirits that you must understand and encourage in ways that make sense to the dog. Your puppy has bestowed on you the highest honor, and it's one you'd never receive from a human: a lifetime commitment to respect your judgment and abide by your rules. You need only to show him how.

In order to show your puppy how to respect you and your rules, you need to remember three key things that a good dog trainer does:

- ✔ Accepts and modifies his own personality
- ✔ Never blames the pup
- ✔ Recognizes the pup's unique personality

Recognize and modify your personality

Now's the time to analyze yourself. Take out a pen and paper and write down three adjectives to describe your personality. What kind of person are you? Demanding? Sweet? Forgiving? Compulsive? Be honest. Then compare your personality with your pup's character (refer to Chapter 4 for puppy personality types).

If you discover that you're demanding, and your dog is sweet, someone's going to have to change. Making too many demands on a sweet dog will only frighten him, and he'll shut down or run away when training begins. If you're compulsive and you have a laid-back dog, you'll be laughed at. Have you ever seen a dog laugh at his owner? It's quite embarrassing. For you to be a good dog trainer, you must modify your expectations to better suit your dog's personality.

Never blame the pup

Believe it or not, puppies don't react out of spite. Your puppy's behavior is directly related to your own reactions whether they're positive or negative.

So how do you handle unruly situations? The first step is to stop blaming the dog.

Never run at your puppy. Racing headlong toward a puppy is scary. Visualize someone two to four times your size barreling down on you. Talk about overwhelming. Even though your puppy may collapse in fear or run from you, he won't take anything from the situation. Consider other options, such as using treat cups, which is described in Chapter 11.

Recognize the pup's unique personality

Yes, puppies have personalities, too. If you've had more than one pup in your lifetime, I'm sure you know exactly what I'm talking about. Many of my clients have started their sob stories with the same line: "My last dog was so easy!" I respond with a smile, and then say, "But, this isn't your last dog. This dog is unique. And to train him, you must begin by understanding his personality."

No matter what his personality, your pup needs to interact and be understood. Puppies love to share their secret language with you, and they're content staying close to you as long as you include them in your daily activities.

The Five Stages of Puppy Development

In Chapter 14, I break down lessons, games, and fun activities you can do with your puppy stage by stage. Though you may be dreaming of an agility champion, setting him on course before he's housetrained is like pressuring a toddler to balance your checkbook. Like children, your puppy's mind will develop along a predictable course. Knowing this course will help you understand what you can expect and what you should teach your puppy and will help define your expectations and bolster your puppy's success rate.

Infancy (8 to 12 weeks)

Life for a young puppy is centered on the five basic needs: eating, drinking, sleeping, eliminating, and playing. Even though your puppy is capable of learning, don't expect too much at this stage. You should be feeding your puppy three to four times a day, taking him out constantly, and letting him sleep when he wants to. Your puppy will learn best when training is incorporated into playtime. Show him the basic stuff: Hang out with him, use his name, and introduce the leash. Discipline will only frighten your puppy and erode your relationship: He's simply too young to comprehend it. Have fun and take lots of photos because your puppy will be all grown up before you know it!

The terrible twos (12 to 16 weeks)

As your puppy matures, you'll notice his personality developing. He'll get a bit bolder and braver and will be harder to impress. By 12 weeks, his brain is fully developed and he's ready to learn. He's old enough to understand and remember your direction, but he's also still too young to take matters into his own paws.

Puppies at this stage are starting to learn things, whether they're guided or not. If you don't train your puppy, he'll train you.

The budding adolescent (16 to 24 weeks)

Suddenly, you may notice that a strange dog, who looks just like your puppy, is slowly taking over your house. Welcome to adolescence. Be prepared and consider yourself warned: You're about to enter the bratty zone. Try not to panic — all of your puppy's behaviors are normal. As much as you may want to hide under the couch for the next three months, don't! This is the best time to start training. Because this stage lasts about eight weeks, lessons are broken down week by week. Breaking lessons down allows your puppy to feel successful and allows him to master each exercise before you apply it in his day-to-day world. This concept is similar to letting children master the alphabet before expecting them to spell.

Puppy puberty (6 to 9 months)

Puppies at this stage go through a major transformation called growing up. You remember growing up, with all its hormones, rebellion, confusion, and curiosity. Ah, puberty. It's never a pretty sight. On top of these typical growing pains is the awakening of breed-specific instincts that tell herders to herd, hunters to hunt, guarders to guard, and pullers to pull. This stage is utter canine chaos and all while they're still cutting their baby teeth! So here you have this puppy/dog who's full of hormones, high spirits, and anxiety. It's no wonder he may give you the puppy equivalent of a teenage eye roll when you give him a command.

The trying teen (9 to 12 months)

Your first milestone is in front of you, but it's not over yet. A puppy at this stage usually calms down and manages better on his own. He'll chew his bone quietly, potty where he ought to, and listen most of the time. Okay, sometimes he'll still ignore you, but please understand: Puppies at this stage want to behave, but their teenage genes are relentlessly telling them to make one more glorious attempt for Top Dog status.

This stage brings with it a subtle campaign of defiance. You may not think a sloppy, sideways sit is a very big deal, but your dog makes a little mental check mark every time you let him get away with something. You can't relax your efforts just yet!

Chapter 7

Socialization and Civility

. . . .

In This Chapter

▶ Calming your puppy during socialization

▶ Conditioning your puppy to accept people of all sizes, races, and genders

▶ Introducing your puppy to wild animals, noises, and other interesting objects

▶ Handling a pup's wary or defensive response

. . . .

Your puppy is hard-wired with a prime socialization window. During this window, which is between 8 to 12 weeks, her brain is developing and she's receptive to new experiences. She's constantly looking to you for your interpretation of these experiences. This is the time to introduce her to everything she will encounter throughout her life, from objects and people to noises and other animals.

Even though some of your early excursions may be restricted until your puppy is fully inoculated, make every effort to expose her to a variety of stimulants so that she'll be more relaxed when she's presented with something new.

If your puppy is older than 12 weeks, don't despair. Even though your puppy has passed her impression window, she's still open to your example when she gets overwhelmed or excited. A noticeably defensive or wary reaction simply indicates that your puppy has no conscious memory of such an occurrence and isn't sure how to act. In these circumstances, your reactions to both the situation and the puppy are important. Placating, soothing, or corrective responses actually intensify a puppy's reactions by focusing attention on the inappropriate behavior.

Wondering just how to handle your puppy during this formative time? This chapter is here to help.

Calming Your Puppy Based on Her Age

Puppies, like children, go through developmental stages, and each stage brings with it a new perspective. In the earliest stages, everything is new, and your puppy's trust in you is innocent and faithful. As she ages, however, she's prone to challenge and question your opinion while still being unsure of life's variety. Maturing puppies, especially those going through adolescence and puberty, have their own set of opinions and must be consistently persuaded to mind you. All this makes for a creative approach to socialization.

Acclimating a young pup (8 to 12 weeks)

When she's very young, your puppy will mirror your reaction in all new situations. If you're nervous, she will be too. If you get excited, uncomfortable, or edgy, she'll follow suit. Expose your puppy to new experiences under controlled circumstances so you'll be centered and prepared to deal with your puppy's reaction.

Young puppies generally react to new situations in one of four ways:

- **Fearfully:** Noted by a hesitant body posture, these puppies pull back or scurry to leave the environment. Often they scratch to be held or acknowledged.

- **Calmly:** These pups are patiently observant and have a relaxed body posture and mild curiosity.

- **Actively:** Because they're very interactive, these puppies explore the new stimulation with gusto and may be hard to calm down or refocus.

- **Defensively:** Puppies who act defensively may back up, hold still, or run forward. Or they may do all three maneuvers and bark or vocalize their feelings in some way. Their ears may be flattened against their heads, and they may hide behind your legs or try to climb up into your arms or lap.

Any attention given to a puppy reinforces her reaction, which is fine *if and only if* your puppy is reacting calmly. Other responses need redirecting. Read on to find out how.

Instilling confidence in a fearful pup

Fear is a common response that shows your puppy doesn't like to make interpretations alone. Because of your pup's dependence, new situations will demand your guidance and direction.

Finding the Red Zone

If your puppy has an intense reaction (one that's fearful, overexcited, or defensive) to a new situation or person, determine her Red Zone: the distance from the stimulus where she can stand comfortably. Stand just outside this zone and handle your puppy calmly using commands, toys, or treats to keep her focus.

Don't coddle your puppy if she has a fearful reaction. Your immediate attention indicates submission, not leadership. Your lowered body posture and high-pitched tone convey the message that you're afraid, too.

A better response on your part is to stand tall, either ignoring your puppy or kneeling at her side. *Brace* her by clipping your thumb under her collar and holding her in a sitting position. Above all else, though, you need to remain calm and assured: Your puppy will be impressed by your confidence.

Capturing the attention of a calm pup

A relaxed reaction is a good sign that your puppy will take everything in stride. Some puppies are so relaxed, however, that they don't register the distraction you're introducing, such as a grate surface or a uniformed police officer. If this sounds familiar, use treats to bring your puppy's attention to the situation at hand.

Containing the excitement of an active pup

The puppies in this energetic group love life. To them, new experiences hold endless possibilities. Even at a young age, passion emanates in everything they do. The goal in new situations and introductions isn't to bring these pups out of their shells. Instead, the goal is to successfully contain their excitement. To displace their enthusiasm, use toys and the bracing technique.

Defusing a defensive pup

An early defensive reaction (before 12 weeks) should be noted and taken seriously. If the tips in this book don't lessen your puppy's intensity, hire a professional. The onset of adolescence, with the release of adult hormones, will intensify an aggressive response. Deal with this behavior immediately.

In the meantime, fit the puppy with a head collar (see Chapter 5), and keep her at someone's side in all new situations. The direction "Stay" should be repeated as this puppy is braced.

Catching up an older pup (12 weeks and older)

A puppy past the critical socialization time may have a more pronounced reaction to new situations, especially if she has no similar experience in her memory bank. For example, an older puppy who hasn't navigated a stairway or hardwood floor may actually be terrified at the prospect. How you handle such a situation determines her future attitude. A dog who is fearful of specific things is more leery of new situations throughout her life.

Discover your puppy's body language and take it very seriously. Focus on her eyes, body position, tail, and mouth. Even though she can't talk in words, your puppy will tell you everything if you listen with your eyes. Check out Table 7-1 for guidance.

Table 7-1	Reading Your Puppy's Body Language				
Body Part	**Fearful**	**Undecided**	**Relaxed**	**Active**	**Defensive**
Eyes	Squinting, darting, unfocused	Focused or shifting	Focused	Attentive, focused	Glaring, hard
Body	Low, arched, pulled back and down	Shifting from forward to pulled back, approaching but then immediately avoiding the person	Relaxed	Comfortable posture, moving side to side	Pitched forward, stone still, tense
Tail	Tucked under belly, wagging low	Tucked under belly, arched slightly over back, fluctuating between the two	Still, gently swinging above rump	High, wagging enthusiastically	Still above rump or arched above back in a tight repetitive wag
Mouth	Pulled back, often in a semi-smile	Terse, trembling	Normal	Panting, normal, may be parted in a vocalization	Tight, unflinching, may be parted in a growl or vocalization

Turn your "can't do" puppy into a "can do" dog by being the example you want her to follow. When your puppy's response is pronounced, you need to stay very calm. Keep your eyes focused on the situation at hand (not on your puppy) and interact with the stimulus — be it a person, situation, or object — in the manner you want her to mirror.

If you look at your puppy or even glance back at her, your posture and visual confirmation may get misconstrued as insecurity. For example, think of playing on a team: The captain wouldn't shout a direction and then look to the players for confirmation. The same rules apply with your pup. When directing your puppy, stand confident and focus on the situation at hand.

Teaching Your Puppy to Be Accepting of All People

Regardless of your puppy's age, her ability to relate to others around her will be determined by three variables:

- ✔ Breed influences
- ✔ Socialization experience
- ✔ Your example

Even though your puppy's breed drives are predetermined, you can vastly shape the future through socialization and positive modeling.

Socializing your young puppy (8 to 12 weeks)

A young puppy will look to you to interpret everything in her life. How you interact with and greet people from all walks of life will be her greatest example. Disciplinary issues evolve when too much excitement is present during greetings. These issues evolve because your puppy interprets this excitement as hyperactive play, and though it can be fun initially, it gets old fast!

A better plan is to actually have a plan. Expose and introduce your puppy to as many new people as time allows. You should follow the same routine whether the person is 9 or 90, dressed down, uniformed, or in costume.

Mothers are right when they say good manners start at home. When greeting your puppy, be very casual. Even though you may be beside yourself with delight, stay calm and interact with your puppy only when she's calm too.

Condition your puppy to a leash and collar, and keep these items on her when meeting new people. Use them to guide her, as if you're holding a young child's hand. When possible, ask people to ignore any extreme reactions, from hyperactivity to fear or defensiveness. Simply put, when she reacts extremely, act as if your puppy isn't even there. When applied for a few minutes, this approach will de-escalate any concern and will condition your puppy to look to and reflect your reaction.

After the new person is an established presence, which takes about one to five minutes, kneel down next to your puppy, *brace* her by clipping your thumb under her collar, and hold her in a sitting position (see Figure 7-1). Repeat "Say hello" as the person pats your puppy.

Figure 7-1:
Bracing reassures your young puppy when meeting unfamiliar people.

If your puppy is fearful or tense, ask the person to shake a treat cup and treat her so that she shapes a new and more positive outlook.

Shaping up older puppies

Is your older pup out of control or poorly conditioned to greeting new people? Don't give it another thought. She may become hyper when the doorbell rings, react defensively to men in uniform, or act warily around toddlers, but you can reshape her focus with patience, ingenuity, and calm consistency.

When left unchecked, such behavior may result in a dog who's permanently wary of children or defensive with the delivery man. Consider living with this erratic behavior for ten or more years — I guarantee it won't be fun. However, this is one of the few times you have the power to reshape your future.

Remember the following three key things, regardless of her pre-established habits, when introducing your puppy to new situations and people:

 ✔ Whoever is in front is in charge.

 ✔ A confident and calm body posture conveys confidence and self-assurance.

 ✔ A steady voice will be followed.

No matter what your puppy's behavior is, it developed in large part because of your attention. Puppies repeat anything that ensures interaction — they don't care whether it's negative or positive interaction. If your pup is hyper, you likely tried to calm her by grabbing her fur, pushing her, or holding her. When a defensive or wary reaction results in a soothing and high-pitched "It's okay," the translation is that of mutual concern. What this puppy needs is a human example of confidence, which is conveyed with clear direction and a calm, upright body posture.

To resolve this greeting dilemma and recondition your pup, do the following:

 ✔ Create a greeting station in sight of, but at least 6 feet behind, the greeting door (as detailed in Chapter 13).

 ✔ Secure a short 2-foot leash to the area and repeat "Back" as you lead your puppy and attach her before opening the door.

 ✔ Ignore your puppy until she has fully calmed down.

Though it may be difficult to ignore her initial vocalizations and spasms, it won't take long for her to discover that a relaxed posture gets immediate attention.

Encourage everyone in your home to respond in kind: No one gives the pup attention until she's considerably calmer. You can leave a bone or toy at her greeting station to help her displace her excitement or frustration.

If your puppy is defensive or fearful, put a head collar on her. This head collar automatically relaxes your puppy because the weight placed over her nose and behind her head stimulates the same pressure points her mother would use to calm her.

Also, in order to help her become used to new situations and people, take your puppy out and socialize her with as many new people as you can find.

Teach and use the directions "Let's go," "Stay," "Down," "Wait," and "Back" as described in Chapter 14. Here's what these commands teach your pup:

- ✔ **Let's go:** Instructs your puppy to walk behind you and watch for your direction.

- ✔ **Stay:** Stresses impulse control and focus. Precede this direction with a "Sit" or "Down" direction.

- ✔ **Under:** Directs your puppy to lie under your legs or under a table. These safe places reinforce that you're her guardian and protector.

- ✔ **Wait:** Instructs your puppy to stop in her tracks and look to you before proceeding.

- ✔ **Back:** Directs your puppy to get behind you and reminds her that you're in charge.

If your puppy is wary of a person, ask him or her to ignore the puppy and to avoid all eye contact. Eye contact is often interpreted as predatory or confrontational and will often intensify your puppy's reaction.

Introducing your puppy to people of all shapes and sizes

Getting your puppy comfortable with life needs to start with introducing her to the variety of people she'll meet in her lifetime. Each person will have a unique look and smell. So that your puppy doesn't mature into a dog that singles anyone out, you need to socialize her early on with the whole spectrum. Check out Table 7-2 for guidance.

The use of a creamy spread (such as peanut butter, tofu, cheese, or yogurt) encourages a gentle interaction. Infrequent use means that your puppy will be enamored with any situation that produces this delight.

Table 7-2		Meeting New People			
Human	*Directions*	*Leash*	*Position*	*Treat Location*	*Comments*
Baby	"Gentle" and "Stay"	Yes, if excitable	Braced to prevent jumping	On the floor, or put a creamy spread on the baby's shoe	Using a creamy spread on the baby's shoe will direct your puppy to this body part. Say "Ep, ep" to discourage facial interaction.
Child	"Sit," "Down," "Back," "Stay," "Gentle," "Follow," and "Say hello"	Yes. Consider two so the child can direct if the dog is trustworthy.	Braced or "Back" behind your feet	Ideally, the child gives the pup a treat. It can also be thrown if your puppy's wild or wary.	A creamy spread in a tube or on a long spoon can be extended to a calm puppy in a "Sit" or "Down" position. Teach your puppy a trick (Chapter 22) to encourage a happy interaction.
Opposite sex	"Follow," "Stay," and "Say hello"	Only as needed in public or if your puppy has an extreme reaction	Braced or at your side if your puppy's reaction is inappropriate	Other person gives the treat unless your puppy is wary. Then treat can be tossed or given by you in close proximity to the other person.	Be calm and comfortable, not unnaturally excited or affectionate. Puppies sense feigned affection and find it odd and unconvincing.
Costume	"Back," "Stay," and "Under"	Absolutely. Costumes are scary for puppies, and the leash gives you the ability to "hold your puppy's hand."	Braced in the "Stay" position. Kneel in front and hold her steadily. Don't pet her until she's calm.	Yes, initially.	Wear the costume yourself. Place it on the floor and surround it with treats. Allow your puppy to watch you put it on.
Ethnicities	"Back," "Stay," and "Say hello"	In public and when unmanageable within the home. Otherwise, no.	Braced during a greeting. Use a ball or toy to encourage a normal response.	Yes, when meeting the person directly. Otherwise, no.	Dogs aren't racist, but some will notice variations in skin color. Seek out different environments to expose your dog to.

(continued)

Table 7-2 (continued)

Human	Directions	Leash	Position	Treat Location	Comments
Shapes and sizes	"Back," "Stay," "Follow," and "Say hello"	Use a dragging leash and hold the leash if your dog is startled or reactive.	Braced during a greeting. Use a ball or toy to encourage a normal response.	Yes, when meeting the person directly. Otherwise, no.	A trip to town will expose your pup to a variety of body shapes and sizes.
Uniforms	"Follow," "Stay," and "Say hello"	Leash initially and always in public.	Walk by nonchalantly and say "Follow." Brace if unsettled. Use "Stay" direction to stabilize reaction.	Use treats to encourage your puppy's focus on you when this person is present.	Wear a hat or costume if your dog is overtly reactive. Expose early and often, especially to delivery people.
Sporting Equipment	"Stay" and "Sniff it"	Yes	Discover your puppy's Red Zone (see sidebar earlier in this chapter). Observe at a distance and gradually bring your puppy closer.	Use treats or a toy to encourage your puppy's focus.	Lay the equipment on the floor and encourage your puppy to "Sniff it" as you explore together.
People holding equipment	"Stay" and "Sniff it"	Yes, unless you're holding the equipment.	Discover your puppy's Red Zone (see sidebar earlier in this chapter). Observe at a distance and gradually bring your puppy closer.	Use treats or a toy to encourage your puppy's focus.	Lay the equipment on the floor or hold it yourself. When you see another person holding equipment, do treat exercises at a distance.

Conditioning Your Puppy to Life's Surprises

Socializing your puppy to all of life's surprises is just as important as training her during the first year. Though a puppy may know a four-star stay in your living room, if she falls to pieces once you hit the road, you won't be able to take her anywhere. And your puppy has so much more in store for her than a variety of different people. Exposing your puppy to all of life's surprises will encourage calm acceptance and healthy curiosity to anything new the two of you may encounter.

Other animals

I recently worked with a 1-year-old terrier-whippet mix who was rescued from New Orleans after Hurricane Katrina. Not only was snow a new concept to her, but squirrels were riveting. Sweet and demure, she turned 180 degrees when facing the prospect of chasing a yard full of busy, gray tidbits. Three directions were needed for this pup: "Back," "Sit-stay," and "Wait." Impulse control was the order of the day.

Whether your pup is young or old, she must learn impulse control when she notices other animals in her surroundings. When you notice a critter before your puppy does, instruct her by saying "Back" and guide her to your side. Then kneel down facing the critter and use the command "Sit-stay" to encourage your pup's containment. If your puppy's radar alerts first, however, you'll notice it in her ears, which will be erect and riveted. She'll orient herself toward the distraction. When she does, direct "Back" and kneel down to brace her. Finally, instruct "Stay."

As your puppy's impulse control matures, encourage her to follow you by using the "Follow" direction. You can discourage any interest with a quick tug of the leash. Praise and treat her for resisting the temptation.

Weather patterns

Your puppy's first thunderstorm may be a memorable event. The best thing you can do is absolutely nothing. Emotional reassurance on your part will get misconstrued as mutual fear, and your puppy could quickly develop a phobic reaction to the situation. By staying calm, reading a book, or laying low, you're setting an example of how to act in a storm. Also consider taping a storm and playing it at low levels during play or feeding until your puppy is conditioned to the sound.

If your puppy has already developed a fearful reaction to storms, fit her for a head collar and guide her on the lead through each storm, acting as though nothing is happening. When possible, stay on the ground floor, offering your puppy nothing more than a flavorful bone. Pay attention to her only when she's relaxed. Her reactivity will improve in time. Speak to your veterinarian about medication if the lead training doesn't work.

Some puppies don't like going outside in the rain and others don't ever want to come in. Even though your puppy is unlikely to change her mind about the rain, you can try winning her over by leaving her inside as you play outside in the rain — but make sure you play where she can watch. If you have no luck, it's time to get a big golf umbrella and plan quick outings with your pup.

Snow and cold present another issue, especially for tiny or thin-coated breeds. When the temperature drops, your puppy's muscles contract. This contraction includes your puppy's bladder muscles, which makes elimination difficult, if not impossible. Consider a puppy coat and, dare I say it, booties when faced with cold weather. If your puppy is small, consider teaching her to go on paper exclusively or in addition to eliminating outside. If you don't like the papers inside your home, consider putting them in the hallway or garage and using them only when the weather's bad. Flip to Chapter 12 for more on paper training.

Objects

You're walking down the road, whistling and strolling happily along when suddenly you notice three gigantic black garbage bags wafting in the wind. You visually assess the situation and are quickly done with the thought process. It's not, however, so easy for your puppy. Puppies assess new objects with their mouths and can't emotionally settle until they've had a good sniff. Whenever possible, approach the situation like a grown dog. Doing so will provide a confident, assured example for your puppy to follow.

Let the leash go slack when safe and hold the handle as you approach the object. Kneel or bend down to your puppy's level and pretend to sniff the object confidently. Wait patiently as your puppy assesses your reaction. When she approaches, speak calmly, petting her and tucking her into your side when she's comfortable.

If you can't approach the object, simply kneel at your pup's side and brace her as you remind her to "Stay" and then "Follow."

Various noises

Included on my list of important noises to socialize my puppy, Whoopsie, to were fireworks, trucks, construction noises, sirens, and a baby's cries (because I was pregnant at the time). Each time I either approached a loud situation or set one up, I kneeled and braced Whoopsie. If she was startled, I would back up until she was more at ease and then would repeat the handling technique. When she could comfortably face the distraction, I would calmly instruct her to "Stay." Gradually we moved closer and eventually the instruction to "Follow" was enough to assure her because she had integrated the noise into her stimulus memory bank. I encourage you to follow this same approach with your puppy.

If your puppy has a more startled reaction, or if your puppy is older and unfamiliar with a noise or situation, you need to craft your approach to limit the intensity. If your pup looks like she might attack or run from a distraction, she's clearly in a state of panic. Retreat from the situation immediately and figure out your puppy's Red Zone (refer to the sidebar earlier in this chapter). Work on treat- and toy-based lessons, brace her, and gradually move closer to the distraction.

If a specific sound is unsettling to your puppy, tape-record it. Play it at gradually increasing volumes while your puppy is playing or eating. If she's still startled by the noise, lower the volume and play it in a distant room.

Places

You'll have to wait until your puppy is inoculated to go on field trips. However, when your vet gives you the green light, go, go, go! Away from her home turf, surrounded by the unknown, your puppy will suddenly grow hyper with impulsive excitement, fearful, or defensive. Each reaction gives you the perfect opportunity to step in and direct her by using all the techniques found in Chapters 16 and 17. Even though these techniques initially take a commitment of time, you'll have the lifelong freedom to take your dog along with you wherever you go!

Regardless of your puppy's response, use the directions "Let's go," "Stay," and "Wait" as you navigate new places together. By doing so, your direction and posture says to your pup, "I'm the leader, follow me!"

In addition, bring a familiar bed or mat for your puppy to ride on in the car and to sit on when you'll expect her to be still. If you're going to an outdoor restaurant, her veterinarian, or school, bring her mat along and direct her to it. Her mat will act like a security blanket, making her feel relieved, happy, and safe.

Quieting an excitable response

Freaking out with excitement is a common response to a new place for some puppies. Fit this type of pup with a head collar and brace her frequently. If she's motivated by food, use it to focus her attention. Stay very calm and be the example you want her to follow. Brace her securely before people approach you.

You'll have to work hard to teach this type of pup not to jump. If she rolls onto her belly during a greeting, say "Belly up" to encourage that response.

Correcting a fearful reaction

A fearful puppy needs a guardian and protector to step up and direct her: Here's your curtain call! Avoid the temptation to bend and soothe your puppy. Instead, use a head collar to guide her — a neck collar can intensify fears because it may feel as if it's choking her. Brace her when she's most distressed and stave off admirers until she's more sure-footed. When it's time for introductions, bring yummy treats and be generous. Point training is another effective technique that helps build confidence; you can read about it in Chapter 11.

Chilling out a defensive reaction

This defensive puppy takes life a little too seriously. Socializing her will be necessary to calm her intensity. Put a head collar on her and sit on the outskirts of a given activity or social setting. Teach your puppy the term "Back" to mean "Stay behind me because I'm in charge." Repeat "Stay" when necessary, and remind her to "Follow." Over time, your pup's resolve will melt. Make a commitment now to socialize the paw off this puppy. However, remember that it may take many outings to mellow her caution to where she'll become more pleasant to have around.

Chapter 8

Kids and Puppies

One of the hallmarks of my childhood was my dog, Shawbee, who was a Husky-Shepherd mix. She was my constant companion, waiting for me at the bus stop, hanging outside the church while I took ballet lessons, sharing my ice-cream cone on a hot summer day. Nowadays, dogs and kids rarely have the freedom to bond this way. The world today is different from when I was a child. We have computers. Most communities have leash laws. Dogs left outside are stolen. People are even more dog phobic. Unfortunately, times have changed, and new problems are cropping up.

Today, kids are often overstimulated at a young age, and they have less time to hang out with dogs. Riding bikes and running around is often limited to parks where dogs aren't allowed. To boot, young puppies and young kids don't always hit it off. In some circumstances, the puppy views the child as another puppy to bite and bully. I've dealt with situations where the kids don't like playing with the puppy anymore because "he bites too hard." At other times, a child becomes jealous of the attention the new addition is getting, which leads to an all-out war between the child and the puppy.

All this talk may sound depressing, but these are things you must think about. Even though a good child-puppy relationship can happen, it takes time, patience, and understanding. Don't worry. This chapter can help.

Encouraging Positive Interactions between Kids and Pups

Puppies and children are a lot alike. Both like to be connected to adults and like to take direction from others who seem to know more. At a very young age both are astoundingly aware of what gets attention, and they will go to great lengths to either please those they respect or run the show.

As puppies and children grow up, their impulses and hormones mature in kind, spawning egocentric manners, possessiveness, and disrespect. Even though it's frustrating, each experience is a great sign that your beloved is developing normally. As the days pass and adolescence hits, don't be too surprised if either one gives you the eye roll. Adolescence is an emotionally confusing time. When puberty hits, both species may want to disown you completely — remember going through all these emotions when you were that age? It's not fun no matter how many legs you walk on.

To bring out the best in your household, be mindful of where your children are emotionally and what your puppy is capable of at the time. Your child and puppy will be most cooperative when they're understood and you stay positive. In this section, I give you some suggestions.

Use positive catchphrases

Kids don't respond well to nagging. Phrases such as "Don't do this" and "Don't do that" have a tendency to go in one ear and out the other. Like dogs and puppies, kids respond better to a more positive approach.

Catchphrases, such as the following, can be very helpful:

- ✔ **"Four paw rule":** This catchphrase helps the kids remember not to pet Rex until all four paws are planted on the floor. And, this catchphrase sounds a lot better than "Stop calling the dog on the couch." (At which point, I would defiantly do exactly what you said not to do, if I were the kid.)

- ✔ **"It looks like rain":** When the kids come in from school, have them "look for rain" until your puppy calms down — that is, tell them to cross their arms in front of their body and look to the sky (see Figure 8-1). You can also have your kids look for rain when the pup jumps into their laps for attention. This body language will communicate calmly that jumping is an ineffective way to interact.

If your puppy is just too big for the "looking for rain" technique to be effective, use a spray bottle filled with water or a water-vinegar mix to discourage your pup from jumping. Instead of aiming at his face, however, spray the mist in between your child and the puppy.

Figure 8-1:
Kids should "look for rain" until the puppy calms down.

- ✔ **"Kisses":** This trick is fabulous. Rub a frozen stick of butter or peanut butter on the back of the kids' hands, have them extend their hands, and together instruct "Kisses." The trick not only teaches your puppy to kiss a hand that reaches toward him, but it also discourages nipping.

- ✔ **"Thumb clip":** This is a kid's version of bracing (see Chapter 7). Show your children how to clip their thumb over your puppy's collar and fan their fingers across his chest. This technique is a good way to discourage jumping and calm your puppy down.

These catchphrases are just some of my all-time favorites. Get creative and discover some catchphrases that work for you. Keep me informed of new ones because I'm always on the lookout for clever ways to help kids and dogs get along together.

Play groovy games

No tug of war, please! Even though your puppy will bait your children and your kids will like the game, discourage it. Your puppy must learn that when hands are touching an object, teeth let go — period. Tug of war can lead to serious consequences because your puppy most likely won't be able to distinguish between a stuffed toy or leash and an item of clothing (see Figure 8-2).

Breaking the cycle of tug of war

A 6-year-old girl was strangled to death after she was sent out to play with her 3-year-old Golden Retriever. The Golden Retriever was overstimulated in play and tugged on the girl's scarf until she suffocated and died. Even though no words can express the family's sorrow, there is a moral to this story: No tug of war. Your dog must learn never to pull on an object that is worn or held by a human.

Puppies love to tug and wrestle as much as, or more than, children do: Tugging is an age-old developmental game of control and power. It has, however, no place in a child-friendly household. Kids can get easily overwhelmed or overpowered by a puppy who can't differentiate between a toy, an article of clothing, a cherished stuffed animal, a doll, or hands and fingers.

If your puppy is a tugging addict, try the following:

✔ Tie objects to other grounded objects, such as banisters or trees, and encourage your puppy to tug on these. A banister won't budge, nor will a tree — this technique is a great way for your puppy to vent his impulses.

✔ Refer to Chapter 23 to teach your puppy a solid "Give" reaction.

✔ Place your puppy on a drag leash. Doing this enables quick interference if your puppy begins to get noticeably rowdy. If you suspect he's getting riled up, interfere quickly with a tug of the leash as you say "No." Then, refocus him onto another activity.

✔ Use the spray-away techniques described in this chapter to discourage your puppy from tugging with or on your children.

✔ Bait your puppy to play with or grab at a toy. Tug him sternly if he jumps or grabs at the objects impulsively. Regardless of temptation, this quick tug of the leash will teach your puppy not to grab or tug anything held by or worn by you and your family.

Check out the sidebar "Breaking the cycle of tug of war" to find out how to discourage your pup from playing tug of war.

Figure 8-2:
A simple game of tug of war leads to nipping and tugging.

To eliminate tug of war, you must take away the rope toys, shared stuffed animals, and socks. Warn the kids that you will tolerate absolutely no more wrestling, teasing, or chasing the puppy. Jeez, you say, what's a kid supposed to do for fun? Check out Chapter 23, which contains ten great games you can enjoy with your pup.

Monkey see, monkey do. You are your children's best example. If you remain calm and structured with your puppy, your child copies you. If you're frantically confused or you encourage rough play, your child copies that, too.

Inspire motivational projects

There's no question that getting a puppy will add to your life — but in the beginning there's a lot of work to be done. Multiple feedings, hourly housebreak runs, and play, play, and more play. If you get frustrated with your puppy or speak badly of his transgressions, you may notice that people in your household lose their enthusiasm for your new addition. Instead, think through activities that could motivate everyone's cooperation and bring a united front for this newest member of your family.

Try doing the following with your children:

- **Make sticker charts:** Make an activity chart, and every time one of your kids completes a task (feeding, walking, or brushing your puppy), she can add a sticker to her column. If you have more than one kid, you'll need plenty of column space. See Figure 8-3 for an example.

Weekly Fun Chart

Time	Activity	M	T	W	Th	F	S	Su
7 a.m.	Out							
7:15	Feed and Water							
7:30	Out and Play							
8:00 – 11:30	Lead, Station, or Crate, Supervised Freedom							
11:30	Out and Play							
Noon	Feeding and Water							
12:15 p.m.	Out and Play							
12:30 – 3:30	Lead, Station, Crate, Supervised Play							
3:30	Out and Play - Explore							
4:00	Feed and Water							
4:15	Outside							
4:30 – 7:00	Lead, Station or Crate, Supervised Freedom							
7:00 – 9:00	Family Interaction							

Figure 8-3: Make everyday projects fun with a chart like this one.

- ✔ **Create a super schedule:** Kids love to be creative. Ask them to help you write "the SUPER schedule for REX." Include times for everything: feeding, brushing, playing, and napping. Let the kids decorate around the edges, and hang the finished schedule in a place where everyone can see it.

- ✔ **Set up play stations:** Ask your children to help you create a place for your puppy in each room (refer to Chapter 5 to see a typical play station). Furnish the location with a place to lie down, a favorite chew, and a toy. Each time you enter the room, send your puppy to his area using a chosen word, such as "Go to your bed." If your puppy isn't cooperative with staying in his area, secure his leash to an immovable object (see Chapter 13).

- ✔ **Decorate supplies:** Call your children to the table and let their imaginations and creativity run wild. Ask them to help you decorate treat cups, snack packs, and your puppy's dishes. So what if you just spent big bucks on a shiny stainless steel bowl? If your child puts her own stickers on the outside of it, she'll be far more likely to participate in meal times.

Include kids in short, positive lessons

Kids like to help and be involved, but training exercises can bore them to tears. Face it: To a five-year-old, mud wrestling for two hours is more exciting than a two-minute heel. Training exercises are just no fun, and the phrase "It's your responsibility to feed Rex" has a negative spin. The good news is that you can get the kids happily involved, but you must be very upbeat and creative. Staying positive is also a plus. Here are a couple ideas:

- ✔ Your child can teach your puppy to heel using the jumping trick "Over" found in Chapter 22.

- ✔ "Sit" can be a prelude to "Paw" (see Chapters 14 and 22).

Don't make your commands too singsong or whiny: Your puppy will take your tone to mean playtime. Teach the puppy a negative sound for unacceptable behavior, such as nipping, and then use it regularly when you see your puppy becoming too excitable with the kids. I use the sound "Ep, ep."

Daily Discouragements

Let go of the idea that the kids can communicate leadership. Even though some can, usually the responsibility to train your pup will fall (like everything else) in your lap. Young kids can't train puppies until they grow tall enough to stare at you eye to eye — when they're about 12 to 14 years old. Before then, they're just too close to the puppy's height to be taken seriously. Kids also bend and "bark" too much. So, it's up to you to teach the puppy to respect the children.

Set up situations your pup can expect to encounter — such as the kids' running frenzies or their building sets and dolls — to teach your puppy how to handle himself. Use your leash as described in Chapter 13. With the right training techniques, you can remedy many everyday occurrences between kids and puppies — things like mouthing and nipping, food grabbing, and chasing. Take a look at Chapter 16 for details on overcoming these and other daily hassles.

Nipping

A young puppy needs a lot of sleep: 16 to 18 hours until the age of 12 weeks. When overstimulated or overtired, a puppy will nip hard! When he starts getting nippy with the kids, consider separating your puppy calmly to see if he simply needs some quiet time to regroup.

If your puppy is still nippy and wild when the kids are around, secure a leash onto his collar — a more thorough explanation of the drag lead can be found in Chapter 5. He can wear this light leash around the house, which makes for a great way to give indiscrete corrections.

Try as you might, your puppy will consider younger children as sibling puppies. Their play will be different, more facially interactive and impulsive. In the end, your children will have a special and unique relationship with the puppy that will grow as they both age. However, you'll need to teach your puppy how to interact with your children or he'll make up his own rules.

Avoid yelling at your puppy when energy escalates. He'll think you're part of the play or, worse, that you're being confrontational. Instead of yelling, check out Chapter 16, which outlines a more thorough age-appropriate approach to resolving nipping.

Clothing assault

Life can get a little boring for a puppy because he's always looking up and only able to focus on objects that move by at his nose level. When a fuzzy slipper or dangling sweatshirt passes his line of vision, it's virtually impossible for him to ignore. If you notice your puppy mounting an all-out assault on your child's outer wear, you'll need more than one approach to refocus his excitement.

Encourage before you discourage. Find a toy or object you can place on the floor to refocus your puppy after a correction. Within short order, he may start going for this new item before assaulting the kids! Play with this toy or object both before and during misbehavior so he'll associate the toy with interaction and group attention.

Come up with one cue word that indicates your child needs your help. "Help" always works under my roof. When you (or any other grown-up) hear this cue, grab a spray deterrent, such as Bitter Apple spray, and move to the rescue. Don't run, however, or you'll give yourself away. Walk quickly and quietly, and then discretely spray the clothing your puppy is targeting, whether it's in his mouth or not. After your puppy has released, refocus him on a toy. You may also need to take care of a need if one is pressing, such as potty, hunger, or play.

If your child is older, she may be able to successfully handle the spray correction on her own. Instruct her to quietly get a spray deterrent and say "No" while spraying the item of clothing your pup is targeting.

If your puppy is repelled by a distasteful spray, douse the coveted item and leave it out for the pup to find. He'll learn on his own to avoid chewing or pulling on it.

Also consider using a drag lead inside and out to enable you to redirect your puppy's focus before it goes astray. Move quickly and quietly and say "No" as you tug the leash.

Chasing compulsion

They dart, they spin, they stare, and they bark. Wow, those little two-legged creatures are just like puppies. This next exercise will help your puppy learn not to chase and nip them when they go zooming past. It requires a few volunteers — little volunteers, that is. If you don't have kids, borrow some. Then practice these steps:

1. **Start inside. Place your puppy on a leash and go to an open room.**

2. **Ask the children to run in front of you while you watch your puppy. See Figure 8-4.**

3. **The second you see that gleam in your pup's eye, just as he prepares to bound after them, say "No" sternly and quickly tug back on the lead.**

After you've conquered the chasing exercise, it's time to try out distance control. Using your long line or Flexi-Lead (see Chapter 5), repeat the procedure again. Tell your little volunteers to race around in front of you (but no circling behind). Correct all thoughts of a chase by tugging back on the lead, saying "No," and praising your pup for resisting temptation.

Figure 8-4:
Stage
setups to
curb your
puppy's
impulse to
chase.

Struggle of toys

"Mine!" This popular lament is common in all toddlers — whether they walk on two legs or four. If you're experiencing this daily frustration, you're not alone. You must, however, transfer the control of the situation to your child, basically teaching your puppy that when your child touches an object, the puppy must remove his mouth. Following are some suggestions:

✔ Use the "Give (or Drop)" section in Chapter 23 to teach your puppy the proper response to the command "Give."

✔ Encourage your child to leave the puppy alone when he's chewing his toys. Also, ask your child not to shriek when the puppy picks up one of her toys, though I wish you good luck — your puppy may be easier to train than your kids!

✔ Place treat cups (see Chapter 11) all around your home. Anytime you see your child approach your puppy when he's chewing an object, shake the cup and say "Give." Treat your puppy if he obeys and praise him lavishly.

✔ If your puppy is showing signs of possessiveness, and you're unable to convince him to defer to your child, call a professional dog trainer or behaviorist for help. This type of behavior can lead to a serious situation: one in which you'll have to give your puppy up, or if he bites badly enough, euthanize him.

Mounting

Some puppies mount kids (and even adults) when they get too excited. Don't be too embarrassed. Mounting is more a sign of dominance than sexual preference. Knowing this makes it no more acceptable, however. Mounting dogs are bossy dogs who get overstimulated in exciting situations. To rehabilitate your mounting pup, do the following:

1. **Leave a 4-foot lead on your pup inside or out.**

2. **When the mounting starts, calmly grasp the short lead and tug down firmly.**

   Don't face off to a mounting puppy. Also, don't make eye contact, and don't push him away. These reactions may ignite a confrontational response, escalating your puppy's reaction instead of calming it.

3. **After your pup is grounded, stand very tall, glare at him, and say "Shame on you!" in your most indignant tone.**

4. **Station your pup for 15 minutes with no attention.**

5. **If your dog acts aggressively, terminate the corrections and seek help from Chapter 18.**

Chapter 9

Living with Your Puppy in the Real World

In This Chapter

▶ Being a good neighbor

▶ Helping your puppy adjust to life changes

▶ Traveling by plane, boat, or automobile

*Y*es, life beyond your four walls holds endless possibilities, and you should take your dog with you wherever life leads. The key is in knowing how to direct your puppy so that she's a welcome presence everywhere you go. Knowing how to manage every nuance that life can throw at you — from greeting other people and pets to curbing the chasing instinct as well as welcoming new people or animals into your home — is what this chapter is all about.

Thinking of taking your puppy along with you for an overnight or extended trip? In this chapter, you get the skinny on everything from packing to making airline accommodations. Are you adding a new pet or baby to your family circle? Your puppy may be less than thrilled with the intrusion. Not to worry though — I give you some tried-and-true techniques to spin her disgruntlement into joy. Sound like fun? It can be with the right approach!

Life in the 'Hood

"It's a beautiful day in the neighborhood . . ." until, of course, you hear the constant serenade of a barking dog! I love my neighborhood dearly, but one quiet summer day my neighbors left for the beach and tied out their 8-month-old Beagle (bless her little soul). That day, I swore I'd move to Barbados. However, it's not the Beagle's fault. Once, I went over after three hours of the street-dog serenade, only to find her water bowl empty. I gave her a fresh bowl of water and a chew bone, which kept her busy the rest of the afternoon. Finally I had some peace and quiet.

Five signs that you're a bad dog neighbor

1. A neighbor has returned your wandering pup more than once.

2. Your dog constantly barks outside (especially when you leave).

3. Your dog torments neighborhood dogs on walks.

4. Your puppy visits neighbors' yards to relandscape, retrieve their papers, and potty on their lawns.

5. Your neighbors appear to be afraid of your puppy.

You need to keep a lot in mind when trying to be a good dog neighbor, and fortunately, this section can help.

Respecting your neighbors

Some neighbors get along. They know when to accept those situations that won't change. They clean up after themselves, and they're fairly quiet. Others, however, bicker and fight in negative situations. They make messes, and they're loud and intimidating.

The question is: Which of these two types of neighbors do you want you and your puppy to be classified as? The choice is yours, but if you want to be well-respected, it's not difficult — just follow these steps (turn to Chapter 14 for details on these directions):

✔ Instruct "Heel" as you parade around the neighborhood and teach your puppy to follow your lead.

✔ Use the "Wait" direction to teach your puppy to wait at curbs and to wait while you visit or window shop.

✔ Teach the "No" direction to discourage your puppy from going after everyday temptations, such as cars, joggers, and other animals. (You can introduce the concept of "No" when your pup's 16 weeks old.)

If your dog's lunging at the end of the leash and trying to get at whatever has her attention, you're too late to discourage her. Impulse rules, but if you can anticipate her reaction by watching your surroundings for temptations and correct her just before she reacts, you'll be able to refocus her before her instincts take over.

✔ Make sure your puppy potties on your own property. As they grow into adulthood, puppies recognize boundary limits with their noses. Help your pup learn where her territory ends by keeping her close while walking around the parameters of your yard or block. In case of an accident, carry a bag with you so you can remove the evidence from your neighbor's lawn. Don't forget to also dispose of the evidence properly.

Dealing with other neighborhood dogs

Most dogs like to think they own their neighborhoods. The problem is that every block usually has more than one dog. When left to their own devices — free-ranging, so to speak — the dogs establish a hierarchy and get along fine. But neighborhood dogs usually aren't free. Instead, when they greet each other, they're confined on leashes, which is tantamount to holding an eager person by his or her arms. The dogs' struggle to get free from restraint pitches their bodies into an unnaturally confrontational pose that may be unreflective of their personalities.

The leash should be used to communicate leadership — human leadership, that is. Puppies, however, don't always listen to that message. Some puppies think they're supposed to walk their owners. A confident puppy leading its owner wants to approach other dogs, and when she's suddenly restricted by a choking feeling around the neck or chest, she gets very defensive. She pulls harder and gets more intense. As she grows up, she threatens from afar when she sees other dogs. A better approach is using the direction "Heel," which teaches your puppy to look to you for direction and in turn helps her to feel safe and guarded (see Chapter 14).

A cautious puppy, on the other hand, feels intense panic when approached by another dog. Because no one has communicated leadership to this pup, she collapses in a state of panic, often scurrying back and hiding under her owner's legs. Even though this behavior may seem endearing, a puppy hiding under your legs is like a child clinging to his mother's skirt. This puppy needs training to learn that you're there to direct her in all situations. A head collar or no-pull harness (see Chapter 5) is ideal for this personality type because both tools allow you to guide your puppy calmly without the feeling that you're trapping her by the neck.

A normal greeting involves a mix of excitement and respectful submission or puppy play. Puppies normally submit to older dogs by rolling onto their backs, laying their heads down, lifting a paw, and pulling their lips back or licking the lips of the approaching dog. When two puppies meet, they often get excited and paw and mouth each other quite a bit.

Resist the temptation to soothe a frightened puppy. Your intentions are pure, but because a puppy views the soothing as submissive and fearful, you're only reinforcing your pup's concern. Act brave and calm, and speak in directional tones. Kneel down and brace your puppy as described in Chapter 7, and use familiar directions to help contain her fears.

When your puppy approaches or is approached by another dog, remember the following:

- ✔ Don't look at the other dog.
- ✔ Walk by the dog at a brisk pace.
- ✔ Keep your dog behind you at all times.

What if you want to let your puppy play with her new canine acquaintance? Keep your pup at your side while you cross the street or while the puppies approach each other. Then release your dog on a loose lead with a command such as "Okay."

If you and your on-lead puppy are approached by an angry, off-leash dog, walk swiftly from the scene, correcting your pup so that she doesn't face off to the aggressor. If either of you makes eye contact with the dog, you may be attacked. If your puppy is small enough, pick her up calmly and swiftly leave the area. Cup your hand gently over your puppy's muzzle to discourage squirming.

Leaving your pup home alone

To be a good neighbor, you need to keep your puppy quiet when you're away from home. No puppy enjoys being left alone — she's sociable by nature. Don't be surprised if she thinks of some activities to pass those lonely hours — digging, chewing destructively, or barking.

Don't worry. Just because you have a dog now doesn't mean that you'll be stuck at home for the next decade. You have a lot of options for when you need to leave your puppy alone. She can stay inside or outside. You can confine her in a room or let her roam around. You can tie her up or fence her in. What's best, you ask? Put yourself in your puppy's paws. Outside is okay — she'll have fresh air and sunshine — but being confined outdoors can be stressful because she needs a companion to protect her, interpret events, and help her enjoy life. Most puppies would rather stay inside with a cozy blanket and bone to chew.

Preparing for your departure has lasting benefits. Before you leave, do the following:

- ✔ Exercise your puppy for ten minutes.
- ✔ Follow playtime with a two-minute training session.

- ✔ Leave a couple of chew toys and scent them by rubbing them in your palms.

- ✔ If you leave your puppy indoors, leave her in a dimly lit, confined space with an old shirt or blanket and a radio playing soothing tunes.

- ✔ If you leave your puppy outdoors, provide her with access to a shaded area and plenty of fresh water.

If you're expecting inclement weather, don't leave your puppy alone outside. Go with her to her potty area and bring her directly back inside after she's done.

If your puppy suffers from separation anxiety and is a _gulper_ (which means that she eats things she shouldn't), crate or enclose her in a small space with a large bone and no bedding. You don't want to leave bedding for your pup because she may eat it when she becomes upset that you've left.

Picking up your puppy's messes

Make a habit of cleaning up your puppy's elimination the moment she goes potty. Aside from the obvious sanitation element, when your puppy sees you picking up her mess in the right location, she's more likely to go again.

Yes, there is an art form to picking up dog poop. You can spend a chunk of change on a fancy hand-held bull-dozer design, but remember that taking these types on the road with you is difficult and cumbersome. My suggestion? Take an empty plastic bag, put your hand in it, grab the poop, flip the bag inside out, and tie the knot. Voila! I use empty grocery or newspaper delivery bags, but you can find perfumed blue bags at the pet store if you fancy!

A couple of guys in my area opened a business called Poop Patrol. These guys are forever dedicated to keeping yards free of puppy messes. There's a business idea for all you entrepreneurs!

Dealing with the chasing instinct

Chasing is an instinctive behavior that goes back to the canine ancestor — the wolf — who had to hunt for a living. Even though owners offer their puppies all the luxuries of retirement (read: a free buffet of kibbles two times a day), many still think chasing (anything, but especially cats) is a great pastime.

Chasing the neighborhood cats

When a new puppy approaches a cat, one of two things happens: The cat runs, which leads to — you guessed it — a free-for-all, or the cat stands its ground, often hissing or batting at the persistent pup. Regardless of the cat's reaction, you want to steer clear of the interaction. Yelling and chasing a wild puppy only positively reinforces her chasing behavior.

If your puppy has already formed the chasing habit, don't fret. You can still resolve things. Follow these steps:

1. **Secure a light 6-foot nylon leash to your puppy's collar.**

2. **Focus on your dog's ears as you walk (ear perk is a sign that a chase is in your pup's future).**

   To influence the chasing problem, you must correct the thought process, not wait until the chase has begun. Dogs' ears act like built-in radar systems. They can pick up sounds in every direction. Unfortunately, if your puppy's ears are alert to every other distraction, she's not focused on you. So, in this case, training is definitely in order.

3. **If your dog's ears lift when the cat saunters by, tug the leash quickly and say "No!"**

   Don't look at the cat or the puppy at any time during the interaction. Eye contact means interest.

4. **Walk away from the cat confidently. Encourage your puppy to come along with the direction "Let's go!"**

5. **Continue to quickly tug and release the leash and say "No" until your puppy focuses on you.**

   Don't drag your pup away from the object. Instead, tug and release, and wait for your puppy to follow you willingly.

Chasing the neighborhood cars

Chasing cars is one scary problem. Young puppies are usually hesitant about cars until their fourth or fifth month. Around that time, fear turns to fascination and moving objects are best when chased. To nip this problem in the bud, you need to think a few steps ahead of your dog. If your puppy is very young (less than 12 weeks), act scared when you see a car. Whimper like a puppy and retreat to the roadside.

After you begin formal training (16 to 18 weeks), follow these steps when you see a car:

1. **Instruct your dog with the command "To the side" and run to the curb quickly.**

2. **Tell her "Wait" as the car passes, bringing her behind your heels.**

3. **If she looks at the car, say "No!" very sternly and tug the lead quickly.**

Use this same technique with bikers and joggers. Correct your dog the second she thinks about chasing something. After she's in motion, you're too late.

Adapting to Life Changes

Change is a part of life. Even though many changes are for the best, all changes are stressful. I'm not just talking about humans — dogs experience stress, too. The difference between their stress and ours is how they display it. Sure, I may pack in some extra calories when I'm feeling anxious, but I don't destroy the couch; your puppy might, though. And do you know what happens if you correct an anxious pup? She gets more stressed and destroys other things — perhaps your rug or the bed, for example. Other signs of stress are aggression, barking, hyperactivity, and extreme withdrawal. Is she being bad? Not necessarily. She's just confused and worried, and she needs your help to adjust.

Moving in to a new home

Moving is one of life's most stressful changes. First, the financial decisions may bring about more theatrical conversations than you have on the average day. Then you have the packing, shipping, and traveling back and forth. When the big day finally arrives, your energy is spent, and you've reached a new peak of exhaustion. My heart aches for you, but it bleeds for your developing puppy. Chaos really throws her. Due to her biological nature, she depends on predictability to ensure her safety. During this change, you may notice your puppy resorting to early puppy behavior: She may become hyper, demand attention, nip, jump, or chew. Forgive her, and vow to help her cope.

Following are some suggestions that you can use to help her:

- **Play some classical music while you debate and discuss your big move.** It'll calm everyone.

- **Include your dog in your packing activities.** Don't isolate her in the backyard. If she gets in the way, station her with a bone to chew, and pet her when she settles down.

- **If you're traveling back and forth to the new house, lead your puppy in the home using familiar commands, such as "Wait" and "Let's go."**

- **Create stations in your new home using familiar toys, leashes, and bedding.**

- **If you're spending the day at your new house, don't forget to pack some dog food and water.** Bring her familiar bowls.

- **Keep your dog with you while you're unpacking.** Let her sniff the collectibles as you remove them; she identifies objects with her nose and will feel happy to recognize something.

The first time you leave your puppy in your new home, she may stress out, resulting in destructive chewing or excessive barking. Confine your puppy in a small room or crate with one of your old shirts and a favorite chew toy. Don't correct your puppy if she demolishes something. Your corrections only increase the anxiety and destruction. Puppy-proof the area ahead of time. If you come back to destruction, ignore it and clean the area up later when your puppy is occupied.

Don't let your puppy off-leash in your new yard unless it's fenced in or she's secure on a long line. She'll be disoriented for a few weeks and may get lost if she wanders off. Was your old place fenced in? If your dog was accustomed to running free in a yard but can't anymore, you need to make up for the loss. Use a long line or a retractable leash and discover some good games to burn off that energy. Flip to Chapter 5 for more info on leads and long lines and to Chapter 23 to discover some fun puppy games.

Are you moving to a new climate? Going from extreme cold to hot or vice versa can be alarming for your pup. A sweater may be in order in colder climates, and a big bowl of water is a must if the weather is suddenly blistering.

Mourning the loss of a loved one

I've lost two people very close to me in my lifetime. In both cases, I was in a trance for weeks. Emotionally, I had to drag myself out of bed. I lost my zest. Sure, my dogs felt confused by the passing, but I think they were more confused by my mental state. Here are some things I did to help them out:

- I asked a friend to walk them in the morning and had the neighbor's kid come by in the afternoon.
- I set my alarm clock to ring at their mealtimes.
- I set aside five minutes per day for an obedience lesson.
- I bought them new chews and tried to play kick the bottle (their favorite game) with them in the afternoon.

Losing a loved one isn't an easy place to be in. Your world is forever changed, and yet daily demands continue — especially from those who depend on you. Get through one day at a time, ask for help when you need it, and find life in the love you share.

And baby makes three: Expanding your family

Whether you're getting another pet, giving birth to or adopting a child, or inviting relatives to move in, your puppy will notice the shifting dynamic. All spell out generally less attention for her. With some forethought and cooperation, you can reverse the inevitable and show your puppy that this new addition is generally in her favor.

Preparing your pup for the new arrival

A new baby in the house can be one of the coolest changes of a lifetime — for people, that is. Puppies, on the other hand, often feel shafted and like they've been moved to the back burner. To ensure that your four-legged pal doesn't feel left out, start planning for the new arrival.

Imagine the baby has moved in. He's a cute little creature who's just weeks old. Your parenting instincts are in full throttle. Now enters your beloved puppy. Is she used to lounging on the furniture or jumping up for attention? Does she order up a back rub by pawing, barking, or nudging you? Can you see the problem that's developing here? She won't stop this behavior just because you're holding a newborn. Don't shout at or isolate her — she'll just grow leery and jealous of your new fancy. Fortunately, you can take a few steps ahead of time to ensure that nobody gets left in the doghouse:

- **As early as possible, socialize your puppy with small children.** Put some cereal (cereal has fewer calories than dog biscuits, so it's okay if kids are very generous) in a cup, and shake and treat until your pup associates the sound with a reward. Then invite over some friends who have children and ask them to shake and treat. Stay calm while they visit, but keep your dog on a leash if you're uneasy. Dogs are very telepathic, so your emotions come across loud and clear.

- **Take your puppy to a playground.** Keep her on a 6-foot lead, and if a parent and a child approach together, ask the child to take a break and give your dog a treat.

  If your puppy shows any signs of aggression, call a professional. Your reaction can make the problem worse. Petting or soothing reinforces the behavior, and disciplining makes your puppy feel more threatened.

- **Establish an exercise schedule that will be realistic with your new responsibilities.** Mornings may be rough, so help your puppy look forward to afternoon romps instead.

- **Establish a station in or just outside your baby's room, and get your pup accustomed to settling on command.** Tell her "Settle down" and secure her on a 3-foot lead if she seems restless.

- **Walk through your daily routine with a stuffed doll.** Allow your puppy to sniff it regularly. When changing your baby (both the doll and the real thing), practice the directions "Wait" and "Stay" (see Chapter 14). When putting your baby down for a nap, guide your puppy to her station while saying "Settle down." When nursing your baby, give your puppy a special chew and place her mat or bed near your feet.

- **Watch your words.** Phrases like "What a good girl" must be changed to "What a great dog!" If the phrases you use for baby and dog are too similar, your pup will get confused.

- **Set new furniture rules.** Dogs shouldn't be allowed on the furniture near a new infant. If you wait to spring this rule on your pup after the baby's home, the puppy may feel shafted, so lay down the law now. Keep a short leash on your puppy's buckle collar, and if she hops up, quickly tug the lead handle and say "No." Remember, pushing is interactive and suggestive of a game.

  If you must have your dog on the furniture, give her the luxury on command only. Tell her "Up" and pat the cushion when you want her there. Use "No" with a leash correction if she comes up uninvited.

- **Get your puppy used to one hour of the cold shoulder every day.** Yes, I want you to ignore your puppy completely. You can break it up into two 30-minute or three 20-minute segments, but get your puppy accustomed to life without your doting. If your puppy can get your attention wherever and whenever she wants it, she'll be upset when you're focused on the baby.

- **Stop all confrontational games, such as tug of war and wrestling, and eliminate all in-home chasing matches.** Play games outside, and teach your puppy calm household manners.

- **Consider your child's toys and how they may compare to your puppy's favorites.** Give your puppy a couple of objects to chew on or play with, return them to your puppy's bedding when displaced, and use a calm approach to discourage her from going after the child's toys on the floor. Avoid theatrical reactions when your puppy chooses the wrong object; simply approach calmly, remove the item, and encourage her to find her toy. If your puppy can't resist snatching forbidden items, place her in her special space (room, pen, or crate) with her toys and wait until she's calmed down (or you've cleaned up) to bring her out again. See Chapter 16 for a more detailed description on how to discourage chewing.

- **Grab and tug on your puppy as you treat and praise her.** Babies and small children like to grab and pull, and your dog may be startled if the baby's tug is the first one she experiences. So tug on her coat, pull her tail, and hug her tight. What a wonderful puppy. Isn't this great? Don't forget to make some baby sounds, too, for the full effect.

- **Don't give your dog shoes, socks, rags, or plastic or stuffed toys.** If you do, she'll think anything in that category is fair game. Oops, already started that habit? Well, you should stop cold turkey. Stay calm when your puppy gets confused, remove the object without fanfare, and use it to teach your puppy the concept of "No" as described in Chapter 14.

When it's time for baby to come home

The day will come. Your baby will come into the world, and your life will never be the same. To help your puppy adjust, follow these steps:

✔ **Ask the nurse if you can bring home some bed sheets or blankets from the nursery.** It may seem like a strange request, but I'm sure yours won't be the first. Ask a friend or family member to place these items in your puppy's play station or crate and around the area where you plan to nurse. Praise your puppy for sniffing them, but discourage chewing or tearing. (Keep your puppy on leash, if necessary.)

✔ **Brush up on obedience lessons while Mom's in the hospital.** Puppies love structure.

✔ **Hire a dog walker if the house is empty.** Isolation is stressful for puppies.

✔ **Introduce puppy and baby on neutral ground.** If possible introduce the two as you're leaving the hospital or outside your home. Exercise your pup before the meeting and bring along some peanut butter to distract your dog's interest if you're nervous. *Don't* choke up on the lead or shout at your puppy — it's unsettling and makes a bad first impression.

✔ **Plan your homecoming.** Keep your puppy on leash and let her welcome the baby, too. Use the same techniques as the first meeting to ensure a smooth arrival.

✔ **If your puppy's too boisterous, give her leash a quick tug and say "No ma'am."** Spread some peanut butter on your hand and say "Kisses."

The butter trick also works as you establish a bond between your baby and your puppy. Dab some butter on your baby's hand and say "Kisses" (see Figure 9-1).

✔ **Let your puppy drag a leash and use it to correct all mouthing or jumping behavior.** Look at and praise your dog when she's calm.

✔ **If your puppy is restless at her designated stations, secure the 3-foot lead and hook her up while you direct her to "Settle down."**

Figure 9-1: Use butter or peanut butter to teach your puppy to give the baby kisses.

Puppies like diapers, so don't be surprised if you find yours nibbling on one. My suggestion? Get a super-secure diaper bin and spray a little Bitter Apple spray on the outside to discourage her interest. Last, but not least, use the setup outlined in Chapter 16 to correct this behavior when you catch your puppy near the bin. Say "No," pull her off the bin, and shout at the bin, not the pup: "Bad, bad diaper bin!"

New infant resentment syndrome (NIRS) is exactly what it sounds like. If your four-legged friend is suddenly excluded from normal daily activities, she'll feel resentful and may take out her alienated feelings on the new arrival. If your dog growls at the baby, call in a professional to assess the situation.

Bringing home another dog or pup

Getting another puppy may seem really exciting to you, but your resident pup may be less than thrilled. Some puppies take to new paws on the carpet, but others don't. To make the transition as smooth as possible, follow the advice in this section.

First introductions

Ideally, you should introduce dogs in a neutral place, such as a park or parking lot. If the meeting place is in the open, place both the puppy and the new dog on 20-foot lines and stand back as they check each other out. Whether you can organize such an encounter or not, how you approach the interaction will influence their future relationship. Remember the following:

✔ **Stay cool.** With or without a leash (the tightening of which conveys tension), if you shout directions at or scold either dog when they're first greeting each other, both dogs will be nervous wrecks, and nervous dogs are likely to attack.

✔ **Even a young puppy may do a lot of body and vocal bluffing at the initial meeting.** When two dogs meet, there may be a lot of posturing and growling. Don't be alarmed — it's very natural and necessary. It's the equivalent of "Hi, how are you? What do you do for a living?" Her hair may stand up, and she may even growl. Meeting anyone for the first time can be a little scary. If you interfere, though, the dogs may fight. Just stand back and ignore them. Interact with them when the initial tension has subsided.

Some dogs just don't get along. If you bring together two dogs of the same sex or two dogs who have both become used to being "only children," they may fight. Be prepared: Have two people handy to take the leads and run in opposite directions.

Hints for happy two-puppy households

When you add two puppies to your household, you definitely have your work cut out for you. The next year is going to be quite the balancing act. Resolving housebreaking, chewing, nipping, or jumping habits in two pups can be double the workload. You have to pay close attention and be very consistent. That said, raising two puppies can give you hours of entertainment watching them play and experience life together.

When left alone 24 hours a day, your puppies will form a strong bond to each other, which is good. However, that means they'll also be less attached to you, which makes it difficult for you to influence their behavior. To prevent this bonding, separate them at least twice a day and if possible, let them sleep in separate bedrooms. Use individual crates for housebreaking, chewing, or sleeping difficulties.

Here are additional hints for making life a little easier for everyone in the two-puppy house:

- **A puppy is a puppy is a puppy.** Truer words were never written. Certain similarities string all puppies together. However, like humans, each one has her own unique personality and temperament that affects the way she relates to her world. In a multidog household, everyone must be sensitive to the needs of each individual puppy.

- **Let your dogs establish their hierarchy.** Personality affects the way puppies relate to one another. Groups of two or more puppies form a hierarchy, with the most outgoing, assertive one assuming the leadership role.

    Puppies don't base hierarchy on who's the biggest, or who came first. Nor do they base it wholly on who's the toughest. Hierarchy is based on who's the most responsible. The puppy with both the brains and the brawn wins out. Regardless of your feelings, you must support their arrangement.

- **Give the royalties to the leader.** You must support the hierarchy your puppies set by giving all the household royalties to your leader. She should be fed, greeted, pet, and allowed out first. If you pay more attention to the subordinate dog, you may cause discontent among the ranks, which can lead to fighting.

    Although young puppies are submissive, they may challenge the leadership status as they mature, and although it may go against every loving impulse in your body, you need to reorganize royalties based on their decision of who's the leader.

- **Remember the discipline rules.** If you don't know who did it, you can't correct either puppy. That's the rule. If you find a mess after the fact, forget it. Correcting both pups only weakens your connection to them and strengthens their resolve to one another. For suggestions on specific problems, see Chapters 16, 17, and 18.

✔ **Wrestling is okay, to a degree.** Teach your puppies to go to certain areas of the house or outside to play. If they tend to get out of hand, leave short leashes on them in the house to enable interruption and redirection. Say "Shhh!" as you separate them and then instruct them to go "Outside" or to another area to play. If you don't have enough space for this technique, instruct "Sit," and refocus them on chew toys. Crate or secure them at a station if they don't calm down.

✔ **Play the name game.** Teach your puppies two names: their personal names and a universal one that you can use when they're together, such as "Dogs," "Girls," "Boys," or "Babies" — whatever works for you. Using a single name makes calling them easier; "Girls, come!" rolls off the tongue easier than "Buddy, Fi-Fi, Daisy, Marlo, come!"

✔ **Feed your pups separately.** Place your leader's bowl down first. If you're having difficulty keeping the puppies separate, create two separate feeding stations (see Chapter 5).

✔ **Don't start a toy war.** I know, you want them both to have a toy. But one puppy keeps insisting on having both. You give it back to the other puppy, and she takes it away. The giving and taking could go on all day. Remember your leadership rule: If the leader wants both, the leader gets both. Period.

✔ **Whatever you do, don't yell during a dog fight.** Yelling is perceived as threat barking and actually makes the problem worse as your puppy matures. If you have a dog fight, the best thing to do is walk out of the house and slam the door. No words or discipline — just leave abruptly. It's usually your presence that prompts an argument. You can also try breaking up the fight by dumping a bucket of water on their heads or turning a hose on them momentarily if they're outside. Also, an excellent product called Direct Stop is useful in fight situations; it's a fierce spray of citronella that's not harmful but is startling enough to break up the dogs. You can find it in stores or online.

After things are calm, review your actions. Were you supporting the underdog? That's not good. After the fight fizzles out, isolate the subordinate and praise the leader. I know it sounds cruel, but if the leader feels supported, she won't challenge the other dog. Additionally, if you catch a fight before it begins, shame the underdog and reward your leader with attention. I know it feels unnatural, but remember that your dogs aren't human, and they don't think you are either. If the situation repeats itself, call in a professional.

Trips, Tips, and Travel

Everybody likes a vacation. The most depressing part, however, is parting from your beloved pal. Her soulful stare can stay with you for hours. Why not take your puppy along? Having your pet with you can be great fun, but you'll also come across some risks. To help you make your own decision, I go over some hard-and-fast traveling rules in this section.

Packing an overnight bag

A lot of planning goes into a trip. You have to remember everything right down to your toothbrush and socks. It's understandable that your puppy's needs may get overlooked. However, familiar objects are as soothing to your puppy as a fuzzy, warm security blanket is to a child. So, don't forget to pack an extra suitcase — one for your puppy, that is!

Here's a quick checklist of your puppy's needs:

- A familiar mat or other bedding
- Regular food that's separated for each feeding, plus an extra meal or two just in case
- A selection of familiar bones and toys
- Food dishes
- Water, if you're visiting an environment where bottled water is recommended for human consumption
- Housetraining bell, if your puppy uses one

Taking your puppy on a plane

I'm leery of planes, so you can imagine how neurotic I get thinking of a dog in the belly of one of those steel babies. Personally, I'd avoid taking any pet on a plane if I didn't have to. Even if only 1 dog in 90 dies, I don't want to be the one holding the empty leash. Sometimes air travel is unavoidable, however, so here are some guidelines that can make the plane trip go more smoothly.

Taking some preflight measures
Follow this preflight advice to make your puppy's trip as smooth as possible:

- Plan direct flights late in the evening or early morning to minimize the amount of time your puppy spends in holding. The cargo areas where pets are held before and after their flights are neither heated nor cooled. Please respect the airline rules regarding flying your dog in extreme heat: Suffocation is the biggest risk in airline travel.

- Make your puppy's reservation when you make your own. Planes only accept so many four-legged passengers.

✔ Book a direct flight in a large plane. Large planes have better air circulation than smaller ones.

 If you can't fly direct, book a flight with a layover that's long enough for you to reunite with your puppy. Take her out for a stretch, drink, potty break, and hug.

 ✔ If you're planning to take your puppy with you overseas, check with the embassy of the country that you're visiting to find out about regulations and required paperwork. In addition, check with the agriculture department in your state for the heads up on regulations regarding your dog's return home.

 ✔ Airlines require health certificates and proof of vaccination, so you need to get them from your veterinarian and forward a copy to the airline immediately. Carry one with you the day of the flight, too, in case any questions arise about your dog's clearance to travel.

Getting your puppy set to go

Follow this advice to make sure your puppy is as comfortable as possible during her flight:

 ✔ Purchase a sturdy USDA-approved travel kennel custom fit to your puppy's size. Make sure the kennel is only large enough for your puppy to stand up and turn around in.

 ✔ Get your puppy comfortable with her kennel quarters a few days before departure.

 ✔ If you have a teenie-weenie puppy or dog who can come on board, buy a crate that fits under the seat.

 ✔ Write "LIVE ANIMAL" in 1-inch letters on top of the crate and on each side. Tape on huge arrows to indicate the crate's upright position.

Wanting to go by train? Sorry!

I've looked high and low and can't find a rail service that's dog friendly. Of course, they all allow service dogs on board, and my local metro train allows small, well-mannered dogs on off-peak hours. But traveling by rail with a pup is definitely pretty limiting.

- On the top of the crate, in ½-inch letters, write the flight's destination, including your name and the name, address, and phone number of the person or place you're visiting.

- Remove all training collars. Your pup should wear a well-fitting buckle collar with identification tags.

- Don't feed your puppy within six hours of the trip.

- Prep the crate for takeoff with light bedding and paper (taped down) in one end to absorb mistakes. Affix two manufactured kennel bowls inside the crate. Freeze water in one so your puppy can have a drink while in flight.

   If your puppy is a champion chewer, you may need to nix the bedding. Some puppies are so stressed by air travel that they'd chew the shirt off your back if you were sitting next to them. If you suspect that your puppy will be distressed, ask your veterinarian for a sedative.

- If the flight is longer than 12 hours, tape a bag of food to the outside of the crate with feeding instructions. Don't be too disappointed if no one's available to feed your puppy; all you can do is hope.

- Allow your puppy to potty right before you put her in her kennel. Most puppies can't hold their bladders for very long, so be prepared with paper towels and water to clean the kennel and your puppy when you're reunited.

- Never padlock the kennel. You don't want your pet trapped in case of an emergency.

Upon arrival, go immediately to the baggage area and insist on seeing your puppy. Kick and fuss if you must. Sitting in a holding area is stressful for your pet, especially if she turns out to be an escape artist. Imagine watching your puppy tearing down the runway trying to herd a jet. That's one time when "Fido, come!" just isn't going to work.

Road trip! Traveling by car

I've never owned a puppy or dog who didn't love a road trip. I know some dogs have less than enjoyable experiences, but even they can be transformed with some patient car conditioning (see Chapter 13 for details).

Taking a few precautions

Cars can be a dangerous place for dogs, so you must take certain precautions:

- ✔ **Don't leave your puppy in the car on a warm day.** Even with the windows down, your car will bake like an oven, leaving your puppy uncomfortable or dead. Nothing is worth that.

  Keep an extra set of keys in the glove compartment in case of an emergency. If you must leave your puppy, keep the engine running with the air conditioning on full-blast and lock the doors. Keep the second set of keys with you so that you can get back into the car.

- ✔ **Got a pick-up truck? Let your puppy ride in the cab.** On a leash or off, the bed of a truck is no place for a dog.

- ✔ **Keep the windows cracked but not wide open.** Some people think that letting a dog hang her head out the window is cool. Actually, though, it's dangerous. Dogs can get hurled from the car in an accident or have debris fly into their eyes, causing permanent damage.

- ✔ **Never allow your pup to ride in the driver's seat.** Not only are both you and the puppy in jeopardy, but so is everyone passing you on the street! You can't drive and bond at the same time.

Rules for the road

Your puppy must have structure in the car. If she doesn't, she'll think she owns it, which can lead to a cascade of problems, the least of which is barking at everything that moves. You have some options:

- ✔ **Put your pup in a crate during road trips.** Crates are cumbersome and can be a little big, but they keep your puppy contained while you drive. Buy a strong, wire-mesh type (for good air circulation) that's sized for your puppy's weight and breed. Line the bottom with a mat, cloth, or similar bedding to provide a surface your puppy can sink her paws into while you're driving.

- ✔ **Put up a barrier.** Barriers enclose your puppy in the back compartment of a wagon or sport utility vehicle. Aesthetically, they're not too appealing, and the cheaper models collapse easily, but a good one can effectively keep your puppy safe and contained.

- ✔ **Use a harness.** Harness gadgets secure around your puppy's body and keep her buckled in (see Figure 9-2). The only drawbacks are that they're tough to put on and that dogs are often less than thrilled to be buckled in.

- ✔ **Secure your puppy to the seat belt.** Give your puppy her own area when traveling. Tie a short lead (no more than 2- to 3-feet long) to the head rest or seatbelt and secure it to your dog's traveling harness (which you can find at a pet store). Decorate her area with a mat and toys to keep her comfortable and occupied during the drive. This simple organization takes minutes to set up and will ensure a lifetime of calm travels because it keeps your puppy safe while you take care of the driving.

Figure 9-2:
This pup's
secure and
ready for
the road.

Guidelines for long trips

Are you planning a long journey? Traveling with a puppy can be a joy or a nightmare; how you organize the adventure will greatly influence the outcome. Following are some guidelines to ensure that you both get to where you're going safely and soundly:

- ✔ **Check your pup's buckle collar to ensure that all identification tags have been updated.** If you're planning an extended stay, make a temporary tag with your temporary phone number. Most pet stores have machines that make affordable tags in next to no time.

- ✔ **Keep your pup's diet and feeding times consistent.** A change can upset her system — and that's one discomfort that you can easily avoid.

- ✔ **Avoid traveling in extreme heat unless you have a good air-conditioning system.** If you're in extreme heat, plan to travel at night or early in the morning.

- ✔ **Never leave your puppy unattended in the car.** If the weather's extreme (either hot or freezing), make an extra set of keys so you can leave the climate control on while you lock the car and take care of your business.

- ✔ **Keep your puppy on a leash at *every* pit stop.** When traveling, a puppy's homing device shuts down. If she wanders off or gets momentarily distracted, she may have trouble finding her way back to you. Traffic is also a danger, so be safe, not sorry.

✔ **Give your puppy water and exercise at every rest area you stop at.**
Feed her before you walk her, and allow her ten minutes to digest her
food before hitting the road again.

✔ **If you're planning a hotel stay, ask about the hotel's "welcome dog"
policy when you make your reservations.**

If you're searching for places that accept pets, you have a few resources.
Many books are dedicated to just that subject, so check the pet section
of your local bookstore. You can also pick up guidebooks offered
through AAA and Mobil Oil that list accommodations that welcome pets.

✔ **Help your puppy adjust to her new surroundings by using a leash and
by stationing her at night on a familiar blanket with a trusty ol' bone.**

When you arrive at your destination

Even though you may be ecstatic to have the trip behind you and to see friends
or family, stay cool until your puppy gets used to the new environment. Plan
ahead if you know your pup will have to meet another dog or other pets when
you arrive. Decide in advance where and how you'll introduce them (pet-to-pet
introductions are covered earlier in this chapter). When you enter a new home,
make sure your puppy stops at the door and allows you to enter first. Give her
a few minutes to "sniff out" the new space. Don't be too surprised if your puppy
eliminates. This is her way of saying "I pee, therefore, I am." Don't make a fuss,
and clean it up discretely. Watch her closely, and if she continues to eliminate
indoors, supervise her freedom and review the routines you established at
home.

If your trip lands you in an unfamiliar climate, be patient. Your pup may react
in ways you can't predict: Snow cover can put a damper on housetraining,
excessive heat can drive even the most adventurous dogs indoors, and rain
can eliminate all hopes for outdoor adventure. If you're introducing water or
snow activities, keep your puppy leashed so that you can direct her calmly.
Chasing, shouting, or physically handling your puppy in a new situation can
overwhelm her and prompt her to run off and perhaps get lost.

Part III
Training Your Puppy

The 5th Wave   By Rich Tennant

"You know, you're never going to get that dog to do its business in your remote control dump truck."

In this part . . .

Are you beginning to think that your puppy is as much work as a child? You're right. Both need training and structure. Both need help containing naughty impulses. Both must be socialized properly. And, well, you may need some help to make it all come together.

In this part, you get the scoop on basic training lessons — from teaching your puppy some control and manners to teaching your puppy basic commands. You also get hints on problem solving and guidance in finding additional help if you need it.

Chapter 10

Getting Everyone Involved

. . . .

In This Chapter

▶ Encouraging consistency among your family and friends

▶ Creating a clan of helpers

▶ Comparing puppy schools and private trainers

. . . .

*B*ringing up a well-rounded puppy in today's society is definitely not a one-person job, even if you do live alone. However, if you're surrounded by family members or friends, striking a balance between consistency and cooperation takes some effort. You soon find out that sometimes your puppy is easier to train than your roommate. Finding outside help — from a veterinarian and dog walker to a fun, informative puppy teacher — is paramount too.

A Team Effort: Getting Help and Buy In from Friends and Family

The mere fact you're reading this book proves that you have knowledge and common sense on your side when you try to get your friends and family involved with the training of your puppy. However, this doesn't mean that everyone agrees with your chosen approach. In order to get your friends and family to go along with your approach you have to do the following:

✔ Set your boundaries early on.

✔ Show effectiveness through example.

✔ Communicate your methods positively (positive-reinforcement training isn't just for puppies anymore!).

Making sure your family and friends are consistent with your pup

If I could pick one paragraph out of this book to give to families, this one would be it. Inconsistencies can be oh-so-confusing for a puppy. Imagine being a puppy in these scenarios: One person says "Sit in my lap," while the other shouts "Get off the furniture!" One discourages jumping, and the other wants to dance. One refuses to give me any human food, while another is sliding tidbits under the table.

Mixed messages often create maniac rituals — especially when new people arrive. Instead of having one clear thought or a solid understanding of how to respond, the puppy must now dance around trying to determine what this new person's rules are.

Please spare your puppy this mass mix-up. Sit down with your friends and family and create a consistency chart. Table 10-1 shows one from my house.

Table 10-1		Consistency Chart	
Behavior	*Routine*	*How to Extinguish Bad Behavior*	*Directions Given*
Greeting	Pup must sit, roll over, or get toy	Fold your arms over your face or tug on pup's drag leash	"Sit," "Belly up," or "Get your toy"
Barking for attention	Find another way to get attention	Ignore your pup's behavior completely	"Get your toy" when barking stops
Nipping	Pup must lick or prompt a need	Slip your finger under your pup's collar or take leash and tug away	"Kisses," "Out," or "Go to your mat"

Engaging in some interior decorating

Okay, you don't need to be an interior decorator to raise a puppy, but you've probably discovered (or may shortly) that anything at floor level is fair game for your puppy's chewing. By leaving valuables within your pup's reach, you're inviting mischief, which surely can arouse chaos and confrontation. Prevention truly is worth a pound of cure. Start by redecorating your home: Tidy up and put everything out of reach of your puppy. Then put everyone in charge of their own stockpile. If your partner's favorite slippers are destroyed, you can say "I told you so!"

After you've cleared the floors, have your family help you organize a play station in each room (see Chapter 5 for info on creating play stations). Place all your puppy's toys and bones at the play station. Your puppy quickly bonds to this area if it's a center point of attention and treats.

Let your example be everyone's guide — your puppy is happy and responsive knowing that he has his own special corner.

Creating a cause-and-effect chart

To help your family see the effects of their interactions with the puppy, create a cause-and-effect chart. Just the slightest modification in behavior can help your puppy understand and can keep your family motivated in the training process. Table 10-2 shows an example.

Table 10-2	Cause-and-Effect Chart	
Behavior	*Encouraging Reaction*	*Discouraging Reaction*
Jumping in greeting	Push, shout, or interact	Ignore, look away, or fold arms over face
Nipping in play	Physically correct or jerk hand away	Leave a leash on your puppy and pull him off; determine if a need is pressing; play a game or isolate for a nap
Stealing an object	Yell, chase, and capture	Walk out of the house, or shake a treat cup while pretending to eat the treats yourself as you walk away
Barking at the door	Yell or physically correct	Leave a leash dragging to interfere casually — redirect pup to your side; use a treat-oriented lesson to refocus
Piddling when excited	Yell or stick his nose in it	Ignore your puppy until he has calmed down; externalize his focus with a toy or treat cup

Naughty behaviors can become habit through well-meaning, but nonetheless interactive, attention.

No, you shouldn't have to bribe your family to take part in raising and caring for your puppy. But, you might have to anyway. Do whatever it takes to get your puppy through his first year with your sanity and his spirit intact. And who knows — after your family sees how much fun hanging out with your puppy can be, they may just vie for walks, feeding, and play time!

It Takes a Village: Enlisting Outside Help

No matter what your political affiliation is, you probably remember Hillary Clinton reiterating the quote: "It takes a village to raise a child." Well, in today's society, with all the hustle and bustle, the same holds true for your puppy. Take time to surround yourself with a happy clan of outside helpers, and be sure to keep their numbers close at hand because you lean on these people more than you think! The following sections give you an idea of who needs to make up your clan.

Your veterinarian

Think of your dog's veterinarian as being on par with your own doctor or your child's pediatrician. Medical knowledge is essential, but a good bedside manner is the cherry on top of the sundae. Speak with the receptionists and bring your pup in for a cheerful social call before your initial visit. Talk to the doctor like she's a neighbor. Do you feel comfortable sharing all your canine concerns with her?

If you're unsure of which veterinarian to use, ask around. You can narrow your search by asking your friends and family who they use and why.

Puppies can be very impulsive — they often swallow things that look edible before even considering whether they actually are. So, at your first veterinary visit, ask the doctor if she has a recommended method for inducing vomiting. You should also find out the poison-control hot-line number and always keep it by your phone in case of an emergency. As well, seek out a 24-hour emergency veterinary hospital in your area. Keep the hospital's number by your phone also. Accidents can happen during off hours, so have a plan.

Dog walkers

Whether your life demands consistent hours away from the home or circumstance steps in to temporarily rearrange your schedule, knowing a dog walker can make the difference between a happy puppy and a stressed out one. Puppies are like human babies in that they have a strong need dependency. Even though an adult dog can hold it until you get home or can survive until a late meal, your puppy may very well eat your walls if you get stuck in traffic. A reliable dog walker can be a real godsend in times like these.

Ask around and interview a couple of dog walkers before you actually need one. Being prepared ahead of time makes crisis situations that much easier. When interviewing dog walkers, remember that reputation counts, as does your puppy's reaction, so be sure to ask for references and allow your puppy to interview the candidate. Tail wagging and kisses are equivalent to a double thumbs up!

Groomers

Groomers have a tough job, so I give them a lot of credit. Many dogs backpedal before they even reach the door. Many growl when approached, and some even need to be muzzled. It's often a thankless job. You can greatly shape your puppy's opinion of the groomer by exercising your puppy before bringing him in, keeping him combed between visits (to keep painful knots at bay), and introducing him to their handling techniques.

When deciding on a groomer, visit each facility ahead of time, and ask to see where the dogs are stationed while they're waiting their turn or drying. What vibes do you get from each place? Do the dogs already there seem happy or stressed? Is it clean and _almost_ odor free? Would you want to get a haircut here if you were a dog?

Watch the groomer's handling techniques. Groomers need to be rougher than you would be, but cursing or harsh corrective techniques are unnecessary. Ask the manager what the pay structure is and find out their recommended drop-off and pick-up schedule. Also inquire about what they do when a dog needs to, or does, eliminate in the holding area. Don't accept anything less than "We remove the dog and clean immediately."

Doggie day care

I love the concept of day care for your dog, especially if you work all day. The vision of a bunch of dogs running helter-skelter through a yard or matted room is exhilarating. When deciding between doggie day care centers, ask the following questions of each center:

- How are the dogs/puppies grouped?
- What do they do in case of a dog fight?
- Who is the veterinarian on staff? If they're off location, where is the doctor located?

✔ Do they kennel overnight?

✔ What plans are in place if you're delayed?

✔ Do they offer auxiliary services, such as grooming, training, medical care, or medicating?

Bear in mind that your puppy may be exhausted after his visit to day care. If training, walks, and bonding are high on your priority list, plan these events for another day. Your puppy may be blissfully brain-dead when he gets home.

Puppies, like kids, pick up both good and bad habits from their friends. If you notice your puppy roughhousing or being uncharacteristically defiant, ask to meet the dogs he plays with. If his playmates are rubbing off bad energy, you may consider asking whether your puppy can be placed in another group. Or, consider taking a break from day care until your puppy is more mature because an older puppy or dog is less likely to acquire bad habits.

Puppy kindergarten

A great kindergarten program is worth its weight in dog biscuits. Social time mixed with structure and training blend for an experience that's fun for everyone involved. Look for a program that welcomes families (if you have one you want to bring along), that limits enrollment to four to eight puppies, and whose teacher you're comfortable talking to. If the teacher seems nice with your puppy, but is rough or distancing with you, look for someone else. You're being trained as much or more than your puppy: You should look forward to class too!

Puppies are impulsive and excitable. Find a class whose teacher takes excitability in stride and doesn't single out any one puppy as problematic. Your puppy is who he is: The goal of puppy school is to discover your puppy's personality and how to modify *your* approach of communicating with him.

Free play is the time during a kindergarten class when the puppies get to race about and get to know the other puppies and people in their classroom. Free play is a very big part of my puppy kindergarten classes. Even though some get overwhelmed at first, they integrate by the third free play and are consequently more comfortable in different social settings. To ensure that your puppy can get this socialization, ask prospective kindergartens if free play is a part of their curriculum.

Chapter 11

Using Cool Tools and Groovy Gadgets

*B*elieve it or not, you can solve more problems with positive feedback than with discipline. I've used every technique in this chapter, often simultaneously, and I guarantee that these fun approaches are more effective. By creating an atmosphere in which cooperation is fun and learning is natural, your puppy's days will be stress-free and her reactionary mischief almost nonexistent. I'm as eager to share this information as, I'm sure, you are to discover it.

Your puppy's behavior is determined by what gets your attention, and she doesn't care whether the attention is negative or positive. Select one or all of the techniques in this chapter (from clicker training to targeting and snack packs) to highlight what your puppy is doing correctly, and those activities will rule your days. Teaching your puppy many skills will dramatically improve her focus and mental well-being — you're in for a tremendous surprise!

Using Positive Reinforcement to Encourage Happy Cooperation

Imagine being a puppy. You're small, inexperienced, and often bored, as all young, restless minds are. Day after day, you're stuck watching this giant group of two-legged dogs (as humans are to them) bustling about. Human talking and chitchat is nothing but noise to your puppy's ears. Activities, from television to phone chats and cooking are relatively incomprehensible to her. Take a minute to think of your life from your puppy's perspective: What exactly is she thinking?

The one highlight that makes a puppy's day complete is your interaction with her. Dogs like being plugged into group activities. They want to know what's going on and want to be included in your thought process. Puppies are sharply aware of what behaviors get a reaction, and they quickly adapt their behavior according to your behaviors and routines.

For example, have you noticed your puppy repeating anything that guarantees even a moment's recognition from you? Think about it: All that whining, stealing, jumping, and nudging is done for your engagement. Staring, drooling, and pawing puppies can be so creative when sifting through behaviors that get your attention. Now what if I told you to use the same logic to encourage good behavior?

Whatever puppy behaviors you pay attention to, you reinforce. Focus on a good dog, and that's what you'll have. Get carried away with the negative, and you'll have a horror show.

With the smallest effort, you can teach your puppy to share objects rather than steal them, to sit for attention rather than jump, and to bring a ball to entice play rather than bark in your face. You see, the choice is up to you.

I can just imagine what you're thinking — "Well, I've done all the wrong things. Can this confusion now be reversed?" The answer is a resounding "Yes." Simply remember that your puppy prefers cheerfulness over stress. The following sections guide you down the path to a better-behaved pooch.

If your puppy has already developed bad habits, use Chapter 16 to reorganize your environment, discourage her interest, and restructure her activities to ensure that all her needs are met.

Emphasizing Good Habits with a Little Indulgence: Treat Cups and Snack Packs

The age-old question is "To treat or not to treat?" My opinion is to treat and to treat often. For the record, though, I started out in the business very anti-treat. And anti-treat training can be done, but it's not much fun. In a life filled with daily responsibilities and stress, you may as well enjoy the process of teaching and learning with your puppy. So, feel free to use treat cups and snack packs galore.

Treat cups

Treat cups are easy to make and fun to use. Find an empty plastic container, cut a small hole in the lid, and fill it half full with small treats or your pup's food. Shake it and give treats until your puppy associates the sound with getting a reward. Shake, treat, shake, treat, shake, treat . . . soon the sound of the cup will bring her running. Then, you can use this sound to highlight positive moments between you and your puppy and to encourage your puppy's happy association to important words and people.

Create multiple treat cups and spread them all around — in every room of the house, in your car, and at Grandma's house. You can never have too many treat cups. However, remember to put them out of your puppy's reach so that she doesn't overindulge herself!

Have children? Make it a family project by decorating your treat cups with construction paper, markers, and stickers.

Using treat cups for problem solving and conditioned learning

Use your treat cup to shape your puppy's happy and willing cooperation. By creating a calm, understanding environment, your puppy will develop into a calm, easy dog. Trust me, it works. For example, if you want your puppy to sit but she's jumping up, hold the treat cup out of her reach. When she finally calms down, praise her and give a treat. The same method works with her favorite toy, as you can see in Figure 11-1.

Figure 11-1:
If your puppy jumps, lift the toy or treat cup out of reach. Treat for civil sitting.

Making an object exchange with a treat cup

Each time your puppy puts something in her mouth (good or bad, her object or yours), find the treat cup and shake it. Say "Share" as you approach her calmly and exchange a treat for the object in her mouth.

I've heard this argument about 10,000 times: "But doesn't the treat cup reward bad behavior?" Hear me out. A young puppy will mouth everything. She'll chew whatever feels nice to her, whether it's a rawhide, boot, or tissue. Yelling at her will only create tension and stress, leading to — you guessed it — more chewing and destruction. To top that, yelling conveys prize envy and often leads to catch-me-now antics or, worse, aggression.

Shaking a treat cup and encouraging your puppy to share will teach her only one thing: to bring you what she's found, undestroyed. Focus positively on her objects, and that's what she'll settle for in the end.

Treat cup fun and games

Use your treat cup to play fun, recreational learning games, such as the following:

- **Runaway-Come Game:** Shake the cup as you run away from your puppy. Shout her name cheerfully as you run away and say "Come" as you treat her for being near you.

- **Treat Cup Name Game:** Send your puppy back and forth between two or more people. Use her name as well as each person's. Soon your puppy will know everyone on a first-name basis, including herself!

- **Quick Sit Game:** Shake the cup and position your puppy into the sit position. Soon she'll be conditioned to sit quickly each time she hears the cup being shaken — and no words will be necessary. When your pup has mastered the Quick Sit Game, use it when company arrives.

Snack packs

Not to be confused with the pudding-cup treats for humans by the same name, these snack packs are strictly for dogs. To make a snack pack, simply dig a fanny pack out of the bottom of your closet or buy one, and fill it with goodies and a clicker if you're using one (see the section "Clicker-Happy Training" later in this chapter). Begin to treat (or click and treat) your puppy when she cooperates. It won't take long for your puppy to notice where the treats are coming from. Reward her for everything she's doing right — which is to say everything she's not doing wrong.

Saying "Good dog!" repetitively in a high-pitched tone may create so much excitement that your puppy may abandon her good behavior for something more recreational, such as nipping or jumping. If you're using a clicker, click before you treat. If you're not using a clicker, use a sharp, marking word like "Yes" or "Good" to highlight the exact behavior you want your puppy to repeat.

Am I supposed to feel like a Pez dispenser?

Do you feel like a gigantic Pez dispenser when you're wearing your snack pack? Does your puppy come up to you expecting tidbits all the time? Well, good — now you really have the power to shape her behavior. Ignore the behavior you want to extinguish and continue to treat your pup only when she's sitting calmly or behaving in a civil manner.

If your puppy charges you or blocks your path, ignore her. Look away and walk on. If she barks or whines incessantly, don't cave. Also, don't use any eye contact or physical interaction. If she paws at you, don't dole out any snacks or attention. If she's prancing through the living room with your undergarments, ignore her and leave the room. After enough mischievous behavior she'll finally sit or collapse in exhaustion. And when she does, reward her! She'll catch on quickly to what you expect from her.

No rules say that your puppy can't work for her meals. I used to walk my puppy with her breakfast in my snack pack to highlight her off-lead cooperation. When time allows, place half or more of your puppy's meal in your snack pack and run through familiar exercises or directions.

Conditioning your pup to come to you naturally

Most puppies come when they're young, and few stray far because the world is new and overwhelming. However, just as suddenly as life becomes more predictable, wanderlust takes hold, and off they go. Screaming, yelling, or chasing your pooch all unite to make matters worse — your flamboyance is perceived as interactive, *not* directional.

Even though enclosures are a must and long lines irreplaceable, you can use your snack pack to condition your puppy to check in and come naturally. Each time your puppy walks by, click your clicker (see the following section for details) or say your word marker (such as "Yes"), and treat her immediately.

If your puppy seems uninterested in your presence, take out some temptations that are sure to get her attention, such as a treat cup or favorite toy. I've even kneeled down and played with sticks or pretended to find something delightful on the ground: It works every time!

Clicker-Happy Training

If you've never been formally introduced to the clicker, allow me: This small hand-held device makes a sharp cracking sound each time it's pressed. Pair this sound with a food reward and you'll discover power that would make Pavlov proud. Your puppy will alert to the sound, and when she connects this noise with a food reward, she'll be prompted to repeat whatever action makes it snap. Use the clicker properly to condition good behavior in mere seconds. Sounds too good to be true, right? It isn't, and you can get started with puppies of any age.

"Photographing" the moment

A clicker is best used to reinforce good reactions the moment they happen: from sitting or lying calmly and coming when you call to peeing in the right spot. Think of it as "photographing" a moment you want to see again. Your puppy sits: Click and treat. She potties in the right place: Click and treat. She returns with a toy in her mouth (or returns to you with anything): Photograph her behavior by clicking and treating.

To get the most out of the click-treat combination, work on your timing. Click the very instant your puppy accomplishes a task (such as "Sit" or "Down") or during a time when she's behaving well.

You'll soon find out that click timing is a lot like photographing a child's smile: Delay even a nanosecond, and the moment's gone. Also, limit your excitement and praise until after you dole out the treat.

The click-treat formula is one click, one treat. Any other formula would be inconsistent, and inconsistency is too confusing for your puppy. If she makes a gigantic breakthrough, you can give her a handful of treats, a so-called jackpot, but use only one click to highlight her cooperation.

Click and treat: Married for life

Note that each time I tell you to click, I follow it with the word "treat." I use these words together because they're married for life. No prenup necessary: The two shall never part. Your puppy will count on this association: Empty clicks will snuff her enthusiasm. The lone click becomes the number-one canine disappointment.

You don't want to become clicker dependent, so later in this section, I detail how to phase out the clicker's use. You need to phase out both the click and the treat as one unit.

Clicker specifics

Are you ready to start using this wonderful tool? You can use it around the clock to condition good behavior or at specific "lesson" times to target your goal. Even though I would rather use the clicker around the clock, I find that using it to highlight specific actions (such as housetraining) and during lesson times is more realistic for me. (Besides, I've got a 2-year-old who loves to copy, and a clicker in her hands would leave us all a little stressed out. . . .)

Around-the-clock reinforcement

If you want to use the clicker throughout the day, attach it to a bracelet key chain or a lanyard around your neck. Stuff your pockets or your snack pack with goodies so that you're never without them, and click and treat away.

Clicker-happy lessons

Another option is to limit the use of the clicker to set times or organized lessons. You're less likely to become clicker dependent when using this approach, but you also run the risk of having a puppy who only listens when you have a clicker in hand. To avert this pitfall, use directional words and hand signals at all times; if your puppy ignores you, simply position her using pressure points discussed in Chapter 14.

If you decide to use this approach, set aside time to do between one and four ten-minute clicker lessons per day. Focus on one or two skills, and click and treat any cooperation.

Top ten clicker-happy associations

Here are the top ten behaviors and directions that benefit from the use of a clicker-happy association:

- **Name:** Call out your puppy's name. If she looks to you, click and treat. If not, ignore it and move on.

- **Sit:** Each time you expect civility, encourage your puppy to "Sit." Some preferred times of civility include before you give her a treat or toy, before you toss a stick, and when entering and exiting the home. Click and treat the instant her bottom hits the floor.

- **Housetraining:** Click and treat the moment your puppy eliminates in the right spot.

- **Down:** Using the techniques described in Chapters 14 and 15, guide your puppy to lie down. Click and treat the moment her elbows hit the floor, and say "Down" as she lowers herself into position.

- **Greeting:** When greeting your puppy, ignore her until she's sitting at your side or until she fetches a toy. Reward both behaviors with an instant click and treat.

- **Give or Drop:** To help your puppy learn to spit out toys or other objects on cue, hold out a treat when she has something in her mouth. Say "Give" and click and treat the instant she spits it out. If she debates the issue, use a more tantalizing tidbit.

- **Come:** If you want your puppy to return to you reliably, click and treat whenever she's nearby. With this click and treat combo, she won't stray far.

  Rewarding a puppy for being nearby is different from trying to lure your puppy to come to you. Though many have tried to use the clicker to entice their puppy to come, the cooperation is short lived — especially when the temptation to stray is stronger than the temptation to snack.

- **Extinguishing impulse chasing:** To discourage your puppy from chasing your children, cats, or other temptations, use the leash corrections found in Chapter 8, and then use the click and treat association to refocus her attention on you.

- **Contained barking:** No one minds when a puppy barks a little, but when it turns bratty or incessant, well, that's another story. Use the click and treat method to reinforce your puppy's alert barking and arrest any ongoing chatter with a quick tug of the leash (Chapter 17 goes into more detail about how to handle an overly talkative puppy).

  Pay close attention to your timing when encouraging your puppy to quiet down. If you click when she's merely taking a deep breath or a long pause, your click and treat combo will only inspire more ruckus. Wait until your puppy has fully quieted down and is focused on you to reward her cooperation.

- **Settled down and chewing a bone or toy:** Ah, finally a moment's peace: Your puppy is settled down and is quietly chewing a bone. Now is the time to lavish her with attention and praise. For Pete's sake — this is a moment to highlight.

Phasing out the clicker

No, you won't be dependent on the clicker for life. You're only temporarily using it to positively condition word/behavior memory. However, orchestrating the clicker's disappearance will take some ingenuity, lest your puppy forget what she's learned. The key phrase to remember is *unscheduled reinforcement,* which means phasing out the clicker gradually so that your puppy is unable to track its predictability. This system peaks her motivation and interest until each new direction gets encoded into her behavioral memory — click or no click!

Following is a set of steps you can use to phase in and out your use of the clicker. I use the direction "Sit" throughout the example.

1. **When introducing the first direction, "Sit," use continual reinforcement for a week — click and treat each time you say this direction.**

   You may use your treat to lure your puppy into position, but you'll begin to witness your puppy's quick association. In fact, soon all you'll have to do is show her the clicker or the treat and she'll sit automatically. That said, you may also notice that your puppy is less focused if the clicker and treats are absent.

2. **After a week of reinforcing the "Sit" direction, introduce another direction, such as "Down," with continual reinforcement. At the same time, you should begin to phase out using the clicker with the "Sit" direction by replacing the click and treat with verbal praise.**

   Don't stop using the clicker with "Sit" cold turkey. Instead, vary the click-and-treat reinforcement with praise. For instance, click and treat two responses, and then go two or three with praise only. Click and treat three in a row, and then praise the next one. Over a week's time, tip the scale: Click and treat one, praise three. Within two weeks, your verbal appreciation will be incentive enough for your pup to continue the good behavior.

As you phase out the continual reinforcement phase of a specific direction, introduce continual reinforcement at other times throughout the day, such as before you feed your puppy, toss toys, or give her a bone. Light bulbs will start blinking, and your puppy will associate this direction with praise and rewards.

As you phase out the clicker, don't forget to praise your puppy. Eventually, when all the lessons are understood, you'll shelve the clicker, and the only thing motivating your puppy's good behavior will be the sound of your voice.

Targeting

You can choose from three targeting skills, which can be used individually or in unison, to improve your level of communication and your puppy's enthusiasm for learning. See Table 11-1 for details on these targeting choices.

Table 11-1	Targeting Skills		
Type of Training	*Skill Puppy Must Use*	*Tool*	*Lessons*
Point training	Focusing	Your finger	All obedience directions and "Go to" (a person or object)
Target training with a wand	Following	Targeting wand	All obedience directions and "Go to" (a person or object)
Target training with a stationary disc	Standing; staying	Targeting disc	Stationary directions such as "Stay," "Wait," "Go to" (bed or crate), and "Go out"

The concept behind targeting is simple: Using verbal and food reinforcements, you teach your puppy to move toward the point of your finger, a hand-held wand, or a stationary target (which can be anything from a lid to an index card or a book of matches). Used separately or in unison, these tools encourage your puppy's interaction and help you highlight her cooperation the moment it happens. With these simple skills, the sky is the limit.

Point training

As a whole, the human species is more focused on verbal directions. Your puppy, however, pays closer attention to visual cues. *Point training,* which involves directing your pup with the point of your finger, enables you to be in constant communication with your puppy. Hand signals also quickly increase your puppy's visual awareness and dependency on you.

Have you noticed how much your puppy looks to you for guidance? Young puppies check in throughout the day for some simple directional cues. If you ignore this opportunity to give her direction, your puppy may grow up thinking that you need help with everyday decisions. But point training your puppy will make the difference between raising a puppy who feels included in day-to-day activities and one who feels ignored. Pointing quickly enhances a puppy's understanding of all directions, from "Sit" to "Come" to "Go say hello." It even helps shy puppies overcome inhibition and aggressive puppies get in check.

To teach your puppy point training, you have to follow three phases (shown in Figure 11-2a–c) in order to achieve your end result (shown in Figure 11-2d). The first two phases use food as an incentive, and the third works to wean the pup off treat dependence. The whole process takes ten days to two weeks.

a

b

c

d

Figure 11-2:
This simple signal helps your puppy feel included rather than ignored.

Phase 1: Instant gratification

This step introduces the hand signal and concept behind pointing. Though your long-term goal is for your puppy to follow your signals without needing food rewards, this first step rewards her instantly every step of the way. Follow these steps:

1. **Place or line up ten treats on a high table. Use either a clicker or marker word (such as "Yes") to highlight the moment your puppy alerts to the point of your finger.**

2. **Point your index finger straight to the floor, and curl your other fingers into your hand.**

3. **Tuck one treat into the palm of your hand.**

4. **Hold your pointed index finger 3 inches from your puppy's nose.**

5. **When she reaches out to touch your finger, say "Yes", and then click and treat by flipping your hand around to reveal the snack.**

6. **Repeat this simple exercise until all the treats are gone.**

After you get through the first ten treats, vary the format just slightly. Hold your hand farther away from your puppy's nose, and have her touch your finger twice before relinquishing the treat. Signal your puppy into a "Sit" or "Down" position, treating her the moment she moves into position.

Keep the lessons short and snappy, practicing one to four times each day for five to ten minutes.

Phase 2: Delayed gratification

Follow the steps as in Phase 1, but instead of holding the treats in your hand, place them in your pocket. Your puppy will experience an obvious delay in the time it takes you to reach the treat, which in turn will peak her curiosity and awareness of your presence. Vary this pause to increase her focus. The big lesson for your pup here is patience.

Begin the same way as in the first step of Phase 1 above. Then, hold a treat in front of you and vary the position, increasing to multiple points. Use your pointer finger to direct your puppy's position.

Phase 3: Gradually phasing out treats

Indiscriminately phase out rewarding each point, and integrate pointing into your daily direction. Going upstairs? Point the way. Releasing your puppy to greet someone? Pointing a "Go say hello" at your puppy's eye level will further discourage jumping. Sending your puppy to her crate or bed? Keep on pointing. Each time your puppy cooperates, praise her cheerfully. Life is so much fun when you can communicate with each other!

Targeting wands

Think of a *targeting wand* as an extension of a point. You can use a kitchen utensil, metal office pointer, or tent pole. Pick your tool, and teach your puppy to mark the end by rewarding her interest. Follow these similar steps as discussed in the point training section:

1. **Point the end of the wand to the floor and hold it inches from your puppy's nose.**

2. **The second your puppy reaches out to sniff it, say "Yes" and then click and treat.**

3. **Continue simple touches until your puppy's reaction is familiar and reliable. Then vary the distances and the angle of the wand.**

4. **Increase the number of touches between rewards and increase the directional cues to include the following:**

   - **"Let's go":** Hold the wand next to your side and give this direction as you walk along.

   - **"Go to":** With a partner, direct your puppy back and forth between the two of you using the "Go to" direction. Two target wands may be used.

   - **"Down":** Signal "Down" as though your target stick were an extension of your finger. In this case, the targeting wand allows you to increase the distance between you and your puppy.

   - **"Follow":** Use this direction when teaching your puppy to move away from your side. This cue is ideal for confidence-building exercises and off-lead adventures, such as agility, pet therapy, and competition obedience.

   - **"Come":** A targeting wand is an ideal attention-getting and directing tool for off-leash, distant comes.

Targeting discs

Targeting discs can be useful for helping your puppy better understand and cooperate with your vision. Make a disc out of a heavyweight paper, or use the top of a plastic container. This technique requires some ingenuity and patience. Follow these steps:

1. **Place a disc on the floor.**

2. **The moment your puppy shows interest in the disc — even so much as a sniff — say "Yes" and click and treat.**

   Continue this association until her interested is piqued when she sees the disc.

3. **Then wait until she touches the disc with her paw (see Figure 11-3) to reward her interest.**

   It may take some time initially, but you need to wait for her to figure it out. Positioning her foot doesn't lead to understanding and may have the reverse effect. The moment she steps on the disc, say "Yes" and click and treat. Gradually increase her understanding until she steps on it with her entire paw.

4. **When your puppy comprehends the task, repeat it often to cement her understanding. Begin to associate the word "Disc" with this behavior.**

5. **Now begin to move the disc between sequences.**

   Practice three moves per lesson.

6. **The moment your puppy steps on the disc, instruct her to "Wait." As she cooperates, use a lightweight leash or short leash to steady her as you introduce familiar directional cues.**

   Start with stationary directions like "Sit" and "Down." If your puppy is familiar with "Stay" use it, too. Gradually increase the time you expect your puppy to be still.

7. **Position the disc increasingly farther from your side.**

When your puppy's showing a real connection to the disc, place it on her bedding, and send her there by saying "Go to your disc."

Figure 11-3:
Target disc in action! Teach your puppy to stand on the disc wherever it's placed.

Who could resist this Basset Hound's ears and smoochy face? This puppy will mature into a sociable yet stubborn dog with a cheerful air yet independent ways. Are you game?

These three Saint Bernard pups playing peek-a-boo under the covers look adorably small and cuddly. Don't blink too fast, though. This giant breed grows quickly, and before you know it, they'll be taller than you! (See Part I for the lowdown on choosing your perfect puppy.)

This Alaskan Malamute looks adorable and sweet! Though this breed is certainly both, their thick coat, independent nature, and high energy level makes them most ideal for people who will respect and nurture their needs.

The Welsh Cardigan Corgi is a short breed with a strong spirit! Bred to maneuver cattle, it will stand on its own and respect only the most confident directions.

Cute and stately, the Cavalier King Charles Spaniel is a small breed with a sporting heart yet a secret love for pampering.

These two Sheltie puppies look so sweet you may be tempted to adopt two puppies simultaneously. Think long and hard because raising two puppies together is a much different experience than raising one.

If you're attracted to spots, these Dalmatian puppies are sure to make you smile. Before adopting this high-energy breed, however, understand their watchful nature and be sure you can commit the time to early training (Chapter 14) and socialization (Chapter 7).

Chihuahuas are taking their turn as a highly popularized breed. They're easy to spoil, but pamperers beware! These pups are born with a strong sense of self and can be bossy and bratty when treated like a stuffed animal.

This collie pup, beautiful and refined, will never settle for being a mere decoration. His need for exercise and direction surpasses the commitment to grooming, so make sure you have the time to raise and train this lovely herding breed.

Kids and puppies: What could be a better mix? Before selecting a breed, analyze your family structure taking into account your children's age and their hobbies, as well as their interest in being a part of the puppy training experience. Chapter 8 provides good guidelines to follow.

Is there any wonder the Yorkshire Terrier has consistently been one of the most popular toy breeds around? Just be prepared for lots of grooming! When these pups become full-grown, their hair gets considerably longer.

Though there is little else as adorable as a litter of look-a-like Golden Retriever puppies, each one has a unique spirit and personality that can be tested for at a young age. Use the personality tests and temperament evaluation (Chapter 4) to determine which puppy will fit best into your lifestyle.

Beagles are a group-oriented, sweet breed that still have a mind of their own. Lessons will always be secondary to a wafting aroma. But just look at that face!

This Cocker Spaniel pup couldn't look more endearing if she had ribbons tied to each ear. Loyal and loving, this breed acclimates well to family life but won't enjoy time spent alone.

Shopping for a big dog in a small package? Look no further. The Pug is a breed to satisfy big dog lovers who may not have the time or space to commit to large breeds.

These adorable toy Papillons will grow into cheerful companions who are still driven with a purposeful spirit. Born of a gun dog lineage, these puppies want to be far more than a household decoration.

This large-and-in-charge Rottweiler is a composed and focused puppy. He will grow rapidly and test your role as leader. Be firm, and you'll have his respect.

If you want to adopt a breed that is as much a comedian as it is a cuddly lap dog, these Shih Tzu pups are more than happy to oblige.

Lining up these seven English Cocker Spaniel puppies is one photo-op moment indeed! Although a bit more mellow than the American Cocker Spaniel, these dogs are every bit as driven to interact, follow, and retrieve as their cousins.

Labradors are America's number one breed, and its no wonder; they're good natured, athletic, easy to care for, and great family dogs.

These three Schnauzer puppies are looking quite content resting in the flower bed. As they mature, their energetic and feisty spirit will keep the mice at bay and bedazzle everyone.

Though Bull Terriers were originally bred as fighting dogs, this vigor has been diminished due to mindful breeding and a lack of employment. If you decide to adopt one, however, ensure his congeniality by socializing him with other pets and people.

Chapter 12

Housetraining for Success

1 wish I had a nickel for every time I heard "He knows it's wrong! Just look at his eyes — guilt's written all over his face." Interestingly enough, even though puppies know when you're mad, they can't connect your reaction to their own actions, even if they happened only a few short seconds before.

Dogs shouldn't soil the house, but some do — especially young pups. I know — a puddle or poop on the carpet is a wrenching sight to see, but think about it from your puppy's perspective: By virtue of his species, he's genetically predisposed to cave life. Left outside, he'd never mind using the nearest tree or bush as a toilet (or as a toy, depending on the current need). In general, a puppy doesn't care about what kind of shape your home, furniture, or solid oak floors are in. At this point in his life, he's more focused on his needs than on your décor.

Sure, you want your puppy to respect your home and hygiene, but certain respect-garnering approaches are frustrating to your pup and can impede learning and create more tension. To be effective, you simply need to understand and empathize with your puppy's dilemma. Then you need to work to condition habits that jive with your puppy's instinctive tidiness (or lack thereof).

So, if housetraining has got you down, cheer up. Even though puppy housetraining is a project that requires consistency and cooperation, it is, by all means, very doable. If your efforts are proving to be less than effective, you need a fresh approach that's outlined start to finish. You need a program that you can apply whether your pup's target is grass, papers, city cement, or gravel. Housetraining your puppy is just a matter of time.

Understand Your Puppy's Natural Potty Impulses

Believe it or not, your puppy's potty activities have a pattern. For example, young puppies go consistently after they do the following:

- ✔ Eat
- ✔ Drink
- ✔ Rest or emerge from isolation
- ✔ Play
- ✔ Chew

Even though my suggestion that you take your puppy out after each activity sounds like a lot, a very young puppy (8 to 10 weeks old) can't control his impulses. However, establishing a routine early on can cement his understanding of "holding it" until he's reached his potty place.

It may help you to know that your puppy's bladder muscle is the last to develop: Flimsy and small, it fills up very fast and, until social maturity (around 5 months), it needs to be emptied often. Asking your puppy to "wait just a second" while you tie your shoes may just not happen.

Your puppy will often let you know that he needs to go out before he eliminates. Like a child, he's driven to communicate physical discomfort, but rather than crying for attention, he'll nip excessively and become restless. Correcting the nipping will only result in confusion. Instead, consider a bathroom run when he gets ornery and always remember to direct him with familiar words. Hang a bell on the route to his potty spot and within no time, he'll be ringing to clue you in to his potty needs (see "Helping your pup communicate his need to go," later in this chapter, for more).

If you find that your puppy has no capacity to hold his urine — he's even going in his crate or when stationed — he may have developed a urinary tract infection. If you think this is the case, take a sample of your puppy's urine in and ask your veterinarian to check it. To collect a sample from your pup, take a plastic container outside and catch a spray of morning urine by holding it under your puppy as he goes. Either race over and drop it off at your veterinarian's within an hour or refrigerate it for preservation.

Direction versus Correction

Correcting a puppy's accidents generally falls flat as a housetraining tool. Puppies really have no clue what you're trying to get across. I've felt your frustration, believe me (I had a dog who still had accidents when she was 9 months old!), but your puppy really doesn't understand your goals. Delightfully self-centered and absorbed in the nuances of his world, your puppy will jive with your routine only if it's presented in a clear, matter-of-fact manner.

Have a small puppy and a large house? If you don't restrict his freedom, he may develop a habit of running into an unoccupied space to potty instead of interrupting you. Yes, it's a polite thing for him to do, but it's obviously not a pleasant thing. To stop him, limit his freedom and be patient until proper habits are more firmly established.

If you're having trouble finding the time to present a consistent routine, your puppy will have trouble focusing on your plan. Housetraining takes time, direction, and consistency. Paying attention to these three ingredients will get you far.

Time

If you've never potty trained a child or housetrained a puppy, you're in for a surprise: It takes time. In the case of puppy training, it takes time to secure a leash and navigate to his area. Then, it takes time to wait for the elimination light bulb to go off in your puppy's head. Let all expectations go, because housetraining could take days, weeks, or months.

Commit to the time housetraining takes, and make doing it right a priority. Your attitude can ease your puppy's misunderstanding, but if you let frustration creep in, your tension will stress him out.

Direction

Your puppy won't arrive knowing where you want him to go to the bathroom. Even if he's housetrained, you'll need to outline where you want him to go. Pick an area inside or out, and direct your puppy there with a specific word each time you bring him to the spot. Direct him again and again, and further help your puppy by associating the "act of eliminating" with another direction, such as "Get busy," which you say while he's in the process of going. Soon he'll know when and where to go simply by hearing these directives. How handy is that?

Make a clicker-happy connection

If you want to put the hurry on your puppy's housetraining connection, employ a clicker. The clicker, which is described in detail in Chapter 11, highlights the moment your puppy cooperates with a sharp click. You follow the click with a yummy snack. For example, discover a dog treat that your puppy will do flips for, and then reward him postclick the moment he eliminates in the right spot.

Pick a potty area that's in a discreet location either close to the house or in a quiet room. Like people, dogs don't like to potty out in the open, nor should they learn to wander to eliminate. Because eliminating puts puppies in a vulnerable position, privacy is best.

Consistency

Consistency is the bedrock of creating any habit — including housebreaking! Tell your family and friends the following:

- Where to take your puppy to potty
- When to take him to potty
- What his behavioral signs are (from pacing to quick exits or frantic nipping rituals) before he potties
- Your route to the potty area, including any sound cues, such as a word or ringing a bell
- Your catchphrase that's said during the potty ritual, such as "Get busy"

Establishing Structure and Routine

You can train some puppies in days. But with others, training may take months. The best way to housetrain your puppy is to establish a strategy and follow a routine. To create a consistent routine, use the following guidelines:

- **Regulate attention and walks.** Number one on the hit parade is to realize the importance of delaying reconnections. For example, you know your puppy lives for his relationship with you. But when your puppy gets up from a nap or is released from isolation (at any time of day), don't greet, cuddle, walk, or chat with him. Simply direct him with the appropriate command, such as "Outside," "Elevators" (if you're in a high-rise), or "Papers." Reconnect lovingly only after he has pottied. Continue this ritual until he's fully housetrained.

✔ **Blaze a trail.** Always follow the same path to the potty spot. Encourage everyone to follow this route. Go out the same door consistently until your puppy is fully housetrained. See Figure 12-1 for an example.

If you have a small dog or young puppy, don't carry him to his potty area. Let him walk so he can learn how to navigate the path on his own.

✔ **No roaming.** When you arrive at the area, ignore your puppy until he eliminates. Don't walk around letting him sniff or potty around the neighbor's house. A human parent would never toilet train a child by sending him to the neighbors, so don't do the same with your puppy.

✔ **Create behavioral memory.** As your puppy is eliminating, use a second command such as "Get busy!" After a month of saying this phrase while he's in the process of pottying, your puppy should be able to go on cue.

✔ **Don't be stingy with the praise.** When your puppy's done, greet, praise, and walk him as usual.

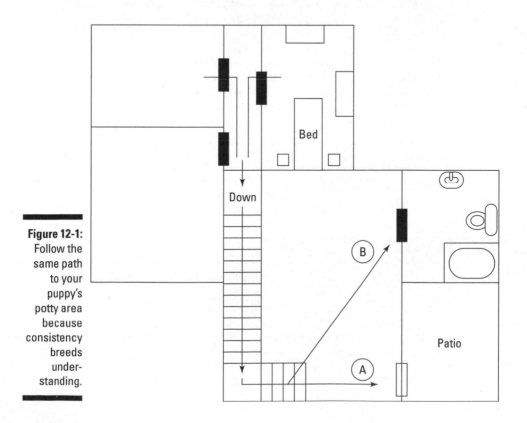

Figure 12-1:
Follow the same path to your puppy's potty area because consistency breeds under-standing.

Getting on a potty-time schedule

So, just how many potty breaks does your puppy need per day? Well, that depends. Really young puppies — younger than 12 weeks — may need to go outside every hour or two. Older puppies can hold out quite a bit longer.

Use the following general guidelines for your puppy:

Puppy's Age	Number of Potty Breaks a Day
6 to 14 weeks	8 to 10
14 to 20 weeks	6 to 8
20 to 30 weeks	4 to 6
30 weeks to adulthood	3 to 4

Based on the preceding guidelines, you need to set up a daily housebreaking schedule. If you're able to be home during the day, follow the schedule shown in Table 12-1. If you work outside the home during the day, follow the schedule shown in Table 12-2. *Note:* In both tables, the italicized events may not be necessary as your puppy grows up.

Dogs of all ages need interaction between the times listed in the tables, so remember that playtimes are extremely important throughout the day. If you work outside the home, try to come home for lunch or hire a dog walker to split up your dog's day. If given a good run midday, your dog should be able to tolerate confinement while you're out.

Table 12-1 Housebreaking Schedule for Work-at-Home Owners	
Time of Day	**Potty Time**
Early morning wake up	Go outside
Breakfast	Go outside after breakfast*
Midmorning	*Go outside*
Afternoon feeding	*Go outside after eating**
Midafternoon	Go outside
Dinnertime (4 to 6 p.m.)	Go outside after dinner*
7:30 p.m.	Remove water

Time of Day	Potty Time
Midevening	*Go outside*
Before bed	Go outside
Middle of the night	*Go outside if necessary*

* A young puppy may need to eliminate after isolation; if you find your puppy uninterested in his meal, take him outside for a quick bathroom run before each feeding.

Table 12-2	Housebreaking Schedule for Owners Who Work Outside the Home
Time of Day	Potty Time
Early morning wake up	Go outside
Breakfast	Go outside after breakfast
Lunch break feeding and walk	Go outside
Midafternoon	*Young puppies must go out*
Arrival home	Go outside
Dinnertime (4 to 6 p.m.)	Go outside after dinner
7:30 p.m.	Remove water
Before bed	Go outside
Middle of the night	*Go outside if necessary*

If you work outside the home, take heed: If you expect your puppy to hold his bladder while you're gone during the day, you'll be disappointed. Puppies lack the bladder muscles necessary to accomplish such a feat. If you have to leave your puppy all day, create a space that allows for a good stretch as well as a place to potty. However, remember that your puppy will be confused if you expect him to go outside when you're home.

If you work outside the home, here's a way to help safeguard against messy accidents. Select a be-alone space — a small room, for example — or invest in a puppy playpen, which you can find at most pet stores (make sure the flooring in this space is non-absorbent). Place your dog's bedding, bowls, and toys in one side of the space. Cover the other side of the space with papers or absorbent pads. Initially cover more area than necessary, taping the corners or buying specially-made pad brackets if your puppy is prone to shredding the pads. In most cases, a puppy will choose to eliminate in the absorbent area, which is very handy. Take your puppy outside when you get home and follow the scheduled routine outlined in Table 12-2. To discourage accidents inside, don't allow access to the be-alone space when you're home.

When possible, plan your puppy's homecoming around your vacation time. This initial bonding a training period is an ideal way to kick off your life together!

Changing the routine

As soon as you have the routine down pat (give it about a week), interrupt it. Instead of chanting "Outside!" lead your puppy to the door. Encourage his signal (for example, barking or ringing a bell — see the next section). Is your dog a subtle signaler? Call him back to you and pump him up: "What is it? Outside? Good dog!" Show him the bell or bark with him, and then let him out. Repeat the process in rooms farther and farther from the door or his papers, running enthusiastically to the door with him and leading him to the spot on leash.

Gradually phase out the bathroom escort by letting the leash drop on your way to the spot. Initially walk next to him, and then stop three-quarters of the way there, halfway there, and one-quarter of the way before stopping and allowing him to proceed to his spot on his own.

Helping your pup communicate his need to go

A young puppy's needs can confuse him. Just before he eliminates, he knows something is going on down there in bladder-land, but for the life of him, he just can't identify what. After all, he was just born.

When a need presses, a young puppy often whines, circles, or nips. Nipping is the most common reaction — think of it as a healthy way to reach out for your help. Even though you may want to teach him a more civilized signal down the road, for right now, be mindful that a young puppy's nips may highlight his need to potty. Direct him with "Outside!" or "Papers!" Whatever you do, don't correct him.

As he matures, your puppy will have increased bladder control and will be able to identify a need when it's pressing.

To help your puppy learn more appropriate signals, teach him to do the following:

✔ **Ring a bell or chime:** Secure a bell or chime at your puppy's nose level, raising it as he grows (see Figure 12-2). Tap the bell just before you go on a bathroom run. If your puppy has access to the door, hang it there. Otherwise, start by hanging it next to that gate, stairway, or banister that encloses him. Ring the bell for or with him for a week. If he doesn't catch on, discreetly smear butter or cheese on the prompter before you approach it first thing in the morning. When he goes forward to lick it, open the door immediately and reward him with a treat.

Figure 12-2:
Teaching your puppy to ring a bell when he needs to go out is easier than you think.

✔ **Bark near his area:** If your puppy is a barker, teach him to bark on cue. As you approach the exit area for a potty outing, encourage him to "Speak." When he does, praise him lavishly, and on you go outside. Good puppy!

Using Papers versus Going Outside

You may decide that you're going to paper train your puppy. In other words, you want him to go potty in a spot inside your home instead of teaching your puppy to go outside.

Paper training is a good option if you have a small puppy, you live in an apartment, you're physically challenged, or you're just not the outdoor sort. It has several similarities to outdoor training (see "Establishing Structure and Routine," earlier in this chapter):

✔ Consistently use the same bathroom spot (inside or out).

✔ Use a word or phrase — such as "Papers" — when you lead your puppy to the area.

✔ After you bring your pup to the area, ignore him until he eliminates.

✔ As your puppy's eliminating, use a word or phrase such as "Get busy."

✔ Don't use the place as a play or interaction area.

Paper training does have one main difference from outdoor training, however: namely, that the papers are within the home. If you're paper training, keep the papers away from your pup's food and water bowls and sleeping areas. Place the papers in a discreet location, such as a corner of the kitchen or bathroom, on a nonabsorbent surface (tile, linoleum, or wood), and make sure they're easily accessible to your puppy, even when you're not home.

Cross-Training: Going Inside and Outside to Potty

You may wonder whether you can cross-train: have your puppy pee inside when paper is present but go outside when it's not. This scenario is ideal for working parents or for zones that are hit with extreme weather patterns. (Housetraining a husky in the middle of winter may not present problems, but asking your teacup Chihuahua to piddle in subzero frost just isn't going to happen.)

This cross-training option is slightly more difficult for your pup to comprehend, but any routine can be established as long as you're consistent. Just be clear on your expectations — that he eliminates on paper when you're out or during inclement weather and outside all other times — and he'll eventually learn to follow the routine. Following are some suggestions:

✔ Establish a routine for going outside when you're home and in all but extreme weather.

✔ Get your puppy to ring a bell to alert you when he needs to go and routinely take him to a predestined spot near the door or exit way.

✔ When you're not home, secure your puppy in a small room or playpen with papers or pads. Clean these pads in front of your puppy (to reinforce eliminating in the right place) calmly when you return home and return to business as usual. Keep your puppy confined near you if he tries to venture off to potty elsewhere in the house.

✔ During inclement weather, place the papers down in a distant room in your home, preferably the garage or mudroom, hallway, or by the exit door. As you approach, call out "Papers!" and lay them down.

If your puppy doesn't eliminate within 5 minutes, either carry, crate, leash, or otherwise confine for 5 to 15 minutes before trying again. Not only will this prevent an accident, but it will also help your puppy build his bladder muscles and ability to "hold it." Whining, nipping, and carrying on are all signs he may need a potty break.

Be a good dog owner: Pick it up!

Regardless of where you live, picking up after your dog is a good idea. Stools attract bugs and worms. In the city and many suburbs, cleaning up after your dog is the law. Retail scoopers are available at pet stores, or you can do what I do:

1. Place your hand in a plastic bag.

2. Clasp the mess with your bagged hand.

3. Turn the bag inside out.

Because bags are easy to carry on walks, you should never have an excuse for not cleaning up after your pooch.

Quick Tips for Housetraining Success

Further cement your puppy's understanding by following some basic tips. If you outline your ritual and highlight your plan to anyone involved in the process, your puppy will be housetrained in no time! Here are my quick tips:

- **Start with a small confinement area.** Puppies are den animals, and the classic den wasn't more than about 90 square feet. Most young or untrained dogs won't soil the area right around them, but if they can race upstairs or into an adjacent room, they're more than happy to relieve themselves there.

  So keep your puppy confined. Crate your puppy at night and when you're out, or station him as outlined in Chapter 5. After he learns the rules, you can grant him more freedom, but not now. Before letting your puppy run willy-nilly through all the rooms in your home, review Chapter 5 for tips on a more gradually integrated approach.

- **Clean up accidents privately.** Don't let your puppy see you clean up his mess. Doing so signals a nurturing acceptance that encourages a repeat performance. Isolate your puppy in another room or with a family member as you clean it up.

- **Neutralize the odor.** Your puppy has a very sensitive sniffer. He'll automatically return to areas where his smell is concentrated. Use a pet store formula or a 50:50 mixture of water and vinegar to remove the scent.

- **Know when corrections count.** If you catch your puppy in the process of eliminating in the house, startle him. Clap your hands as you say "Ep, ep, ep!" Jump up and down like an excited chimp or abruptly slap the wall with your palm. Once you've interrupted your pup, relax your posture and calmly direct him to the elimination area as if nothing happened. When he's done, praise him for finishing.

Special confinement issues for pet store pups

Pet store pups often have a rough go of the *don't-soil-your-area* concept. After all, they had no choice in that early impressionable time away from Mom. If the puppies were from a puppy mill, they more than likely had to go in their kennel space, and they were probably stacked on top of other dogs who were forced to do the same thing. If any mother dog had her way, she'd teach her pups to move far away from their sleeping area to go potty.

If your pet-store puppy is having a problem with soiling in his sleeping area, the crate may not be the best option for housetraining because it symbolizes a potty area. At night, a young puppy can sleep at your bedside in a large open-topped box or secured on a leash to your bedside (after he's leash trained and comfortable with daytime stations). During the day, keep your puppy with you or confine him in a small room, taking him outside or to the papers as often as your schedule will allow (ideally within half-hour to two-hour periods). Take him to the same area, over and over, following the routine described in the housetraining sections ("Establishing Structure and Routine" and "Using Papers versus Going Outside"). Having another dog eliminate in this area is helpful because the scent can give your puppy the right idea.

✔ **Know when corrections don't count.** As much as you want to think your pup's human, he isn't, and your frustration and anger toward your puppy just make you look foolish. Even though I've heard the idea a thousand times, I'm still not convinced that a "puppy understands the meaning of a correction." Sure, you can frighten a puppy into a fearful posture, but scaring him isn't the point you're trying to make.

If you catch your pup soiling someplace other than his designated area, you can interrupt the process, but lay off all other corrections.

✔ **Maintain a stable diet.** Avoid changing dog food brands unless your veterinarian directs you to do so. Your puppy doesn't digest food the way you do: His intestine is small and unable to process and absorb a varied diet.

✔ **If your puppy is pooping in the house, lay off food treats.** If you give food sporadically throughout the day, his elimination habits will be random.

✔ **Watch the water intake.** Puppies, especially young ones, drink water excessively if they're bored or nervous. If your pup is having housebreaking problems, monitor his water intake by giving him access to his water bowl during meal times and as you take him to his area.

Be careful not to dehydrate your pup. If he's panting or very lethargic, give him a bowl of water. Remove water after 7:30 p.m. If he needs a drink after that time, give him ice cubes to play with or a small amount of water (¼–½ cup) to quench his thirst.

Chapter 13

Teaching Everyday Etiquette

Awell-behaved puppy is a welcome social guest, a plus at parades and picnics, and an added fan at after-school sporting events. Unfortunately, your puppy won't train herself to be well-mannered and well-behaved, and she'll be influenced (positively and negatively) by everyone who surrounds her.

The key to etiquette training is to set your goals in mind and share them with family and friends — and even strangers. Think of this chapter as sending your puppy off to "Miss Sarah's School of Etiquette," which is a short-term course with long-term freedoms and rewards.

Civilizing Your Pup Room by Room

Giving your puppy full freedom of your house before she's civilized just might be a big mistake! Are you envisioning yours running wild, toilet paper streaming, cushions flying, food stolen off the counter all while you're dodging left and center trying to get a good grasp on the wriggling ball of fur? Well, this can become a sure reality if you don't introduce your puppy to your household mindfully. For the best results, you need to civilize her room by room.

Unless you want your puppy to view your home as one big playground, prepare a spot for her in each room and take a few days out of your schedule to guide her through your expectations. Do this on leash, so the temptation to bolt doesn't takeover. Gradually allow your puppy freedom, but introduce this freedom by allowing her to move about with a drag leash attached to her collar (refer to Chapter 5).

Though the first days of etiquette training involve keeping your puppy secured to a leash, think of it less as controlling and more as holding your puppy by the paw. These techniques will teach her how to contain her impulses and gently ease her into household freedom.

Leading

Leading involves guiding your puppy around the house on a leash. You may secure the leash around your waist or hold it comfortably in your hand, using specific directions as you navigate together. I call these frequently used words *foundation directions*. Eventually, your puppy will respond without the leash. However, until then, you have to give her direction.

Years ago I patented a training leash I call the Teaching Lead. It's a hybrid between a leash and a belt and secures comfortably to your side to manage your puppy without the constant use of your hands. I designed the Teaching Lead specifically for puppies on the go. One of its functions is leading, but it can be used to station and anchor your puppy as well. You can purchase the original Teaching Lead at www.dogperfect.com or replicate this function by tying the leash around your waist. (See Chapter 5 for more details on the Teaching Lead.)

The sooner you introduce your puppy to your home, the faster she'll mature. Like children, puppies adapt to new experiences more thoroughly when they're young.

The following steps give you the skinny on getting started immediately:

1. **Make sure you're using the right training collar.**

   If you don't know what collar is the right one for your pooch, consider your options by asking your veterinarian, checking out Chapter 5, or visiting me online at www.dogperfect.com. Until your puppy is 16 weeks, use a regular buckle collar, head collar, or no-pull harness.

2. **Hold the leash or secure it to your waist like a belt.**

   Put the clip/knot of the secured leash to your left hip if you want your puppy on the left or on your right side if you want her on the right. Just make sure you tell your friends and family which side you clip your pup to because she can become confused without that consistency.

3. **To teach your puppy proper leash manners, and to prevent pulling, take her to a hallway or cleared room. Walk straight ahead.**

4. **The moment she walks ahead of you, call out her name and turn in the other direction.**

   Praise her, even if you feel a tug.

5. **Continue to turn away from her until she pays attention to her name and stops trying to race ahead.**

   Now you're walking in style. Your puppy will follow wherever you lead her. This is your big chance: All household decisions are up to you. Having your puppy attached to you may seem awkward at first, but soon you won't even know she's there. You may even consider it fun. Remember, you're teaching your puppy to follow you, so if there's a conflict of interest (she wants to go left when you're going right), always go your way and encourage her to follow.

   Some dogs love to walk their owners. They find it enormously fun to drag you down the street because it reminds them of all those tug-of-war games you play together. The first step in correcting this problem is eliminating those tug-of-war games. Also, when your dog takes the leash in her mouth, sharply tug it back *into* the roof of her mouth (not out of her mouth) and ignore her. Focus and praise her when she's cooperating.

6. **As you lead your puppy around, start using your foundation directions (see the upcoming section "Teaching basic commands while leading"). Encourage everyone around your puppy to use the directions, too.**

   When giving directions, speak clearly, give your directions once, and enunciate your syllables because puppies understand sounds, not words.

Everyone who's able to lead the puppy around should do so. You don't want your hierarchy to become a dictatorship. The only unacceptable combination is small children and big puppies. Other than that, everyone in the household should take part. If the lead is too long for a child, he can use a short leash or wear it like a banner across his chest.

Teaching basic commands while leading

Here are six foundation directions to get you started:

- ✔ **"*<Name>*, follow."** Give this direction whenever you start walking or change direction. As you turn, hold your head high and don't look at your puppy until she turns with you.

  If your dog or puppy isn't leash trained, put some biscuits in a cup, place your dog on lead, and shake the cup as you walk around, encouraging her to follow by saying "<Name>, follow!" Then pick up the lead and walk around with the cup. Stop every 10 feet or so and give the dog a treat.

- ✔ **"Sit."** Use this direction whenever you offer your dog something positive such as food, praise, a toy, or a pat. Say the direction only once, helping her into position if she doesn't respond. You should say "Sit" only once because puppies understand sounds, not words, which means that "Sit-Sit-Sit" sounds much different from "Sit."

Saying please (sort of)

No, you can't teach your puppy to literally say please, but she can gesture when she wants something. If you consistently direct your puppy to "Sit" before offering her anything she perceives as positive, she'll sit when she wants something, just as readily as most dogs jump. Here are some situations where you want your puppy to say please:

- When receiving meals, treats, and water

- Before a ball toss or toy offering

- Before doors open to get in or out

- If your puppy wants something on the counter or tabletop

- Before car entrances and exits

- During all greetings

- During introductions to children and older people

If your puppy doesn't sit automatically, simply position her by using the technique discussed in the section "Teaching basic commands while leading."

Is your puppy just learning to sit? To position your puppy properly, avoid pushing on her spine. With your right hand, gently lift the chin or pull upward on the collar, as you squeeze her waist gently with your left thumb and forefinger. This pressure point tucks her neatly into place without pressuring the skeletal system.

- **"Wait" and "Okay."** This duo is a real prize. Imagine getting your puppy to stop before she races downstairs or across thresholds. Each time you cross a threshold or heavily trafficked area, direct her to "Wait" and bring your dog behind you with her lead. She may get excited, so wait until she settles down before you direct "Okay." Make sure your feet cross the threshold first. Leaders must always lead.

- **"Excuse me."** Use this direction whenever your puppy crosses in front of or behind you. Also use it if your dog presses against you or blocks your path. As you say "Excuse me," gently knock your puppy out of your way with your foot or knee (hands are perceived as interactive). Remember, puppies respond to hierarchies, so you need to establish yourself as the leader.

- **"Settle."** Teaching your dog to lie quietly in a new environment is no easy task. Read the upcoming sections on anchoring and stationing, and soon your dog will quiet down on cue.

Dealing with resistance while leading

Some dogs like to imitate mules by digging their heels into the ground in an effort to stop moving while on leash. It's either leash insecurity (addressed later in this chapter) or a passive form of resistance. Your puppy is hoping that you will rush back and give her lots of attention, but don't. Following are two approaches you can use to discourage this habit — which approach you use depends on the puppy and the situation:

- **Keep trucking.** Don't turn around. Skip, hop, and praise the air in front of you and walk a little faster: Your puppy will resist initially but will then run to catch up. When she catches up, praise her happily and continue. This method works well with large breeds that have a reputation for being stubborn.

- **Kneel forward.** If you have a more delicate breed or a puppy with a timid temperament, kneel down in front of your puppy (facing forward) when she puts on the brakes. Tap the floor or shake a cup of treats and encourage her to follow you. When she does, praise her warmly. Then go to the end of the leash again and repeat yourself. She'll catch on soon enough.

Don't give your puppy attention for stubborn stopping, and absolutely never pick her up.

Anchoring

As you lead your puppy around, you may need to sit down to talk on the phone, work on the computer, or entertain guests. If you let your puppy free, she may create havoc during her constant vigil to get your attention. Jumping on the counter and chewing the drapes are real eye-catchers — especially for your guests!

To discourage these habits while you're sitting, I suggest that you use a civilized routine called *anchoring*. Follow these steps:

1. **With your puppy secured at your side, slide the end clip around to your tailbone and sit on the remaining slack of the leash.**

2. **Leave enough room for your dog to lie comfortably behind your feet and offer her a favorite chew toy.**

3. **Instruct "Settle," and pet and praise your puppy when she does so.**

Stationing

All puppies love company, and when given the choice, yours will always want to be near you. Too much isolation is a bad thing, because a puppy gleans her personality from group reflection. Confinement, in turn, creates *hyper isolation anxiety,* a term I coined to reflect the often hyper behavior that results from long bouts of isolation. When possible, use the *stationing* technique to keep her with you, teaching her how to behave in each room and ensuring that she can communicate to you if she needs to go outside.

Your puppy must be at least 12 weeks old before you begin stationing her. Before then, supervision, crate time, and safe-room freedom are best. When puppies are young, they're curious and impulsive and . . . clumsy. They can get into situations out of their control. Enclosures (see Chapter 5) mirror the safety of a den.

Determining how long you can station your puppy depends on her age and mental state. A sleepyhead of any age can handle an hour or more, and an older pup can handle more extended periods. The best gauge is your puppy's behavior — keep her stationed near you and be aware of signals. If your pup has been napping at her station for an hour and suddenly gets up and starts acting restless, she probably needs to go to her potty spot. If your puppy chews on a bone for 15 minutes and then starts acting like a jumping bean, she's probably going through an energy spurt and needs time for a little play.

To station your puppy, you first need to select your areas. Go into each room you want your dog to behave well in and pick a good area for her to settle into — perhaps a place near the couch in the TV room but away from the table in the dining room. Set up the area with a comfy cushion or blanket and her favorite chew toy. Doing so helps your puppy identify her special space, her station. Puppies like to have a special place. Think of it in human terms: When you go into your living room, don't you have a favorite couch or chair?

Puppies fidget, so make sure the station is away from stairs, electrical cords and outlets, or other entanglements. Be sure the object you secure your puppy to is immovable, sturdy, and unable to tip. If you have nothing to secure the lead to, screw an eye hook into the wall and clip the leash through it.

When securing your puppy to her station, limit her freedom to 2 to 3 feet to encourage calmness and deter mischief and soiling. Like a crate, the point of a station is to teach your puppy to settle down or chew on her toys. If your puppy insists on chewing her leash, use a spray deterrent, such as Bitter Apple spray, or a chain lead.

Eventually, your puppy will go to her station naturally. Initially, though, you must secure your dog at her station until she learns her place. When stationing, attach your puppy with her buckle or head collar and never with a training collar. If using the Teaching Lead, hook the lead around an immovable object by attaching the top clip to the opposite end of the leash.

When first practicing the stationing procedure, lead her to her spot by pointing and giving the direction "Settle down." At the beginning of your stationing training, stay with your dog. Make her feel comfortable in the area and encourage her to chew her bone. Leave her only when she's busy with a chew toy or resting.

When you leave your puppy, leave calmly and give the direction "Wait." Short departures are good because they get your puppy used to being left alone and they show her that you won't desert her. If your pup's excited when you return, ignore her so that you don't reinforce that behavior. When she's calm, you can give her attention.

Some dogs panic when initially stationed. If you're concerned about your pup, determine whether her reaction is really a panic attack or simply a persuasive protest. You'll know because panicked dogs don't focus on you. On the other hand, dogs who protest are very focused on you and usually bark. Ignore the protesting dog. If your pup's truly panicked, initially station her only when you can sit with her. Encourage bone chewing and begin to leave her side only when she's sleeping. She'll soon get the hang of it.

Bravely ignore whining or barking, unless your puppy's communicating a need (for example, you've missed a feeding or outing or playtime). If she barks and you soothe her, you're teaching a lesson with headache written all over it. Along the same lines, only release your dog from a station when she's calm and quiet. Otherwise, you risk reinforcing a negative behavior. If she gets out of hand, you can try distracting your puppy by using a fancy long-distance squirt gun. But you must be very discreet. You don't want your pup to know where the water is coming from because the interaction will override the discouragement.

Ding-Dong! Teaching Doorbell Civility

When the doorbell rings, here's what often happens: A puppy runs to the door and with paws flying everywhere she jumps all over the arriving guests. And then, because all eyes are on her, she gets even more wound up — until, that is, the enthusiastic puppy is banished to solitary confinement.

The previous example is a common routine. Nobody's in control and nobody's comfortable, except maybe the puppy. But even her comfort passes when you have to isolate her. Fortunately, there's a better way.

Whoever so runs the doorway, rules the den

At the end of the day, your puppy is still a dog. She may be domesticated, but she still views the world from a wolf's perspective, adjusting to your home as though it were a den. Your doorway is the main thoroughfare to the den and whoever rules it, runs the show.

So, with that image in mind, set the structure. Direct your puppy to "Wait" before entering and exiting as if to say "Please let me make sure the coast is clear." Aside from instilling civility in your pup, you're acting like a leader — and your puppy will know it. After she obeys the "Wait" command, either proceed in front of her or release her into an enclosed yard.

First, be stern with your regimen and firm with your company. They need more training than your pup. Rather than admonishing their adoration for your puppy, ask them to help you teach your puppy the "four-paw rule," or greeting without jumping. The four-paw rule says that your puppy should keep all four paws on the floor.

After you've trained the humans, follow these suggestions for teaching your pup how to behave when the doorbell rings:

- ✔ **Secure a greeting station.** Designate an area by the door to send your pup to when company arrives. Secure a leash to the area and place a favorite chew or toy there. Practice the setups described in the next bullet and secure your pup to the area when the bell rings.

  House rules: Everyone must ignore your puppy until she's calm — even if it takes an hour.

- ✔ **Practice doorbell setups.** Put your dog on a training collar (if age appropriate) and a leash. Position someone at the door and ask him to ring the doorbell ten times at 20-second intervals; tell the visitor that you'll answer the door on the tenth ring. Between the first and tenth rings lead your puppy around as if nothing is happening. Then lead your puppy to her greeting station when you answer the door. Practice these setups twice a day until your dog tones down her reaction.

  If your dog is a real maniac, try the head collar (described in Chapter 5) or discreetly spray a deterrent in front of her nose as you say "Shhh."

- ✔ **Do the reverse yo-yo.** Secure a 4-foot lead to your puppy's nylon collar. Tie a knot in the lead 4 inches past where the lead passes your dog's toe. Before you open the door, step on the knot. Your puppy will still jump, but this rig forces her down. Encourage your company to give the dog attention only when she's calm.

- ✔ **Designate a greeting toy.** If your dog's a real tennis-ball fanatic (or really loves any other toy), withhold that toy from her until you have company arriving. Each time you enter your home or company arrives, wait until your puppy has calmed down, and then after she has, give her the toy and say "Toy." Eventually, she'll get the toy the moment she notes an arrival.

Teaching Your Pup to Take Departures and Arrivals in Stride

When your puppy is isolated, she's likely to suffer isolation anxiety. However, it's nothing to lose sleep over: Kids feel it too as part of life's grand adjustment. Your pup will get over it as long as you remain calm and treat her consistently each time you leave and return. Here's my system for teaching your puppy to deal with your leaving and returning home — use it whether you're leaving your puppy in a gated space or in her crate.

Leaving: No drama, please

When you leave your puppy, be cool and calm. Though parting tears may help you feel less guilty, your stress just might freak your puppy out! If you have trouble corralling your puppy at the last minute, let her drag a 4-foot leash before beginning your departure. When it comes time to go, calmly walk to the end of the leash, lead her to her enclosure calmly, remembering to unclip the leash before you leave.

If you find that getting out your keys or your coat trigger her anxiety, frequently stage a departure, but stay home and play with your pup instead. Soon the sound of the keys will carry other meanings too, and anxiety won't be the only thing on her mind. When you actually leave, reserve a favorite bone that will engage her as you walk out the door calmly.

When you do leave, say a set phrase like "I'll be back" as you calmly lead your puppy to her quarters. You may give her a few treats or caress her lovingly, but avoid dramatic fanfares!

I know — puppies can really pull at your heartstrings with their frantic barking, incessant whining, and soft soulful eyes staring up at you. But unless you can rearrange your life's schedule to stay home with her forever, you have to ignore your puppy some of the time. She will adapt, just as everyone has to do at one time or another. Your calm demeanor will be contagious and will pave the way to your giving your pup full freedom in the house while you're away.

Coming back: Keep it cool

So, you've been gone an hour, or two, or maybe even three. Your puppy can't track time like you do, but a full bladder or hungry belly may indeed be pressing. In all likelihood, she's taken a restful nap and will be delighted to see you. Now you must decide whether you want a frantic ritual — complete with flailing paws, clawing nails, and a slobbery, open-mouth hello — or a simple wagging tail and toy toss or belly rub. I don't know about you, but I'm in the toy-tossing and belly-rubs camp myself.

If your puppy gets excited upon your return, just ignore her. If she's behind a gate (inside or out), she's likely to be leaning on it or clawing at it. Don't look at, talk to, or touch her. Yes, she'll be utterly confused — especially if you've conditioned this behavior by immediately releasing her. But the tides will turn quickly: within days to weeks. When your puppy calms down to a reasonable level, release her, but remain calm and level-headed. Any show of excitement on your part will send her into a tizzy. Kneel down by your pup, caress her, or toss her a toy. If you reunite with her like you want to be greeted waking up from a nap, you'll have a dog whom anyone could come home to!

Dogs around Your Dinner Plate

If your puppy is clearly competing for your dinner plate, you've got some strict civilizing to do here. In Europe it's standard for owners to bring their dogs — no matter the breed, shape, or size — to a restaurant with them. Though I don't think you'll have any luck overcoming the health and safety codes here in the United States, you can still teach your puppy to sit calmly while you dine. Training your pup to be calm during dinner begins with how you organize her own meals and how you condition her to behave around food that is both hers and yours!

For your puppy's mealtimes, teach her to sit and wait as you prepare her food. If she won't cooperate with your vision, stand on her leash — giving her just enough freedom to stand or sit. Ignore manic behavior and put her food down only when she has calmed down.

For your own mealtimes, designate a station area 4 to 6 feet from the table for your puppy to sit or play at while you and your family are eating. If you've already encouraged interruptions, you can be sure she won't stay put initially. So, station her there, as described earlier in this chapter. If she's still having trouble relaxing, exercise and play with her just before you eat, and set aside a special chewy or toy that only comes out when human meals are being served.

Looking at your puppy invites her to the feast. To encourage civility, ignore her while you eat. I know it seems cold-hearted, but in the end you're teaching her that this is the time to snooze or catch up on some undisturbed chewing.

Achieving Calm and Happy Car Rides

Put yourself in your puppy's paws. To her, your automobile is a window box with wheels. Even though passing cars, pausing for bicycles, and braking for squirrels is part of your normal routine, it pushes your pup's chasing and territorial instincts to the max. When she barks or bounces, the predators (cars, bicycles, and squirrels) whiz away. So, the point is that she thinks she's victorious. In her mind, she's the champ. Not only do the predators go away, but they go away fast. If you're hoping for a successful outing, the civility must begin with the trip there. Contain your puppy in the car, distract her with a toy or chew, and you will both arrive at your destination with your sanity intact.

Negative corrections don't work to shape good car manners. Yelling is perceived as barking — as backup, collaboration style. Besides, discipline and driving just don't mix — someone has to keep one eye on the road. To stop wild puppy antics in the car or to train a pup to behave, you need to follow some simple routines.

Getting your pup into the car

Follow this routine every time to get your puppy into your car:

1. **Lead your puppy to the car using the direction "Heel" or "Follow."**

2. **Open the car door and direct "Wait," and then pause.**

3. **Say "Settle" and direct your puppy to a prepared car station or into a crate.**

    A car station is like any other station in your home. Identify it with a mat and toys and attach a leash to a collar or harness to prevent pacing and fidgeting while you drive.

4. **Secure your puppy (see Chapter 9 for options), show her a toy, and tell her "Stay."**

Now you can proceed to your destination. Things always go more smoothly when they're organized.

If your dog barks in the car, restricting her motion will lessen the tension and create a far more subdued ride. Consider a head collar too (Chapter 5) — by the nature of the position it reminds your puppy that someone else is in charge.

Does your dog refuse to hop into the car? If she's a tiny tot, her reluctance is understandable. If, on the other hand, you have a 120-pound Great Dane, you're the one being taken for a ride. You have to take a stand and make sure you never lift her into the car again. If you do, you're forcing her into a state of learned helplessness. Lead her to the car, taking some of her favorite treats along — dog or human — and try baiting her in. If treats make little impression, get in the car and, as you bribe her, pull her gently forward. Still no luck? Bring a friend along, pass the lead to him through the car, and have him gently pull as you encourage her forward. If she still resists, physically walk each limb into the automobile one at a time, but under no circumstances should you lift her.

Getting your pup out of the car

Eventually, when you reach your destination, the time comes to get your pup out of the car. Again, from your puppy's perspective, the situation is pretty exciting — new sights, smells, and faces. If she doesn't notice you or listen to your direction at first, don't take it personally. Getting her focused is the challenge at hand. Follow these directions:

1. **Before opening the door to let her out, instruct "Wait."**

2. **If she jumps forward, catch the car lead, say "No," and tug her back.**

3. **Reinstruct "Wait," and pause until she's calm.**

4. **Secure her to a leash and say "Okay" as you let her exit.**

5. **Instruct "Heel" or "Follow" while bringing her to your side, and then proceed with your adventure.**

Dealing with carsickness and fear

Cars really frighten some dogs. The cause usually goes back to being transported at an early age, but this fear can result later in life, too. If your puppy is afraid of the car, avoid pacifying her or being overly forceful. Both reactions reinforce fear. If you must take her somewhere, pick her up, if possible, or take her to the car while she's napping. Speak or sing softly while you put her in the car. Have the car ready and have classical music playing on the radio. Equip her area with a familiar blanket and a favorite toy.

Some dogs just don't like riding in the car because the motion upsets their inner ear, and, like cats, they prefer to stay home. Because staying home all the time is rarely an option, you need to condition your dog to the car slowly. Follow these steps:

1. **Designate and prepare a place for your puppy in the back seat or cargo area.**

   Using a crate is useful if your dog is anxious about car travel (a plastic kennel is best) and if your car is large enough. Always pad the crate for comfort and to prevent slipping.

2. **Pull your car out into the open and, with all the doors open, use the car as a playground.**

   Climb in and out of the car with your puppy while encouraging her interest with favorite toys and treats.

3. **After a romp, take a break in the car, giving your puppy water and food if it's mealtime.**

4. **Play the "Find the Car" game with your puppy.**

   Tell your puppy to "Find the Car" while you run over to the car. Treat your puppy for following you. Work this routine until the car is something the puppy enjoys being around.

5. **With the engine running, repeat the preceding steps.**

6. **After a playtime, secure your puppy (in a crate or on leash) to her area and go for a short spin in and out of the driveway.**

    Repeat this step until your puppy is comfortable with the situation.

7. **Slowly extend your trips and consider stopping for a cheerful game of toss or a walk along the way to encourage your dog to look forward to your jaunts in the car.**

If you must take your puppy on an extended trip, don't feed or water her much for at least two hours before the trip to avoid either a full belly or bladder. Exercise her before you leave and spread sheets over her area. You can pray that she doesn't have an accident, but I'd bring paper towels just in case.

Hitting the Streets: Working on Your Puppy's Public Image

Going public requires some effort, but before you get started with your pup, keep in mind a few universal rules:

- ✔ **Keep the leash on.** Your puppy's leash gives you the ability to direct her calmly. Don't take your puppy off her leash in public for any reason. There are too many dangers.

- ✔ **Use lots of encouragement.** Cheerfulness is contagious.

- ✔ **Always keep her paws behind your heels.** Remember, you lead and she follows.

- ✔ **Keep the communication flowing.** Direction provides your pup structure and security.

- ✔ **No elimination in public.** Take care of eliminating at home. (But bring a bag just in case of accidents.)

- ✔ **Know when to say "No."** You'll say "No" to both your puppy and other people.

Before you hit the streets for real, you want to practice in selected areas so that you can devote all your attention to your puppy. Eventually, being in public will seem effortless, and you'll both be welcomed everywhere. However, your first trip out may be a real shocker. Are you wondering "If going out in public is such a nightmare, why bother?" Here are three reasons why you should train your pup for going out in public:

✔ It gets easier.

✔ A well-mannered dog is fun to share.

✔ Being out enhances your puppy's focus. You'll be the one looking confident in new, unexplored territories.

I know going out in public sounds daunting, but after you get the hang of it, it'll seem natural. It's all about leadership.

When you get to your destination, the first five minutes is three-fourths of the battle. Whatever practice location you've picked — a park, a town, a friend's house, or a building — first impressions really count. If you take control immediately and give understandable directions, the rest is a tail wag.

For example, suppose you've just brought your puppy to your heel after shutting the car door. Instantly, your puppy will have one of two reactions: She'll either become wild or become a scaredy-cat. Read on to find out how to deal with both reactions.

Controlling the wild one

If your puppy is the wild type, her nose will twitch a mile a minute, she'll pivot toward every new stimulation, and she'll pull on the leash to investigate every blade of grass. Here's a way to control your Huck Finn:

✔ **Direct her to your heel (using the direction "Heel" or "Follow").** Keep her paws behind your ankles.

✔ **Tell strangers to back off until your puppy's trained.** It's embarrassing, I know, but you have to. You don't want your puppy jumping up and giving someone a scratch, even if it's only by accident.

The first-outing blues

The first outing with your new puppy may be utter chaos, but don't be discouraged. Even I had the "first-outing blues" with my pup, Whoopsie. She was a headstrong, lively, and playful puppy that couldn't hold herself back. To make matters worse, she had no leash sensitivity, which meant that no matter how hard I pulled, she just pulled back. She pulled me through puddles, over a bench, and through someone's flower bed — all par for the course.

When people gathered to pet her or another dog was near, she forgot about me completely. But that first outing has passed and Whoopsie has learned that her manners are expected everywhere, whether greeting Aunt Carolyn at the door or ten school children in the park. The eventual compliments on Whoopsie's good behavior overshadowed my initial embarrassment, but I didn't start out with perfection, and you probably won't either.

✔ **Reinforce your requests.** If you ask for a "Sit-Stay," get a "Sit-Stay." Keep repositioning your puppy, holding her still by *bracing* her (I explain this later in this chapter).

✔ **Don't expect too much.** Your puppy may have trouble focusing, so position her when she doesn't listen (no matter how well you're doing at home).

Empowering the scaredy-cat

If you have a passive or scared puppy, the experience of arriving at a new place may be overwhelming. Her tail may disappear (between her legs) and her body may lower, and, when stimulated, she may try to hide behind you or she may unknowingly tinkle. Just remember that if you bend to soothe your scaredy-cat, you reinforce her reaction. I know, soothing her is so tempting. However, just keep saying to yourself over and over "Soothing reinforces fear. Soothing reinforces fear." Instead of soothing her, try the following:

✔ **Look confident and stand tall like a good leader puppy.** Soon she'll mimic you when encountering new situations.

✔ **Bring some treats and a favorite toy — something she can focus her attention on.** Withholding these items at home makes the new adventure seem really exciting.

✔ **Use the "Heel" and "Stay" directions often.** Familiar sounds soothe anxiety.

If she's too nervous to listen, enforce a response by positioning her physically without corrections.

✔ **Keep the situation calm and positive.** Deflect any admirers until she's feeling safe.

Under and back: Helpful commands when you're out and about

Have you ever marveled at the sight of a dog lying patiently under the table or under her human's legs? It's calming on all fronts as the dog is at peace knowing that the person is safe and in charge. Fortunately for you, it couldn't be easier to teach your pup this skill.

Your puppy really wants you to be her guardian and protector. Whether resting at home, with company, or in town at a cafe, your pup feels most secure when tucked safely under your legs (see Figure 13-1).

Figure 13-1:
This pup is calm and safe and patiently waiting for her owner to finish his meal.

To get this result, teach your pup the "Under" command, which calms her and helps her feel secure in social situations:

1. **Sit on the edge of a chair with your legs bent out in front of you.**

2. **Wave a treat to bait your puppy.**

3. **Lead her under your legs.**

   If necessary, use pressure points to encourage her into the "Down" position (see the section "Civilizing Your Pup Room by Room," earlier in this chapter).

4. **Direct her to "Stay" if she's familiar with that direction, and give her a bone to chew or toy to play with. If your puppy is young or hasn't learned "Stay," gently guide her into position and distract her with a bone or toy.**

Another direction, "Back," teaches your puppy to back up and get behind your feet. This direction is ideal for outings and social greeting where her enthusiasm may override her focus. To bait her with a treat, draw it back directly under her chin and press her chest gently as you guide her body behind you. If she sits or lies down, hold her waist up by tucking the flat of your palm under her belly.

Making Friends: Introducing Your Pup to Other Dogs

A well-socialized puppy makes friends wherever she can. Meeting other dogs and puppies will top her list of priorities. However, you'll need to teach her impulse control or she may dart headlong into traffic or rush an unfriendly candidate.

Gaining control when encountering other dogs

If you see a dog when you're out and about, don't approach him immediately. First, gain control of your situation by following these steps:

1. **If your puppy acts excited, bring her "Back" and remind her to "Heel," if these directions arc familiar. Otherwise, tug her back to your side, use "Let's Go," and proceed with the steps as outlined.**

2. **Continue in your original direction and pick up your pace.**

   Your goal is to leave the area in case the dog perceives you as trespassing on his territory.

3. **Don't look toward, approach, or follow the other dog. Your excitement may be misconstrued. Unless you know the other dog well, don't approach him.**

4. **If your puppy continues acting wildly, speed up and keep tugging the leash.**

5. **Praise her for focusing on you instead of the dog.**

6. **Never give in or let up.**

   You don't want to raise your puppy to race away from you each time she sees a potential friend.

What if the training tables are turned?

Suppose that you and your puppy are out taking a walk and you're approached by someone who's out teaching her puppy socialization skills and wants to have her puppy greet yours as a training exercise. Are you obligated to get involved?

No. If you're not in the mood, or your puppy's too hyped, just say no. If you're game, however, get your puppy in control behind you and then release with "Okay, go play!" Call her back to "Heel" when playtime is over.

Go! Giving your pup the green light

After you have your puppy under control, you can permit a greeting by saying "Okay, go play." Before you do, though, make certain the other dog is friendly and the other owner is respectful of your training efforts. When play-time is over, instruct your puppy to "Heel" and move on.

If your friend has a dog and you want to get the dogs together to play, let them first meet each other on neutral ground, such as an empty playground or field. Doing so prevents a fierce territorial reaction. When they first meet, you should expect a lot of bluffs, such as growling, mouthing, and mounting. Don't choke up on your lead. This behavior is natural, and your interference often prompts a fight. Stay calm but observe closely. The dogs must deter-mine a hierarchy. After that's accomplished, they'll settle down on their own. If you're certain a fight has begun, separate them with the leashes. Don't handle fighting dogs.

If you're approached by an off-lead dog, don't hesitate, don't look at the dog, and don't let your puppy look at the dog. Just walk quickly away from the area. Discourage any confrontational attempts your puppy makes. Both of you should avoid eye contact. An off-lead dog defends his territory. However, if you leave without confrontation, he'll stop the chase immediately to harbor his fighting reserves for a more threatening foe.

Introducing Your Pup to People

Meeting people doesn't have to be a hair-raising experience. If your puppy is good on the leash, knows her directions, and is friendly, you have what you need to introduce your pooch to strangers.

Before you venture into the social scene, though, read over the following dis-closures. If you identify with any of them, follow my specific instructions and skip the rest of this section:

- ✔ **First disclosure.** If you're having aggression problems, the only person you should introduce your puppy to for now is a trainer or behaviorist with a specialty in aggression rehabilitation. How do you find such an expert? Ask your veterinarian. It's better to be safe than sued.

- ✔ **Second disclosure.** If you notice your puppy getting nervous or tense around unfamiliar people, join a class or work under private supervi-sion. Don't push the issue alone.

- ✔ **Third disclosure.** If you don't believe that you have what it takes to train your puppy, you won't. Confidence is contagious, but so is a lack of it. Hire some extra help if you need the support.

Following five key rules

When you're debuting that puppy of yours, follow these five key rules:

- **Rule #1.** Make sure your puppy is familiar and comfortable with the setting before you attempt to introduce her to anyone. Don't greet people your first day out.

- **Rule #2.** Human feet should always be ahead of doggie paws. Gently tug her back if she forgets, realigning her if she attempts to scoot forward.

- **Rule #3.** Tell admirers "We're in training," so they respect your efforts and contain their own excitement (hopefully).

- **Rule #4.** Stay more focused on your puppy than the admirer. Tug your puppy back into position if she attempts to break or brace her as described in the next section.

- **Rule #5.** Put faith in your own knowledge. Just because everyone has advice doesn't mean they're right. "I don't mind if she jumps" doesn't hold water. *You* mind if she jumps, so don't give in.

Introducing the wild one

How you handle introducing your puppy depends on none other than your puppy. If your puppy is overly enthusiastic and wild, you need to tame her expressiveness. Keeping her focused on you is the key.

Ask people to wait until your wild one is calm before they approach. Enforce a "Sit-Stay," keeping your feet ahead of her paws. Brace her by placing your left hand, fingers down, along her waist and below the ribs and your right thumb clipped over her collar (facing down). Hold her steady in case she jumps. If the person still wants to, he can pet your puppy. Remind your puppy to "Stay," and don't let up your vigil until the person is gone. Whew! What a workout.

Introducing the scaredy-cat

When introducing a scaredy-cat, ask your greeter to wait until you and your puppy are in position. Teach your puppy the "Back" command to let her know you're in charge, and place her in a "Sit-Stay." Kneel down at her side and, if you can muster a free hand, take the person's hand. Let your puppy sniff the two together. If she won't keep her head up, lift it for her as you gently rub her chest.

If your puppy is a little cautious when people approach, before you start out, place some treats in your pocket (or, if your puppy likes peanut butter, bring along a tube of it) that an admirer can extend to her.

Entering Buildings Peacefully

Pick a building you plan to visit with your puppy: the veterinarian's office, the hardware store, the pet shop, or your kids' school. Your puppy's behavior in those buildings depends on who enters the building first. If your puppy leads you, she's in charge. If you lead your puppy, you're the head honcho. Whoever starts in charge stays in charge.

After you've selected your building, approach it with your puppy on leash and follow these steps:

1. **Bring your puppy to your heel as you exit the car.**

   If she's familiar with the direction, say her name and "Heel." Say "Shhh" if she starts getting excited.

2. **Pause before you open the door and direct "Wait."**

   Don't open the door until she's settled down.

3. **If your puppy lurches forward, tug her back and say "Back."**

   Pause again until your puppy is calm.

How to impress your vet

I'll let you in on a secret: Veterinarians love a well-behaved dog. It makes their job a lot easier. To impress your vet do the following:

1. **Bring your puppy's favorite chew toy in case you have to wait because your puppy will probably be excited or afraid.**

2. **Take charge the moment your puppy hops out of the car. Direct "Heel" as you walk to the door and "Wait" after you get there.**

3. **If you must wait to see the vet, direct your puppy under your legs or at your side on a mat. Give her a bone to chew and tell her to "Stay."**

4. **Instruct "Wait" at the threshold of the examination room to keep her calm and focused.**

5. **Place her mat on the examination table to calm your puppy, which, in turn, pleases her doctor.**

Some puppies aren't wild about receptionists and aren't too impressed by the veterinarian either. Set up a practice run and ask the receptionist to meet you outside. Give her your puppy's treat cup (see Chapter 11), and ask her to avoid making eye contact with your puppy. If your puppy is tense, avoid confrontation. If your puppy wants to approach, have the receptionist reward her with treats.

4. **Say "Okay" as you lead her through the door.**

5. **After you're inside, direct your puppy under your legs or onto a mat positioned at your side.**

   Give her a bone if you expect her to stay put.

Some dogs are nervous when they enter new buildings. If your puppy is, don't reinforce her anxiety. If your puppy's showing fear, you need to show confidence. Don't pet her or reassure her that things will be okay. Instead, take along some treats to encourage her to follow you as you approach the building. If she puts on the brakes, kneel down (don't run back), and encourage her inside with food and gentle tugs.

Chapter 14

Training through Your Pup's Growth Stages

· ·

In This Chapter

▶ Performing basic lessons with infant puppies

▶ Building on the basics with exercises for the terrible twos

▶ Training your adolescent pup

▶ Discovering what to focus on during puppy puberty

▶ Teaching the teen dog

· ·

*W*elcome to school. Puppy school that is! This chapter covers the basic directions that all puppies must learn to feel fully integrated and part of your world. Mutual understanding does more than create dogs who take orders — it fosters a communication bond that is equal to none.

I suggest that you practice each exercise five to ten minutes a day. As you practice, you may notice that your puppy picks up certain directions quickly but that others take more time. Don't fret. That's how training usually goes. After all, think of what you're accomplishing: You're teaching another species your language. My advice is to be patient throughout the many phases because puppies learn best from an understanding teacher.

Infant Lessons: 8 to 12 Weeks

Don't expect too much from this age group. Even though a puppy at this age is capable of learning, his brain won't finish developing until he's 12 weeks old. Your puppy learns best when you incorporate training into his playtime. Hang around with him, use his name as you offer him good things (like toys and treats), and introduce him to the leash — pretty basic stuff. Begin housebreaking at this stage, but don't expect a totally housebroken puppy in four weeks.

Forget discipline at this stage because your pup is just too young to understand it. You succeed only in frightening him and eroding your relationship — and that's not good.

Use your puppy's name

Pick a short name or nickname to highlight your cheerful association and attention. Use it each time you offer your puppy something positive, such as food or praise. When you call to your puppy, speak in a sharp, positive tone that bespeaks camaraderie and direction. Avoid "sing-song" tones because those are translated as whines and will bring sympathy or be tuned out.

For a fun way to use your puppy's name, try the Treat Cup Name Game in Chapter 23.

Start leash training

Put a collar on your puppy immediately. He may fuss at first, but don't worry — he'll eventually get used to it. Next, attach a light leash to his collar and let him drag it around. After a day, pick up the leash and follow him around. As he gets used to having you follow him, start calling out his name and encouraging him to follow you.

Do any number of foolish things to pique his interest. When he starts following you, praise him generously. Say "Follow!" and kneel often to hug him. If he strongly resists following you, don't run over to him; you'd be reinforcing the resistance. Instead, tug the leash gently and lower yourself to the floor while you praise him.

Puppies grow fast, so keep an eye on the collar size and loosen it when necessary.

Work on "Sit" and "Okay"

Say "Sit" as you position your puppy. To position your pup, put your right hand under his chin and use your left hand to squeeze the waist muscles below the ribs.

Use the happy word "Okay" to give your puppy permission. Say "Okay" as you give your puppy positive things: a meal, pat, toy, and so on.

Walk the stairs

Stairs can be a very formidable obstacle for puppies. Some small breeds are just too little to tackle the stairs, so they must be carried up and down. That's okay because in time, they'll be scampering up and down like the big dogs. Some larger breed puppies are big enough to use stairs, but they're afraid because their depth perception isn't completely developed.

If you have a puppy with stair phobia, help him walk the stairs by cradling his belly and guiding his paws. If possible, have someone crouch down a few stairs away to cheer him on.

Work on handling and socialization

When you handle your puppy, you're teaching him that human contact is good. So, without frequent and gentle handling, your pup will grow up to be a dog who's wary of people. Also, puppies who aren't socialized often develop a fear of unfamiliar situations and people. By handling and socializing your puppy, you're helping him grow into a well-adjusted, gentle dog who's comfortable around people and new situations.

Handling

When you're calmly petting your puppy, occasionally play veterinarian. Peek into your puppy's ears and check out what's going on in his mouth and eyes. Press his belly gently and handle the base of the tail. Handle the paws like you're trimming his nails. So that he won't get scared while you're handling him, praise your puppy gently or give him a treat. By getting your pup used to being handled, you help yourself and your veterinarian, who always appreciates a good patient.

Socialization

Puppies at this age are too young to be taken out on the town, but between 8 and 12 weeks is the best age to socialize your puppy with new people and other dogs. So, to socialize your puppy, invite your neighbors and friends over, borrow a group of active kids, or have a puppy play date with another healthy canine.

When you're socializing with your puppy, be sure to either walk him on a leash if you're near a road or let him drag a long line (refer to Chapter 5) if you're allowing him free play in an open yard. When people approach to pet your puppy, encourage him to sit as you brace him into position. Keep him near to your side or just behind you so that your presence is known to him. Ask people to offer treats and handle him so that he becomes comfortable with others too.

Food and toy conditioning

Some puppies are prone to food and object guarding — they'll innately guard these objects from another dog, and may mistakenly view your approach with the same level of defensiveness.

To prevent this mindset: Go to your puppy every other day during one of his meals. Offer him a biscuit and a pat and say "Good boy!" After he anticipates your offering, remove his bowl while he eats the treat and then return the bowl and leave. At this point, if you have children in the house, bring them with you and start the process from the beginning.

Early food-bowl conditioning prevents food guarding later in your pup's development.

Correct mischievous behavior

If your puppy is rough or jumpy during playtime, attach a short leash onto his collar. If he starts misbehaving, take the leash and tug him away from or off the person he's jumping on. If you use your hands, the behavior may escalate because hands are considered interactive, and in your puppy's mind, interaction is the best treat in the world.

When your puppy is attached to the leash, you can correct any mischief without physical interaction. For example, if a puppy puts his front paw in my lap and I push him away with my hands, I'm actually encouraging him to put his paw up on my lap again because, in his mind, pushing is interactive. If, instead of pushing, I grab the leash, tug him off my lap, and ignore him until he's calm, he learns that calm puppies get petted.

Terrible Twos Lessons: 12 to 16 Weeks

During the terrible twos phase, your puppy is beginning to recognize what behaviors get your attention, what games seem to last the longest (and these aren't necessarily the games you want to be playing), and who the boss is (and in his eyes, it may not be you). Even though he may act pretty confident during this phase, your pup still needs direction from you. The advice in this section can help you guide your puppy successfully through his terrible twos.

Keep control

When you're home, always know where your puppy is. If you give him complete freedom, he'll misbehave and you'll end up paying for it — in more ways than one. Unsupervised, a puppy can rearrange your closets, eat garbage, and chew on the chairs.

You're still dealing with a young puppy. Keep yours near you in one of four ways:

- ✔ By using the *leading* and *stationing* concepts (outlined in Chapter 13)
- ✔ By observing him in an enclosed area, such as a gated kitchen
- ✔ By keeping him in a crate
- ✔ By making sure he's always with you around the home (Attach him to a dragging lead that's attached to the buckle collar.)

When he's confined, give him attention for good behavior.

Work on ten basic directions

Your puppy is still very young. Even though he can learn a lot, he's still very sensitive and vulnerable to your impressions. So stay cool. Getting frustrated or impatient only frightens him and makes him less responsive to you.

Following are some suggestions when working with your toddler pup:

- ✔ Keep your lessons short and snappy. They should be no more than a couple of minutes.
- ✔ Speak your directions clearly and enunciate your syllables. Also, give directions only once because repeated directions sound drastically different from single directions (consider the indecipherable "sitsitsitcome-onpleasesitdown").
- ✔ Continue using your directions during playtime.
- ✔ Use hand signals to help you get visual attention. Also use treats with some of the directions. However, after the direction is understood, food rewards should be phased out gradually to avoid treat dependence.

Believe it or not, your puppy can have a ten-word vocabulary by the time he's 4 months old. He already knows his name, so check one off the list immediately. Read on for the remaining nine commands you can teach your young puppy.

Look Up

This game teaches your puppy to respond to his name being called and to focus on you. Stand above him and call out his name as you lift a toy or treat from his eyes to yours. Vary the time he must stare at you before rewarding him, from two to ten seconds. Good boy!

Follow

Use the "Follow" direction whenever you're walking your puppy on a leash or encouraging him to follow you. If he's disinterested in you, start teaching this direction by shaking a treat cup filled with treats or his meals and rewarding him as you go. Gradually lengthen the distance he cooperates between treats.

This exercise is ideal for a clicker if you're using one: Click when he cooperates, and then treat him. See Chapter 11 for more on using this great training gadget.

If your puppy stops dead in his tracks while learning to follow, you should not drag him. Not only could it cause physical discomfort, but it also may frighten him. You may be thinking "What are my options then?" Be creative. You can shake treat cups, skip and bounce, squeak a toy, or kneel down and encourage. However, you must do all of these without looking at him. Reward and face him only when he's near, and near he'll stay.

The "Follow" direction isn't optional. If your puppy doesn't want to go and you stop to cajole him, you reinforce his resistance. Say the direction happily and then skip, bounce, or dart ahead — do whatever you can do to encourage his quick and willing participation.

Sit

Teaching your puppy to sit is like teaching a child to say please. This is a good manner that will last a lifetime, and like kids, your puppy's good manners are learned at home! Practice the following exercise twice a day for four days:

1. **Take your puppy aside with a handful of small treats.**

2. **Place a treat between your index finger and thumb and say "Sit" as you bring the treat slightly above your puppy's nose (see Figure 14-1a).**

3. **When he sits, give him the treat, say "Okay," and praise him (see Figure 14-1b).**

Keep the exercise fresh by practicing it often and limiting repetitions to three or four per session. After a while, you can begin using hand signals, such as lifting your index finger above your pup's nose, to get him to sit. As the days progress and your puppy seems to catch on, try giving the direction and signal outside of a lesson time and without a treat. After about four days, phase out the treat and stop using this direction in lessons. Continue using the direction and signal throughout the day.

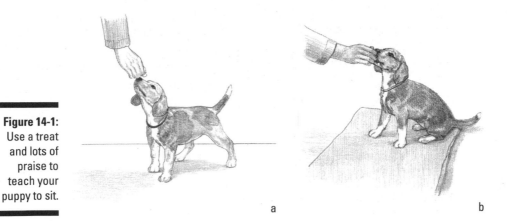

Figure 14-1:
Use a treat and lots of praise to teach your puppy to sit.

a   b

Down

After your puppy has mastered "Sit," begin to use it throughout the day and introduce the "Down" direction during lesson time with these steps:

1. **Take your puppy aside with some treats.**

2. **Placing the treats between your fingers, instruct "Sit." However, before you let go of the treat, drop your hand between your puppy's paws and say "Down."**

3. **Your puppy may not know what to do, so as he looks down, press gently between his shoulder blades with your left thumb and press him gently into position (see Figure 14-2).**

4. **Let go of the treat when his elbows hit the floor, praise him, and say "Okay" to release.**

5. **Repeat Steps 2 through 4 five times.**

The eventual hand signal is pointing to the ground. After four days, phase out hiding the treat in your signaling hand and begin to enforce the direction by gently placing your puppy into position.

Puppy pressure points

If you're having trouble getting your puppy to do what you want him to do, there are several pressure points on your puppy's body that, when gently pressed, will guide him into a specific position. Here are the ones I use most frequently for various commands:

✔ **Sit:** With your index finger and thumb, press your puppy's waist muscles, located just behind his last rib (on either side of his spine).

✔ **Down:** The pressure point for this direction is located between the shoulder blades. With the flat of your thumb, press steadily while lifting out one of his paws (if necessary) to create a tripod effect.

✔ **Stand:** To encourage your puppy to stand, slide your hand between his thigh and belly. Give his belly a tickle with the tip of your fingers if your pup's still down.

✔ **Forward:** When encouraging your puppy to move forward, tuck his tail between his legs and guide his head gently.

✔ **Back:** Back your puppy up by pressing the muscles on either side of his collarbone (located beneath his neck). If this trick causes him to sit, slide your hand along his thigh to prop him up.

✔ **Side:** Take the side of your hand and press his side as you maneuver him to the left or right.

Figure 14-2: Teach the "Down" direction by cradling a puppy's shoulders and pressing him gently into position.

Stand

The "Stand" direction is handy when you want to clean muddy paws and during general grooming sessions. Twice a day for four days, take your puppy aside with some treats and do the following:

1. **Place a treat between your fingers and say "Stand" as you pull an imaginary string from your puppy's nose forward.**

2. **When your puppy stands, stop your fingers and cradle his belly as you repeat "Stand."**

3. **Pause and then release with "Okay" as you allow your puppy to have the treat.**

   Your pup may try to snatch the treat early, but hold it firmly, say a discouraging "Ep, ep," and don't release it until he's standing.

4. **Repeat these steps five times.**

The eventual hand signal is a short point forward from his nose. As the days progress, try this direction out of lesson time and without a treat. After four days, phase out the treats and stop using this direction in lessons. Continue to use the direction and signal throughout the day.

Give

Most puppies enjoy playing with toys, although like young children, they won't get the concept of sharing for a while. To help your puppy along, play the following game. Try it first with your puppy on a leash and with some treats or a clicker in your pocket. Take your puppy into a small, quiet room with a favorite ball or squeak toy and then follow these steps:

1. **Kneel on the floor and praise your puppy happily for nearly a minute before you bring out the toy.**

2. **When you bring the toy out, toss it in the air (and catch it) to encourage his interest and then give it a short toss.**

3. **If he takes the toy, let him keep it for a while.**

   You want him to feel that you're not there to challenge him for it.

4. **Now bring out the treat (and clicker if you're using it). As you offer your puppy the treat, he should spit out the toy. As he does, say "Give" and either click and treat or treat as you praise him.**

5. **Give the object back immediately.**

   This action will highlight your good intentions to play and not steal.

6. **Continue Steps 2 and 3 until you notice that he looks to you as soon as he picks up the toy.**

7. **Encourage him to come toward you with the toy as you run away from him calling out "Bring."**

   Your puppy should release the toy quickly, but if he doesn't, you can encourage him by squeezing his upper muzzle just behind the canines. Praise him for releasing.

8. **Repeat these steps five times and praise him profusely when the game is over.**

Practice these directions in the confines of a small room for five days and then bring the direction into normally populated areas. Phase out the treats gradually.
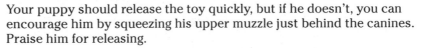

Settle Down

In each room, your puppy should have a special corner or area equipped with a bed and a chew bone. Eventually, you want to be able to send your puppy to this area on direction — a tactic that is especially useful during human mealtimes or when you have company.

To teach him this principle, select areas in each room and then, with your puppy on leash, say "Settle Down" and point to the area with your free hand. He'll probably need an escort, so take him there. If he's unsure, stay with him, eventually securing him to this spot with a short leash. Stay with him until he's engrossed in a chew toy or resting peacefully. The security of having his own spot and being able to consistently go there for toys and attention will prompt his cooperation. Soon he'll naturally go to the area himself when he's tired.

Your puppy must be fully leash trained and older than 12 weeks before you secure him in order to avoid feelings of entrapment, which is common in young puppies. Before you begin teaching this direction, make sure you read and understand the stationing concept. See Chapter 13 for details.

Wait and Okay

When approaching doors or stairs, use the direction "Wait" and bring your puppy behind your feet. This maneuver is best accomplished by bringing the leash behind your back. Pause for a couple of seconds and then say "Okay" as you step out first.

The leader must always lead (that means you!).

Excuse Me

Puppies like to get in the way. Blocking you gets them attention, but it makes you look subservient, and it can be dangerous if you trip or step on them. Whenever your puppy trips you up, gets on the wrong side of the leash, leans, or just gets in your way, say "Excuse Me" and move him out of your way with the leash or by shuffling your feet under his body. Don't yell at or kick your puppy, and don't use your hands (he'll just interpret these actions as an invitation to play). Thank him for respecting you, and soon he'll move with his tail wagging.

Continue to work on handling and socialization

Continue to handle and touch your puppy's paws, ears, eyes, belly, and tail as you would if you were grooming or medicating him. If your puppy will be around children, be sure he can handle it. Act like a kid: Pull his coat gently, squeal, and make sudden movements. Praise your puppy and give him treats during your performance.

And don't forget socialization, because your puppy loves to party. He loves friends with four legs and friends with two legs. If he's too young to be taken out (ask your veterinarian), invite people in — kids included. If you don't have kids, borrow some. After your veterinarian has completed your puppy's shots, start taking your pup out on the town and introducing him to everyone you meet. Take him to three new areas a week.

Ask your veterinarian whether she can recommend a well-managed puppy kindergarten class in your town. Joining a class is a fun way to meet other puppies and people.

Lots of socialization doesn't create a dog who won't protect his home or his people. Socialization simply encourages your puppy to trust your judgment where people are concerned. On the other hand, lack of socialization creates a dog who is overly attached to his family and who is intolerant of visitors. Depending on his breed and temperament, this dog may become fearful or defensive of other people on or off your property. Such dogs are difficult to manage and are a constant concern around people. Spare yourself the agony and socialize that puppy.

Your Budding Adolescent: 16 to 24 Weeks

When you and your puppy reach the budding adolescent stage, you may feel like hiding in the closet. Some days are livable. However, other days you feel like moving. Your puppy won't listen or respond to known directions. He bolts, chases, and nips at everything that moves. He demands your attention and barks or mounts you when he doesn't get his way. He insists on being the center of attention every moment of every day.

Keep in mind that this stage is normal. I managed to live through it, and you will too. During this stage you should start a regimented training schedule. Keep your sessions short and lively, and use each new direction during lesson time only for the first week; after that, you can try it at other times of day.

This process allows your puppy to be successful, mastering each direction before you start applying it to his day-to-day world — similar to letting children master their addition skills in school before asking them to balance your checkbook.

Gradually allow freedom around the house

Continue to organize your puppy's free time in the house with the leash unless you're able to give him your complete attention in an enclosed area.

Knowing the difference between praise and petting

When your puppy learns something new, it's very exciting for everyone. But try to control yourself. When you get fired up, your puppy does, too. Learning takes a lot of concentration, which means that an excited pup won't learn much. As you practice your exercises, remember that there's a difference between praise and petting. Petting comes from your hand — it excites your puppy and communicates play intentions. Praise comes from your voice and eyes and is given from an upright position — it calms your puppy and communicates your leadership. Remember this handy phrase: "Praise between exercises; petting to end them."

If he begins to respond well on his own, attach a short 4-foot drag lead and give him some freedom in the house, gradually increasing this freedom. Don't rush it, though. If he does well for the most part but falls apart when company arrives, put him on the leash when you have visitors.

Continue to teach manners

Continue to use the direction "Sit" throughout the day. Use it before petting him, putting his food down, or offering a treat. Use it when you let him out of the car or house and before his admirers approach.

Give the "Sit" direction only once. If your pup looks at you as though you've never met or he simply ignores you, either tug the leash and say "No" or simply position him. Don't get in the habit of repeating directions because he may never listen!

Add a word a week

As your puppy is developing, both physically and mentally, you need to start teaching these useful directions: Heel, No, Stay, Come, and Stand-Stay. If you work on the "word a week" plan, you'll shape your puppy's understanding and social skills in no time!

Heel

A puppy standing calmly at his owner's side, walking when she moves, and sitting when she stops, is a beautiful thing to watch. Yes, such control can be yours, too, if you're patient. Though it takes awhile to synchronize, eventually you'll be maneuvering through crowded streets and calling your puppy to heel from a distance. Sound miraculous? Use these exercises to train your puppy to stay at your heel.

How many ways were you taught to sit at the dinner table? Most likely you were taught just one. Guess how many ways there are to heel? You're right — one. Picture your puppy at your heel with toes aligned and heads facing in the same direction. Isn't it a pretty picture to imagine?

Do the simple circle

Practice this heeling exercise in an open, quiet place (inside or out). Clear an area to walk in a circle. Position your puppy next to you at your left side, everyone's heads facing in the same direction, and your puppy's paws lined up with your heel (see Figure 14-3). You're ready to start performing the following steps:

1. **Relax your arms straight, keeping your left thumb behind the seam of your pants. Tug the leash back whenever your puppy pulls from your side.**

2. **Instruct your puppy by saying "*<Name>*, Heel" as you begin to walk in a counterclockwise (dog on the inside) circle.**

    Walk in a cheerful manner, with your head held high and your shoulders back to communicate the right attitude.

Figure 14-3: Setting up to do the simple circle heeling exercise.

3. **Praise your puppy for walking with you.**

    If you want to, introduce a click or a treat for his cooperation. Tug him back into position if your puppy's attention starts to stray.

4. **Stop after each circle by slowing your pace and reminding him to "Heel."**

5. **Place your puppy into a sitting position.**

    To position your pup into the sit position when you stop, grasp the base of the leash (where the leash attaches to your puppy's collar) with your right hand and use your left hand to squeeze the pressure point located on his waist.

6. **Practice five circles twice a day.**

If your dog turns to face you when you stop, guess what? He's facing off. He's making another attempt at interaction, play, and misdirection. To discourage this habit, either hold his waist into position as you stop or come to a stop alongside a wall or barrier so that he's unable to move out of position.

A good leash tug shouldn't involve knuckles, shoulders, or chest muscles. Think of your elbow as a hinge. Without the leash, rock your elbow back and forth. Now imagine that I was holding my hand behind your back. Slap my hand without doing more than flexing your triceps muscle with a slight bend of your elbow. Now pick up the leash. Holding the lead behind your back, snap your elbow. Pretend my hand's there and you're trying to hit it.

Float the finish

When you're preparing to stop, slow your pace slightly, lift your left foot high in the air (like you're marching), and then drop it lightly to the floor. This action gives your puppy an added clue that he's supposed to stop and sit.

Change your pace

As you change your pace, keep your leash hand steady and relaxed behind the seam of your pants. Move faster by trotting. Slow your pace by lengthening your stride. Make sure you change gears smoothly and indicate the change by saying "Clk, clk" or "Shh." Remember, your puppy's a canine, not a Porsche.

Do an about face

Walking at a normal speed, say "Heel" and pivot to the right. To help your puppy keep up, slow down as you turn. Cluck, bend your knees, or slap your leg to keep him with you. Walk six paces, stop and position the sit, and then hug your puppy for a job well done. (Remember: Avoid choking him through the turn — that's no fun.)

Heeling practice tips

You know you're ready to practice the "Heel" direction in everyday situations when your puppy responds without pressure on his collar. Use this direction everywhere:

- **Keep a short lead on your puppy around the home.** Pick the lead up occasionally and say "Heel" as you walk from room to room.

- **Use the "Heel" direction on your walks.** If your puppy's young or just beginning to learn, heel him for one-fourth of your walk. Increase the distance over the next month until your puppy is always walking at your side.

- **Practice heeling in a parking lot and other more crowded situations (just make sure they're not too crowded).** Don't allow sniffing or lunging at neighborhood pals and be mindful of your puppy, no matter what the distractions.

Stay calm if things get out of hand when you're in public. If you yell "Heel, heel, heel!" and jerk your poor puppy back and forth, he'll just get more excited. If you have this problem, determine whether you're asking too much too soon. Maybe your puppy simply needs to exercise more before you practice in public.

Be sure to keep your hand behind you — left arm straight and behind your back (see Figure 14-4). If your left hand is in front of your thigh, your puppy is the leader, not you.

Figure 14-4:
The right way to hold the leash for heeling.

Is your puppy too strong for you to manage? Try the *tush push,* which transfers the strain of your leash from your arms to the trunk of your body. Here's how it goes: Slide the leash around your backside and grasp it in both hands. Slide both thumbs together and rest them on your left tush. Keep your arms straight and relaxed, and when your puppy surges ahead, simply push back with your tush.

No

There are a few inconsistencies with the way people use this little word that leaves puppies baffled as to its meaning.

- ✔ **People usually shout it.** Shouting to a puppy sounds like barking. Would barking excite a situation or calm it down?

- ✔ **People use it with their puppies' names.** (In fact, many puppies think No is the second half of their name: "Buddy No!" "Tristan No!" "Molly

No!") You should only use your puppy's name when you're happy, not mad.

✔ **People say it after the action has occurred.** If I yelled at you after you ate a bowl of soup, would you understand that I was upset at you for opening the can? Said at the wrong time, "No" communicates nothing.

✔ **People say it repetitively.** "No, no, no, no" sounds different from "No."

What's an owner to do to teach a puppy not to get into trouble? Fortunately, I have the answer. First, you need to teach your puppy the concept of No by setting up situations to catch the thought process. As you train your pup to understand No, work indoors first and then out.

Indoors, put your puppy on his leash and have someone secretly place a piece of cheese on the floor in a neighboring room (this is your prop). Follow these steps and pay attention to timing.

1. **Bring your puppy into the heel position and casually walk toward the cheese.**

2. **The second your puppy notices the cheese, tug back on the lead and say "No!"**

   Your puppy has a built-in antenna system: his ears. If his ears perk up, your puppy is alert. When teaching No, watch your puppy's ears. Correct your puppy the second he becomes alert to something inappropriate.

3. **Continue to walk like nothing has happened.**

   Remember: You're the boss. No means No.

4. **Walk by the cheese several times to ensure that your puppy got the message.**

If you've been using "Ep, ep" with your puppy, save "No" for major infractions like stealing food from the counter or chasing the cats or kids. You may continue to use "Ep, ep" if you catch your puppy going astray, like when he's sniffing something on the street or considering mischief.

After your indoor training, practice "No" when you're out for a walk. When your puppy notices a passing jogger, car, kid, another dog, or two tidbits climbing a tree, say "No" just like you did with the cheese. Sidestep away from the temptation to emphasize your disapproval. Continue to tug each time the ear-antennas flicker. Praise your puppy for focusing on you and relaxing his radar system.

Stay

If "Stay" is your dream direction, you're not alone. I'm not sure why people have so much trouble teaching this direction. My guess is that they probably rush it. They teach the direction one day and expect their dog to stay while they welcome company or walk into the kitchen for a sandwich. Promise me this: You won't rush. When taught progressively, this direction's a real winner.

Here are a few rules to follow when teaching the "Stay" direction:

- Look over your puppy's head when you practice; never look directly into his eyes. It's too daunting for him.

- Stand tall. When you bend down, you look like you want to play.

- Stay close to your puppy when you start out. You should have about 6 inches from toe to paw. Creating too much distance too soon can be really scary for your pup.

- While doing each exercise, hold the lead directly above your puppy's head. That way, if he confuses "Stay" with "Go," you're ready for a quick correction.

- When you return to your puppy's side at the end of each exercise, vary the length you pause before you release him with "Okay!" This will prevent his "reading" the pattern and encourage a more watchful eye on your direction.

- Resist petting your puppy until you finish teaching him the steps for the "Stay" direction. Too much petting ruins his concentration.

Practice this simplified sequence twice a day until your puppy's feeling mighty fine about his accomplishments.

To prepare for your first lesson:

1. **Take your puppy into a quiet room.**

   No TV. No kids. No cats. Just you two.

2. **Slide your puppy's training collar high near his head and center it between his ears.**

3. **Fold the leash in your left hand to hip level.**

4. **Position your puppy behind your heels.**

Now you're ready to teach your puppy his first lesson. You do six sequences. No more, no less.

To teach the "Stay" direction, stand next to your puppy to start (see the preceding steps) and then follow these steps:

1. **Instruct "Sit" and align your puppy with your ankles.**

2. **Instruct "Stay" as you flash your hand in front of your puppy's nose. Remove the hand signal and pause for five seconds.**

3. **Instruct "Okay" as you swing your arm forward and step out of position.**

4. **Again, instruct "Sit, Stay." This time, pivot to face away from your puppy and pause ten seconds. Return to the starting point and release with "Okay!"**

5. **Back to the start position again. Instruct "Stay." Pivot in front of your puppy. Pause. Now march to create a physical distraction that will teach your puppy how to contain himself.**

   Yes, I said march! March slowly at first, like you're sleepwalking. After your puppy holds still for that, gradually increase your physical motions.

6. **Instruct "Stay" and pivot and pause. Now try jumping and waving your arms.**

   Go slowly at first. You want to ease into your mania. Now make some noise.

7. **Pivot, pause, and then bark at your puppy. Then return, pause, and release.**

   No staring into your puppy's eyes. Instead, keep looking over his head. Add a meow or two when you think he can handle it.

8. **From your starting position, instruct "Stay," pivot in front, and pause for 30 seconds.**

   Stand up tall, relax your shoulders, and keep the leash above your puppy's head just in case he's tempted to break.

9. **When the time is up, return to his side, pause, and release with "Okay!"**

10. **Now you can hug that well-behaved puppy!**

Some puppies have a reduced attention span and initially may not be able to hold still for long. Check to ensure you're following protocol: Are you standing right in front of him as you increase distractions? Are you holding the leash above his head to enforce his control? Are you introducing this direction in a discrete location? Too many distractions make it impossible to concentrate.

Now you're ready to increase the three Ds:

- ✔ **Distraction:** Step up your march, add a new aerobics twist, walk around your puppy full circle, and chant like a chimp. Can you do all these crazy things without tempting your puppy to move?

  Are you wondering why you're jumping around and making noise while your puppy's expected to stay? Eventually, your puppy will have to concentrate while confronted with motion and sound distractions, so you're helping him get accustomed to temptations.

- ✔ **Duration:** Stretch your 30-second stand-still to two minutes.

- ✔ **Distance:** Move out one foot at a time. When you're successful, reintroduce distractions gradually and increase the duration.

Now the two of you should feel like pros.

Hand signals can help your puppy focus

Your puppy can start learning hand signals as early at 12 weeks of age, although I recommend emphasizing signals at 4 months. This visual direction will intensify your puppy's focus — and as you know, if he's taught to watch you he'll not stray far.

Use hand signals in front of your puppy's nose to direct his attention to you. Review the point training lesson in Chapter 11, and then use the point to signal your directions. Here's my list:

✔ **Sit:** Point your finger as you swing your right arm from your puppy's nose to your face, like you're scooping his attention toward you, and say "Sit."

✔ **Stay:** Flatten your palm like a paddle. Flash it quickly in front of your puppy's nose and say "Stay."

✔ **Okay:** Point your finger and swing your right arm out from your puppy's nose as you step forward. Say "Okay" to tell him "Job well done!"

✔ **Come:** When your dog is near you, sweep a pointed finger from his nose to your eye to encourage a happy reconnection. If he's a distance from you, use a sweeping motion to get his attention as you call his name and say "Come."

Come

Now you're ready for "Come," which is another highly desired direction. First you need to ask yourself a couple of things: Have you said "Come" more than once and yelled it repeatedly? Have you chased your puppy and bribed him with his favorite delicacy? If so, trouble is brewing. Your puppy thinks "Come" means disobedience or game time. Fortunately, you can reformat his understanding, but doing so will take time, concentration, structure, patience, and a lot of praise. Read on to find out how.

Going for up-close control first

Teach your pup to interact with you physically so that when he hears "Come," he wants to return to your side. As you instruct him to come from a greater distance, he'll want to close the gap.

The goal when you say "Come" is to have your puppy return and make contact with you. Each time you say this direction, pat, treat, or otherwise handle your puppy so that he learns that "Come" means "togetherness and interaction." To teach your puppy how to come from short distances, follow these steps:

1. **Walk in front of your puppy while he's standing calmly.**

2. **Standing tall, say "<Name>, Come" as you zip your finger up your belly from his nose level to your eyes.**

Make a funny sound to encourage focus: Cluck, whistle, smooch, or make up your own!

3. **If he doesn't look up, cradle his body into a sitting position and pat the sides of his head lovingly. "Come" should be associated with a warm and loving reconnection.**

 To position your pooch, lift up on his buckle collar and tuck his hindquarters into position, squeezing his waist muscles below his ribs as you press down.

 Avoid jerky motions, don't press his backbone, and don't admonish him or repeat yourself as you position. Doing so causes "Come" to be associated with rough handling.

4. **After your puppy makes eye contact, give him a big hug or pat on the head.**

Repeat this exercise throughout the day, whenever you have something positive to share — a pat, a treat, a toy, or even dinner. Make sure your puppy's first associations to this direction are warm and welcoming.

Going for distance control

Before you can teach your pup to come from a distance, he must understand that "Come" means togetherness. After he understands, you're ready to go for distance control. (No, you're not off-lead yet. Be patient.)

Practice this exercise in a quiet room and keep your lesson short and upbeat.

To teach distance control, make sure your pup is wearing a leash and then follow these steps:

1. **Practice three regular Sit-Stays and then return to your puppy's side and release him with "Okay!"**

2. **Leave your puppy in a stay position and walk to the end of the leash.**

3. **Pause. (Vary the duration each time.)**

4. **Call "<Name>, Come!" in a directional tone. Signal it by sweeping your right arm across your body.**

5. **As soon as you issue the direction, scurry backward and reel in the leash.**

6. **When your pup gets near your feet, zip your finger up your belly from his nose level to your eyes and tap your heel to the floor to encourage him to stop and look up.**

7. **Encourage eye contact by standing or kneeling and making kissing sounds.**

8. **Release him with an "Okay," and always remember to praise the good puppy.**

Practice "Come" three times per session. That's all. More than that is stressful for your pup.

Building focus by throwing in distractions

If your puppy gets excited when he hears "Come," you're doing a good job. Now you can start encouraging focus around low-level distractions and increasing the distance from which you call him. Here are some ideas (you can add to the list): Try this exercise in front of the TV, in the backyard, in front of the kids, and during mealtime. In a quiet hallway or garage, attach the retractable leash (see Chapter 5) and increase your distance slowly.

Using the "Come" direction around distractions is more difficult than using the direction in a quiet living room. Most dogs try to pay attention to the distraction and you at the same time, which is impossible. If your puppy's torn, tug the leash and use praise or a treat cup to focus him.

If you're having trouble getting your puppy's attention around distractions, you're not alone. My advice: Stick with it. Don't give up. Think of the direction "Come" as the human phrase equivalent of "huddle" and encourage your puppy with that level of confidence. Convey that "Come" invites reconnection and that togetherness is the safest, most wonderful place to be.

Practice in a quiet room for a day, enthusiastically praising your puppy's focus. Then try it with your TV on by following these steps:

1. **Let him sniff about while letting the leash drag behind him.**

2. **Pause varying lengths of time before you call him.**

3. **Relax your posture and say "*<Name>*, Come!"**

4. **Flag him in.**

5. **Encourage him to sit or lean into you for a hug.**

6. **If you're using food or a click-treat combination, reward him the moment you touch.**

Work up the distraction chain slowly. If your puppy's too stimulated, practice around simpler distractions for a while.

You're not in a rush. Training your puppy isn't a race. And whatever you do, don't get frustrated. Frustration kills enthusiasm.

Use "Come" in two of the following situations daily (you can add to the list, but just make sure you use "Come" only twice a day):

✔ When your puppy's distracted on a walk, during regular teaching, or on a retractable leash.

✔ Additionally, you can run away from your puppy throughout the day to encourage him to check in with you by using your treat cup or a click-and-treat combination to highlight your reconnection.

"Come" do's and don'ts

Here are a few things to remember when teaching the "Come" direction:

✔ **Do use it sparingly.** When you overuse "Come," dogs stop paying attention.

When your puppy understands the direction, avoid using it all the time. Say it infrequently and make it extremely rewarding. (Don't forget about the other directions you have in your arsenal: "Inside" for coming indoors, "Let's Go" for follow me, and "Heel" for staying at your side.)

✔ **Don't chase your puppy if he doesn't respond.** Practice on-lead for now or use a long line to give him more freedom to explore.

✔ **Don't call for negative interaction.** Do you have to brush, bathe, or isolate your puppy? If so, don't use "Come." Also avoid using it when you're angry. You'll only freak your puppy out.

✔ **If your puppy runs away, don't repeatedly call or correct him.** I know the frustration of marching around in the middle of a cold, wet, rainy night looking for your puppy, but if you call or discipline your puppy, you're only teaching him to run from you. If your puppy does run off, here are some measures you may take:

- Call the police as well as neighbors.

- If you can see your puppy, block roads to prevent a mishap.

- Overexaggerate playing with a stick or digging a hole. Stay focused on the activity so your puppy will be intrigued. Calmly reach for him only after he has returned to your side.

- If you've practiced the games listed in Chapter 23, find some props (or carry them with you) to initiate a game to highlight your fun. Your puppy won't be able to resist.

✔ **Don't discipline your puppy when he returns to you.** He won't come back so quickly the next time.

✔ **Do use a different direction to bring your puppy inside.** Coming in from outdoors is a big drag for your pup, no more fun than being left alone or ignored. Using the "Come" direction when you want to bring your pup inside makes it a negative direction. Instead, pick a direction like "Inside." Start using it on-lead when bringing your puppy into the house. Quickly offer a treat or ball toss.

Stand-Stay

The "Stand-Stay" direction is great when you need to wipe muddy paws or groom. Fortunately, if you follow these steps, you won't find this direction too difficult to teach:

1. **Kneel down on the floor next to your puppy.**

2. **Place your right hand, palm out, on your puppy's buckle collar.**

3. **Slide your left hand under your puppy's belly.**

4. **Say "Stand-Stay" as you prop your puppy into a standing position.**

5. **Relax your right hand and slide your left hand so that it rests on your puppy's thigh.**

6. **Vary the pause from two to five seconds — and release with an "Okay!"**

7. **Increase the pause time to one minute.**

8. **Repeat Steps 2–7 from a standing position.**

   After your dog's standing still, you're ready to let go.

9. **Prop your puppy into position.**

10. **Remind "Stay," and slide your left hand away from your puppy.**

11. **After you're successful, slide your right hand from the collar.**

   Remind "Stay" as often as necessary.

After your puppy catches on, begin using this direction whenever the situation calls for it. Does your puppy have muddy paws? Give him the "Stand-Stay" direction. Sure, he may be fidgety. If so, just say "Shhh — Stand-Stay." For brushing, try the same thing.

When introducing this direction for grooming, use peanut butter or another creamy spread slathered on the refrigerator at his nose level. Grooming will be quite the treat for your pup. Eventually, his association will be set, and he'll look forward to grooming activities with or without treats!

Puppy Puberty Lessons: 6 to 9 Months

At this stage, your puppy's world is being shaped by two conflicting forces: the desire to please you and the urge to test his leaders once more just to make sure they can walk their talk. Don't take it personally. After your puppy understands that you most certainly do mean what you say, you'll be in the driver's seat. Here are a few rules to help you through this stage:

✔ **Remain calm.** Don't let your puppy see that you're angry or frustrated. All teens, regardless of species, derive perverse pleasure out of your discomfort.

✔ **Don't let your puppy ignore you.** If your puppy challenges you on a direction and he's on leash, reinforce your expectations. If your puppy is off-leash and he ignores or defies a direction, ignore him and withdraw from the situation.

A graceful retreat isn't a failure.

✔ **Raise his consciousness.** Teach or remind him of the meaning of "No." See the section "No," earlier in this chapter, for details.

Talking to your pubescent puppy

To communicate successfully with your teen puppy, remember these five tips:

✔ **Detach.** Detaching is more a meditation exercise than a dog-training technique. Basically, this technique is for your own benefit, although your mental calmness will affect your puppy too. You appear more centered, and who wouldn't respect that! Breathe in and breathe out and detach yourself from your puppy. Avoid taking his behavior personally. Although you may think all your training has been a waste of time, it hasn't. Remember this: Puppyhood equals patience plus persistence.

✔ **Stay centered.** When your puppy is acting up, use all your energy to stay cool. If you get angry or tense, he knows he's got to you. At that point, you're playing his game and following his lead.

✔ **Watch out for eye contact.** Puppies are very concerned with status at this age: "Am I a leader or follower?"

If your puppy can get you to look to him more than you can get him to look to you, you're the follower. Ignore your puppy's attempts to get your attention. Pet and gaze at him when he's in a calm state of mind. Give him eye contact when you direct his behavior.

✔ **Fall back, if necessary.** Even if you've successfully weaned your puppy from the leash, you'll probably need it again during this stage. When your puppy is overstimulated and unable to focus, connect him to your side or station him for a while with a bone.

✔ **Have alternative plans.** During behavior emergencies — for example, out-of-control door greetings, article stealing, running away, and so forth — use your directions, if they work. Most dogs, however, become temporarily deaf during these situations, so have alternative plans. See the upcoming section "Handling common problems" for alternatives.

Handling common problems

Some problems may surface — or resurface — when your puppy hits puberty. A pup who used to calmly greet guests now goes into a frenzy when people arrive. Or maybe an open door is just too much temptation, and he darts out. Following are some suggestions to help you deal with situations that you may find yourself and your pup in.

Door greeting

Always ask guests to ignore your puppy until he's settled down. Your three solution options include assigning him a greeting station as outlined in Chapter 13, connecting him around your waist to maintain leash control, or if all else fails, crating or confining him with a favorite toy. Bring him out when he's calmed down.

Article stealing

When your puppy steals an article of clothing (or any other item for that matter), leave the area and shut the door behind you. At this age, most puppies are more concerned with playing than with chewing. If you ignore him, he'll lose interest in the game.

Another option would be leaving the house: Putting on your coat and grabbing your keys should be enough to distract him. Take your pup out for a minute or two if you try this trick. Otherwise, he'll start to see right through it.

As a last recourse, follow him around without eye contact or corrections, slowly cornering him in a small area. Calmly remove the object by squeezing his muzzle and instructing "Give." Never correct a puppy while using the "Give" directions, or else he'll quickly distrust you.

Runaway puppy

A puppy running away is more than just frustrating — it's dangerous. You should never let your puppy off-leash unless you're in a confined area. If you want to give him freedom in an unconfined area, put him on a 25- to 50-foot long line so that you can grab the leash for quick control if needed. If your puppy does sneak off, have your plans well thought out. Here are some tips:

- Try a direction or two. If they don't work, stop. Don't panic.
- Try running around like a lunatic (without eye contact), screaming and waving your arms. Drop to the ground in a heap and see whether this strange and interesting behavior brings him running.

> ✔ Try getting in the car. Many dogs can't bear the thought of missing out on a trip.
>
> ✔ If nothing works, follow him quietly to make sure he stays out of danger. Yelling only makes matters worse. Stop traffic if you can, and ask for help if you need it.

Avoid getting angry at your puppy after the fact. Otherwise, he'll learn to be more wary of your ploys. Never use treats as bribery because when used in this way, treats actually reinforce mischief.

The top five directions

When training during this phase, you extend your control on all the directions your pup has learned so far (see the preceding sections). Following are the top five directions that I encourage you to use most often.

Handling walks with "Heel"

Continue using "Heel" to encourage good walking control. In addition, use this direction to call your puppy to your side. To teach your puppy this concept:

1. **Place him on a leash and let him walk ahead of you.**

2. **Suddenly call his name and the direction "Heel" as you slap your left thigh.**

3. **Take a giant step backward as you lead him back to your side as you reel in the leash.**

   Lead him around your left side in a U or to your right around your back. When he reaches your side, make sure he sits before you release him.

After he gets the hang of the "Heel" direction (thigh-slap), begin to encourage him to come to your side around distractions (on-leash at first) and when you're sitting down. Always give the direction positively, enforce a proper sit, and praise him warmly before you release him with "Okay."

Reinforcing manners with "Sit"

Continue to ask your puppy to "Sit" in all situations. This direction is the human phrase equivalent of saying "please." Give the direction only once. If he doesn't respond, give him a tug that says "No" and ask him again. Position him if he doesn't listen.

Using "Down" in all kinds of situations

Continue to work on the "Down" direction even if your puppy doesn't want to cooperate (see Figure 14-5). Position your puppy by pressing on the pressure point located in between his shoulder blades, lifting one paw out to shift his balance. Ignore him if he rolls around wildly on the floor or nips your shoelaces (step on the leash so that he can only lie comfortably). Release him only after he's calmed down.

When your puppy begins cooperating, use "Down" for everything, such as before treating (hold the treat to the ground and direct "Down") and before dinner (cover the bowl with your hand and, as you put it down, say "Down").

Practicing "Wait" with more distractions

Continue using the "Wait" direction to catch your puppy's attention at doorways, cars, stairs, or before entering an area of high stimulation (for example, the veterinarian's office, a room full of children, or a dog-training class). This direction means your puppy should stop dead in his tracks and wait to follow you. If you're successful using this direction in the situations described in the section "Wait and Okay" (earlier in this chapter), begin to practice it when walking your puppy on his leash. Follow these steps when practicing "Wait" with a leash:

Figure 14-5:
Using the "Down" direction with an uncooperative puppy in puberty.

1. **Stop in your tracks as you direct "Wait."**

2. **Pull back on the leash if your pup doesn't stop with you.**

3. **Release with "Okay."**

Taking "No" outside

When your puppy understands that when you say "No" you mean it, begin to practice this direction outside with dogs, bikers, and other temptations passing by. Tug the leash sharply as you say "No" in your sternest correction tone.

Trying Teen Lessons: 9 to 12 Months

During the preceding stage (puppy puberty), I discourage all but the mildest corrective techniques during training. Now that your puppy has become a teen, however, he's emotionally ready to learn that not everything he does pleases you. Your puppy is only acting naturally when he tests your flexibility on the directions he's learned. He wonders whether perhaps the "Sit" for company means something just a little different from the "Sit" for you.

In the previous stages, you labored over the teaching process. You showed your puppy exactly what each direction meant. Now he knows. Every time he doesn't respond or responds in his own way, he's questioning you. If you repeat yourself or position him, he'll never learn to respond on his own. Like teaching a child to tie shoelaces, eventually it must be done independently.

To develop the all-important canine consciousness, you must do two things:

✔ Decide what you want when you give a direction.

✔ Follow through. If your expectations are unclear, your puppy's reaction will be, too.

At this stage, when practicing your directions, avoid repeating yourself or positioning your puppy immediately. If he doesn't respond, tug the leash firmly and say "No" in a corrective tone. If he still doesn't respond, review your tone (is it stern enough?) and make adjustments as needed. If your puppy still ignores you, position him without praise.

If your puppy pivots out of position when you stop in "Heel," inches forward on the "Stay" directions, or moves in front of you during stationary directions, he's testing you. If you position him sweetly, you're actually giving him attention for his defiance. In these situations, tug the leash firmly as you say "No" and position him by maneuvering him into place with the leash. This method may take several tries and a temper tantrum from your beloved pet, but if you let the structure slide, you'll never have a reliable off-leash dog. (Refer to Chapter 15 for info on training off the leash.)

Chapter 15

Graduating to Off-Lead Control

*N*o one can underestimate the pleasure of living with a well-trained dog. In Chapter 14, I cover leash-training techniques; master those exercises before you begin the exercises described in this chapter.

Whether your goal is to have your puppy off-lead around the home or be responsive when you're on a hike at a park, the most considered question is "How will you know when you and your puppy are ready for off-lead-control training?" Well, there's no magic age or season or day: Readiness is something you gauge by experience. If you practice giving these directions and your pup shows signs of stress (licking her lips, hyperactivity, fixated chewing on the lines, or nipping), she's giving you a signal to lower your expectations for the time being. Puppies show readiness with concentrated eye contact and responsiveness that's quick and cooperative. A puppy has her own timetable for readiness: Off-lead work requires impulse control that emerges anytime between the ages of 6 and 18 months. Read on to get started.

Getting Mentally Prepared for Off-Lead Control

To have off-lead control, you must earn it. Remember, dogs are drawn to confidence, so you need to act with authority and self-assurance (even if you have to fake it).

However, as you work toward off-lead control, don't get too bold too quickly. When the leash disappears from around your pup's neck, you may notice a strong lurching fear in the pit of your stomach, and your dog will note that you suddenly have less control. At that moment, your puppy will make a choice: If she doesn't want to come and she's free to run, you may be standing there helpless. Off-lead control means constantly reading and rereading your puppy and being aware that your puppy is also reading you. To have control, you must look like a leader and you must be confident and self-assured so that your dog can trust your judgment.

To further your mental preparation, keep these three suggestions in mind:

- ✔ **Stay cool.** Frustration makes you look weak. As you work toward off-lead control, your puppy may act confused and unresponsive because your guidance is gone. You used to give the direction and guide her with the lead. Now you don't, and it feels awkward to her. Whatever your pup's reaction, stay cool. Any corrections add to her confusion. Jazz up your body language and use some pep talks to encourage her toward you.

- ✔ **Stay focused.** Eye contact communicates control. Your puppy should be watching you. If the reverse is true, you're the follower. To avoid being the follower, make sure you work in a confined area or on a long line so you can ignore your dog when she disobeys. If you're near your house, walk inside.

- ✔ **Step back.** Your puppy is responding beautifully off-lead . . . until someone rings the doorbell, a chipmunk runs across the driveway, or another dog comes trotting past the gate. Then everything she's learned goes out the window, and you're back to being ignored. Let me tell you a secret: Off-lead control takes time. If your puppy is good but is still having trouble in a stimulating situation, review on-lead exercises in distracting situations (see Chapter 14). Using a lead helps control the situation and at the same time conditions more appropriate behavior.

So what goes into making your pup mentally ready? Maturity serves your off-lead goals well. As your puppy passes into doghood, you'll note a calm predictability. Wanderlust and mischief will have most likely lost their thrill. Your dog's joy will manifest in silent teamwork and shared activities. The stages your puppy follows to maturity aren't so different from the ages and stages of a child growing into adulthood. If you think you love your puppy now, just wait — the love continues to grow. Soon, the two of you will be thinking and working harmoniously.

Consider your puppy's breed instincts when working toward off-lead reliability. For example, a terrier, who was bred to follow his hunting instincts independently, is far less impressed with your direction than a Shetland Sheepdog, who lives for the camaraderie and guidance of a shepherd. Hound and Nordic breeds are other pups who must be monitored closely because their instincts can override your direction. Do some research to discover whether your

puppy's breed was bred to work in concert with man or to work independently. Independent thinkers may need more persuasion to focus (a clicker
and some food can work wonders). With an independent thinker, understand
that 100 percent reliability may not be a realistic goal.

Buying the Right Equipment — and Using It Correctly

As you work toward off-lead obedience, you practice exercises that extend
your control greater and greater distances. Before you start, round up these
items (each of which is discussed in more detail later in this section):

- **Retractable leashes:** The retractable leash is invaluable for advanced
  work. Remember — the longer, the better.

- **Indoor drag lead:** This item is a 4- to 6-foot light leash worn around the
  house.

- **Short lead:** This lead should be long enough to grab but short enough
  not to distract your dog (8 inches is a common length).

- **Tree line:** Attach a 20-foot lead to a tree. Use this stationed area to practice distance "Stay" directions. You can use a simple canvas lead, or you
  can make your own out of a clothesline attached to a single-headed clip
  found at most hardware stores. Use the tree line for distance control
  with "Wait," "Heel," "Down," and "Come" directions.

- **Long line:** Purchase a 25- to 50-foot canvas lead or use a clothesline.

Attach all lines to your puppy's buckle collar, not her training collar.

Off-lead puppies aren't created overnight. Training is a step-by-step process.
Use your new equipment to increase your puppy's focus, but don't get itchy
fingers. Just because she behaves well on her retractable leash one day
doesn't mean she's ready for an off-lead romp the next. Take your time. Even
though I explain how to train with each piece of equipment separately, you
can use them interchangeably to vary your puppy's routine to keep her interested, engaged, and on her toes!

The retractable leash

The retractable leash is a great tool for distance training when you're working
alone in an open environment. In fact, that's the only time I ever recommend
its use. This lead allows your pup limited freedom to explore while enabling

you to enforce directions the moment you give them. As a training tool, you can use the retractable leash to reinforce the following directions:

- *<Name>:* Call out your puppy's name enthusiastically. If she looks at you, praise her. That's all that's required — just a glance. If she ignores you, tug the leash, say "No," and then praise her after you have her attention.

- **Wait:** Begin to direct your puppy to stop 3 feet in front of you with this direction. If your dog continues forward, tug the leash and say "No, Wait." Increase your distance to 6 feet, 8 feet, 12 feet, 16 feet, and 26 feet in front of you.

- **Sit-Stay:** Use the retractable leash to increase your distance control. Increase your distance incrementally. (To accustom your puppy to the pull of the retractable leash, pivot in front of her and slide the leash out a few times.)

- **Heel:** Use this direction to call your puppy back to your side. Call out her name and then direct "Heel" as you slap your leg. Praise your puppy as she responds, and then walk a short distance before you stop to release her.

- **No:** Whenever your puppy's focusing on something she shouldn't be concentrating on, tug the leash and say "No." Immediately refocus her attention with a toy, a stick, or another direction.

An indoor drag lead

Use an indoor drag lead (made from a lightweight puppy lead or rope, between 4 to 6 feet long) to keep an eye on your dog in the house. Throughout the day, stand by the lead and give a direction ("Sit," "Down," "Wait," or "Come"). If your pup looks confused, step on the lead and praise her as you help her into position. For example, if you give the direction "Down" and she gives you a blank stare, step on the lead to stop her, and then praise her as you guide her into position. Your understanding can help her overcome her off-lead confusion.

If your puppy gives you some defiant canine back talk (a bark or dodge), step on the lead and tug it as you say "No." Then station and ignore her for 15 minutes — the canine equivalent to being grounded with no TV.

A short lead

After your puppy's reliable on the drag lead, use a short lead to reinforce your stationary directions: "Sit," "Stay", "Down," "Wait," "Heel," and "Come" (refer to Chapter 14 for more on these directions). The short lead adds weight to her collar, reminding her of the security of on-lead direction as well as giving you the ability to guide her calmly should she get confused.

In addition to using the short lead around the house, do a lesson once a day. Bring your puppy into a quiet room and practice a simple directional routine. Initially, hold the short lead but then drop it after you've warmed up. Slap your leg and use hand signals and peppy body language to encourage your dog's focus.

A 20-foot tree line

Tie this line to a tree or post. Secure all knots. Leave the line on the ground and follow this sequence:

1. **Warm up with five minutes of regular on-lead practice.**

2. **Stop your puppy next to the 20-foot line and attach it to your puppy's buckle collar discreetly.**

3. **Remove her regular lead and place it on the ground in front of her; keep your hands free.**

4. **After you direct your puppy to "Stay," walk 10 feet away.**

   Extend your distance as she gains control. Run your fingers through your hair and swing your arms gently back and forth to emphasize that the leash is out of your hands.

5. **As your puppy improves, practice an out-of-sight "Sit-Stay," practice "Down" from a "Sit-Stay," and practice a "Down-Stay."**

You can also practice the "Come" lesson, though you should never call at a distance greater than the line can reach lest your puppy artfully dart away and successfully ignore your direction.

If she takes this opportunity to ignore you and darts for a quick getaway, wait until she's about to hit the end of the line to shout "No!" Return her back into position and repeat the exercise at a closer range.

 If your puppy disobeys, determine whether her response is motivated by anxiety, confusion, or defiance. If she's confused or anxious, her posture will shrink, her tail will lower, and both her eyes and her ears will flicker distressfully. Don't issue a correction: doing so may only create more stress when you're separated. Calmly return to her side and reposition her gently. Repeat the exercise at close range.

 If your puppy breaks defiantly, she'll either trot off ignoring you completely or try to engage you in a game of keepaway. Her head and tail will be held high, eyes either avoiding contact or mindfully baiting you with a defiant focus. Either say "No" firmly as she hits the end of the line, or if she's baiting you, return quietly and tug the leash as you say "No." Either reposition and repeat the exercise at close range or go back to practicing on-lead exercises.

A 30-foot long line

Attach your puppy to the 30-foot long line and let her roam free as you keep a watchful eye on her. Engage her by playing with a stick or ball and investigate your surroundings together. Avoid giving too many commands. Just hang out and enjoy some free time with your pup. Every five minutes, position yourself near the line and give an enthusiastic but clear direction.

If you're issuing a stationary direction, such as "Sit," "Wait," or "Down," stop abruptly as you signal and direct her simultaneously. If you're issuing a motion direction, such as "Come" or "Heel," run backward as you encourage your puppy toward you. If she races over, help her into the proper position and give her a big hug. If your puppy ignores you, quickly step on the line and say "No." (Don't scream; just speak sternly.) After your correction, give your dog the opportunity to right her reaction before lifting the line to tug it or reel her in. End your session with a favorite game.

Gauging Your Pup's Personal Reactions

When practicing various exercises, you'll notice that your puppy is in one of two camps: the excitable explorer camp or the more timid and clingy camp. Neither reaction is preferable. Both warrant gauging if your goal is to enjoy this time together. A radically excitable puppy is difficult to focus and will likely dart away if not taught better impulse control. On the other hand, a puppy who's nervous when you're out of sight won't enjoy the splendor of an off-lead stroll and may appear reactionary to passersby. Keeping your puppy focused on you, regardless of her personality or the situation, is the key to happy off-lead experiences.

If you suspect that your puppy's distracted, do a quick exercise to decide for sure. Either decrease your speed suddenly or sidestep away from her. Does she follow your rhythm and direction or skip to her own beat? Give her a quick tug if she needs a reminder and praise her when she refocuses.

An excitable explorer

You know if you have a puppy with this personality because she's outgoing, social, and insatiably curious wherever you take her. Hesitation isn't in her vocabulary! Before practicing an off-lead exercise with your excitable explorer, tire her out a bit. Play games (indoors or out) that don't require strict conformity to detail. Soda Bottle Soccer and Two-Toy Toss (see Chapter 23) are wonderful options. At first, practice your lessons before your puppy's meals, using either her kibbles or special treats to enhance her focus and cooperation.

Your puppy is watching

Do you know that your puppy can read you as well as, or maybe even better than, you can read her? If your timing is off by a hair or your mind is drifting, she'll notice and modify her cooperation. She takes advantage of you less out of disrespect and more out of her need to learn the rules of this new off-lead game. Practice your lesson only when you can be mindful to detail and use a long line to prevent any mishaps. In case you become truly out of control, have a few backup plans, such as running to the car, mocking a tremendous accident, or shaking a treat cup. Be positive when reunited so that she doesn't lose faith in your reconnection.

A clicker (flip to Chapter 11) can often add a spark to lessons as well. If your puppy is too excited to respond, practice on-lead for half the lesson or return to the basics for a few more weeks.

A more timid pup

If your dog is cautious, she'll be less inclined to romp when you unclip the leash. Her tail may immediately attach itself to her underside, her ears may pin back, and her eyes may dart around looking for a familiar place to hide.

Don't soothe your timid pup. Act with confidence as though nothing's changed — this reaction will impress your puppy. Up until now, her leash has served in the same way that a child's security blanket would — it created a sense of safety until the moment it disappeared. The goal is to help your puppy have faith in your presence and your direction. Try the following to get your pup to have faith in your direction:

- ✔ Increase visual hand signals.
- ✔ Use a treat cup or a click-and-treat combination (provided the sound of the clicker doesn't startle your puppy).
- ✔ Respond in ways that pique her curiosity, such as playing with a stick or toy or showing mock interest in a scent.

Getting the Emergency "Down" Down Pat

Chapter 14 covers the "Down" direction. But for off-lead safety, you need to take it a step further with the Emergency "Down" direction. The Emergency

"Down" (see Figure 15-1) is a high-fired version of the "Down" direction that'll have your puppy hitting the dirt midpace. It can be a real lifesaver. I used it to stop one of my puppies who broke her "Stay" to greet my husband, who was walking home across a busy street.

In the beginning, your puppy may be a little confused, so be patient and positive throughout your training sessions. Don't start practicing this exercise until your puppy has mastered the "Down" direction (see Chapter 14). To teach your pup the Emergency "Down," follow these steps:

1. **Stand next to your unsuspecting puppy.**

2. **Suddenly direct "Down" in an urgent tone and point toward the ground.**

   Use the type of tone you'd use if a loved one were about to walk off a cliff.

3. **Kneel down quickly and help your puppy into position if she looks confused.**

4. **Act like you're being bombed, too, by kneeling down next to your pup.**

Figure 15-1:
The
Emergency
"Down" can
save your
dog's life
time and
again.

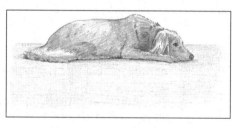

Soon your puppy will catch on. After she does, begin extending your distance from her as you direct "Down" in your most urgent tone.

It's true — the Emergency "Down" really does save lives. Once I was leaving my training classes with my husky, Kyia, when a tennis ball slipped loose and started rolling toward the road. Kyia, the sweet thing, wanted to help and ran innocently to collect it. In a panic, I shouted "Down," and she dropped like a rock. What a good girl!

The Emergency "Down" exercise is very stressful. Limit your practice to one out-of-the-blue Emergency "Down" sequence a day.

Knowing When to Trust Your Pup: FAQs about Off-Lead Training

Before I address frequently asked questions (FAQs) about off-lead training (OLT), let me warn you: It only takes one mistake to lose your puppy. Until she's an off-lead expert, she may get confused. Or she may turn into a little comedian and bound away from you just for fun. So practice all initial training in an enclosed area. Keep the situation safe until she's reliable.

You may be wondering many things about OLT at this point. Here's a list of questions that I'm asked most often:

- **When will I know I can trust my dog off lead?** You should feel it. It's never a smooth road in the beginning; some days you get a quick and happy response; other days feel more like your first lessons together. Stay cool, though — frustration is a sign of weakness, and you can easily lose your dog's respect. You'll gradually notice your dog's hesitation diminish. She'll respond happily and without consideration, and you'll get a fluid feeling that she enjoys being near you and listening to you. Until this point, keep your puppy in an enclosed area or dragging a long line as you practice so that if she starts to act cocky, you can retreat immediately. And don't hesitate to go back to the long-line or on-lead exercises for quick review.

- **I get so frustrated when my puppy ignores me that I sometimes feel like hitting her. Is it ever okay to hit her?** Feeling like hitting is fine. Actually hitting her isn't. If you hit your dog, you erode your relationship and diminish her off-lead trust. If you're really angry, walk away calmly. Remember, a graceful retreat is not a failure.

- **My puppy breaks every time I leave her in a "Sit-Stay" on her retractable leash. What can I do?** Increase your distance slowly. For example, if your puppy gets up every time you walk out 15 feet, practice at 10 feet for a week, then at 11 feet and 12, and so on.

In addition, don't face your puppy as you walk out. Walking backward invites a "Come" response. Instead, walk out confidently, with your back toward your puppy, and pivot at your final destination. Remind her, "Stay."

- **Sometimes my dog crouches and barks at me. How can I make her stop?** Don't look at her. She's trying to turn all your hard work into a game. Ignore her until her antics subside. Work on-lead at short distances if she's being impossible.

Dog-to-dog greetings

If you meet up with an off-lead dog, stay calm. Tensions can get misconstrued, prompting two otherwise peaceful dogs to tussle. Here's what to expect:

✔ **Normal greeting:** When meeting for the first time, it's normal for dogs to posture considerably, which may include raised hackles, tail flagging, jumping, pawing, growling, staring, or mouthing. When two dogs meet in an open space, they'll generally race at an angle to one another and circle, assessing who should be in charge. After the roles are established, the dogs can be expected to get along unless human interference stresses the situation.

✔ **Abnormal greeting:** A dog usually won't make a beeline for another of its own species. This reaction highlights an attack, which may be prompted when a dog is protecting her young or her perceived territory. This reaction is occasionally seen in poorly socialized animals or dogs who have experienced excessive isolation. When this type of confrontation occurs, the only hope may be for the other dog to lie still in complete submission or turn and run away, which may or may not happen. If you have any control over the outcome, retreat from the aggressive dog and the situation immediately. Encourage your puppy to avoid any direct eye contact (and look away yourself), which would be perceived as confrontational.

✔ **Don't the lines get caught around trees and doors?** Yes, they do. Clip all lines to the buckle collar and never leave your puppy unsupervised.

✔ **When I place my puppy on the short lead, I can't get near her. Should I just give it up?** You need to work on your drag lead for another week or so. When you try the short lead again, put it on *with* your drag lead and correct her by stepping on it when she darts away.

You should not do off-lead practice in an unconfined area. Your puppy's a fragile jewel that you must protect.

Part IV
Overcoming Behavioral Problems

The 5th Wave   By Rich Tennant

"Down Skippy, down!! Mike has tried so hard
to socialize this dog so we can have people
over without being embarrassed, but evidently
he needs a few more lessons."

In this part . . .

In this part, you discover how to resolve day-to-day frustrations — from teaching your puppy what to chew and where to potty to basic manners that will make him the most endearing pup on the block. You also get hints on resolving aggression, separation anxiety, and other socially unacceptable behaviors.

Chapter 16

Dealing with Daily Hassles

. . . .

In This Chapter

▶ Finding out how to handle a chewer

▶ Controlling your pup's nipping and mouthing

▶ Dealing with a pup who jumps

▶ Discovering the best way to train your pup

. . . .

No one likes having chewed carpets, scratched doors, or company that hides from a jumping puppy when you open the door. The first step in resolving these kinds of actions is to understand that you and your puppy aren't sharing the same worldview. For example, when your puppy jumps on company, he enjoys every minute of the chaos that follows when you try to keep him down. And while you don't appreciate it, a chewed carpet is usually a sign of boredom, anxiety, or teething. To resolve the behaviors that you don't like, you have to look at them from your puppy's perspective, and then you have to modify *your* behavior to change his reactions.

In this chapter, I cover chewing, jumping, barking, nipping, and the infamous grab-'n'-go. (The serious puppy infractions are covered in Chapter 18.) The process for remedying these behaviors isn't too difficult, but you need a few guidelines to get on the right track. By following the advice in this chapter, you can soon reap the rewards of seeing a change in your puppy's reaction and behavior.

Three Ingredients of a Good Correction

A good correction should never be seen as coming from you. Can you imagine a 400-pound gorilla running, shouting, or pushing you around? Well, that's just how you're perceived by your puppy. When you correct your pup, you don't sense understanding in his expression — instead, you see unadulterated fear. If your goal is to teach your puppy to avoid certain behaviors, pay close attention to how he perceives your reactions, and then modify your response and memorize the following three ingredients of a truly helpful correction:

- ✔ It should be seen as coming from the environment, not from you.
- ✔ It should cause an immediate withdrawal of group interaction.
- ✔ It should consist of a verbal or physical redirection to a more appropriate displacement activity that's rewarded with your reconnection.

If attention (negative or positive) reinforces behavior, you can see why a behavior that causes group withdrawal can be easily extinguished. An environmental reaction may include an unsettling tug of a leash, a spritz from a spray bottle, or a sharp noise, such as a shake of a can of pennies or a loud horn. Specific interruptions are outlined in each section, but always remember to direct your puppy to an alternative behavior that reestablishes your connection.

Stopping the Chewing Frenzy

Chewing is a puppy thing. It's nothing personal. Puppies don't know a stick from a table leg or a doll's head from a chestnut. Just like kids, pups are curious about the world around them, and they love to explore. Kids use their hands to explore, and puppies use their mouths. Additionally, pups between 3½ and 11 months are teething. During this time, your puppy may chew on the furniture or your favorite shoes to alleviate discomfort. To ward off possible destruction, supply and encourage the use of appropriate chew toys. As well, be patient and use some of the tried-and-true techniques described in this section.

Get Bitter Apple — and lots of it

Bitter Apple is nasty-tasting stuff that you can buy at most pet stores. You spray it on things you want to prevent your puppy from chewing. If you notice your puppy chewing on the furniture surrounding his station, spray everything but his bed and bone. Also, if your puppy is chewing household items, such as wires or phone cords, discreetly approach your puppy and spray the object as he's chewing it. You should always provide your puppy with an appropriate chew after discouraging him, so after you spray an object with Bitter Apple, direct him to his bone.

Believe it or not, some puppies like the taste of Bitter Apple. If your pup is a founding member of this club, try some red-pepper juice with a little garlic or Tabasco sauce. Or you can try the new product called Bitter Bitters, which can be purchased only through your veterinarian.

Offer one main toy plus a surplus of surprises

Having too many objects to choose from can confuse your puppy. Pick a bone or toy that satisfies your puppy's penchant for chewing, buy multiples of that item, and spread them around the house for quick access. Here are some other suggestions:

- Keep your supply of play toys in a special place (designating a box or drawer), bringing them out for special interaction times.
- Designate one toy that's only offered during greetings. I use a hollow bone stuffed with peanut butter.

Be aware of prize envy

If you yell at your puppy *after* he's begun to grab an object he shouldn't or after he's finished chewing, you only damage your relationship with him. Yelling afterwards communicates *prize envy* — what's being grabbed is valuable because of the challenge to get it back. If you give the correction too late, your puppy thinks "Wow, what a great prize — everybody wants to take it from me!"

Instead of disciplining after the fact, set up situations so that you can correct your puppy's thought process (see the upcoming section "Correct the thought process," to find out how). Also, you can use treat cups after the puppy has already grabbed something you don't want him to have (see "Use treat cups when your pup's caught in the act," later in this section).

Correct the thought process

Correcting a puppy younger than 12 weeks is tantamount to child abuse. Sure, he may look like he knows better than to chew your grandmother's heirloom hanky, but I've got news for you: He's only terrified. Put the situation in perspective: Imagine a giant monster chasing you down shouting unintelligible epithets. That wouldn't be too pleasant, would it?

Correcting a puppy any age after the fact is ineffective and damaging to your relationship. On the flip side, correcting the thought process — and then shaming the object of interest — puts the negative focus outside your relationship.

Set up a situation with something your puppy's obsessed with — tissues, shoes, a Barbie doll, or whatever else strikes his fancy — and follow these steps:

1. **While your puppy's resting in another room, set the object in the middle of the floor.**

2. **Bring your puppy to the object on his leash.**

3. **The second your puppy notices the object, say "Nope" and tug back on the leash.**

4. **Pick up the object and shout at it — without looking at your puppy (see Figure 16-1).**

Figure 16-1: "Bad Sock!" Shout at the object, not at your puppy.

You read right: Get angry at the object, not at your puppy. You're doing the puppy version of telling a child the stove is hot — the focus isn't on the child's being bad but on the fact that the object is unsafe for her.

Don't even look at your puppy as you mouth off to the naughty thing. Your neighbors may commit you, but your puppy will love you for it.

5. **Walk by the object again.**

Your puppy should avoid it like the plague (see Figure 16-2). If he doesn't, consider his age — he may be too impulsive to absorb this lesson (wait a month and repeat this sequence) or you may be looking at him, or perhaps your timing is off. Say "No" as your puppy approaches the item, and then scold it (not your puppy) sternly!

Figure 16-2: "What sock?" If you scold an object, your puppy then avoids it.

Don't practice this exercise off-lead. If you can't stabilize him, he's likely to dance about and dart away from you, turning this lesson into a game of cat and mouse.

Use this technique to catch your puppy in the thought process. If your puppy already has an object in his mouth, you're too late. Stay very calm at this point and focus on teaching your puppy to share his finds instead of coveting them. You may do so by using a drag lead (see Chapter 5): You can step on the drag lead and calmly open his jaw by squeezing his pressure points (located just behind his upper fangs) to remove the object. Or you can do what I do, which is teach my puppies to share their treasures by shaking a treat cup — for more information, read on.

Use treat cups when your pup's caught in the act

Making a *treat cup* is easy; refer to Chapter 11 for specific instructions. If your puppy hasn't made the connection on what a treat cup is, shake the cup and offer him treats until he associates the sound with getting a treat. Now spread treat cups all over your home. Keep the sound consistent and familiar by using the same kind of cup in every room. Party cups or deli containers work best.

First you need to communicate to your puppy that your approach with the treat cup is a good thing. Therefore, anytime your puppy is chewing on an acceptable object, go over to your pup while shaking the treat cup, say "Give," offer him a treat, and leave. When your puppy's eating a meal, shake the cup, say "Give," offer him a treat, and leave.

After he understands that your approach isn't threatening, the next time your puppy grabs something you don't want him to have, find a treat cup, shake it, and say "Give" as you offer a treat. Praise him when he releases the object and help him find a chew toy. You can say "Where's your bone?" to encourage him.

I can hear some of you already: "Doesn't treating encourage the behavior?" Even though this technique doesn't discourage your puppy's mischief, it does encourage him to share his treasures, which can save you a lot in replacement fees. A delivery system is better than a destructive puppy.

Consider all objects your puppy grabs, good or bad, as treasures, and he'll be much more cooperative. Be mindful to be most engaging when your puppy is playing with his toy. As he matures, he'll be less focused on "things" and most engaged in what brings you mutual satisfaction.

Calmly kiss your puppy-destroyed things goodbye

If your puppy has destroyed something, let it go. Yelling or hitting your puppy only makes him nervous and frightened, which leads to more chewing. Any puppy owner can commiserate, and I know firsthand how angry you feel, but don't take your anger out on your pup. He doesn't know any better.

Your puppy's mouth is equivalent to your hands; if your puppy is nervous or fidgety, he chews. I'm sure if your puppy could surf the Net, scan the soaps, or twiddle his thumbs, he would, but because he can't, chewing has to do.

Controlling Mouthing and Nipping

Mouthing and nipping are two different issues. *Mouthing* is a lesser infraction; it's more of a communication skill to convey need or confusion or to inspire playful interaction. Even though mouthing involves less pressure than a nip and is usually less annoying, it's still not particularly charming. *Nipping*, on the other hand, is a puppy thing; it's interactive and playful. (If you have an older puppy who still nips, though, read Chapter 18's section on aggression.) Nipping puppies are bossy and manipulative and need a firmer regimen.

Mouthing most often communicates a need. However, many times it's used as an attention-getting behavior. If your puppy uses it to communicate a need to go out, respond. If, on the other hand, your puppy mouths you for a pat, ignore it. Pretend he isn't there. If he becomes too annoying, buy Binaca mouth spray and discreetly spritz the body part your puppy is mouthing. Avoid eye contact, comments, or pushing. When you use the mouth spray this way, you're performing a *cause-and-effect correction* rather than using interactive discipline. Interaction involves eye contact and physical manipulation — which are not good, because your pup's getting the attention he wants. Cause-and-effect corrections, on the other hand, result in unpleasant reactions that your puppy will try to avoid.

Follow this cause-and-effect correction with a verbal redirection to a bone or toy, and if you can, take a few minutes to play or take your puppy to potty.

Puppies interpret discipline as confrontational play. Excessive physical corrections result in aggression, so be wise and stay cool.

Nipping is different from mouthing (nipping with sharp little needle teeth can hurt!), and it's another one of those puppy things that you need to refocus. Consider this: When your puppy still hung out with his littermates, he nipped during play and to determine his rank. When you bring your puppy home, this behavior continues.

What your puppy wants to know is who's a puppy and who's not. The answer determines the type of mouthing or nipping he uses: soft or playful. Usually, everyone gets categorized as a puppy. Why? Well, for starters, most people pull their hands away when nipped. To a human, drawing back is self-defense; to a pup, however, it's an invitation to play. Even if you were to correct your young puppy, he wouldn't understand (it's like correcting a 1-year-old baby for pulling your hair). So what should you do? Good question. Your approach depends on your puppy's age. Check out the following sections to find how to correct your pup.

Correcting pups younger than 16 weeks

Young puppies mouth a lot. They mouth when playing, and they also mouth to communicate their needs. If your puppy starts mouthing, ask yourself these questions: Is he hungry or thirsty? Does he need to eliminate? Is he sleepy? Does he need to play? Remember, puppies mouth when they feel needy (just like a baby cries). So, if your puppy won't let up with the mouthing, ask yourself whether he might want something, such as an outing or a drink.

Physical corrections get interpreted as confrontational play, so it's at this point that a puppy's mouthing can escalate to nipping as a defensive reaction to your corrections.

The following advice can help you control mouthing and nipping:

- If your puppy doesn't need anything and he still won't quit, crate or isolate him with a favorite bone. Don't scold your puppy as you isolate him. Calmly place the puppy in his area.

- Whenever your puppy licks you, say "Kisses" and praise him warmly. Encourage licking by slathering your hands with a frozen stick of butter. Yum! With the butter treat, he'll gladly lick your hand instead of mouthing it.

- Withhold your attention when your puppy nips softly. Keep your hand still, because withdrawing your hand is an invitation to play and nip harder.

- If your puppy starts biting down hard, turn quickly, say "Ep, ep!" and glare into his eyes for two seconds. By the mere fact that you don't look at him often, this intense glare will surprise him. Just as quickly, go back to your normal routine. If he knows the direction "Kisses," encourage this to enable a reconnection.

    If he persists, try spritzing yourself with Bitter Apple or putting a leash on your puppy so you can tug the lead sharply to the side when he nips hard. If necessary, place him in a quiet area to cool off.

Correcting pups over 16 weeks

If you have a Peter Pan pup, one who still nips when he's older than 16 weeks, you need to start curbing it now. Although nipping will continue (for a few weeks yet), you need to make clear that it's unacceptable. Following are a few tips to help you:

- **Stop all challenge games.** These games include wrestling, tug of war, chasing your puppy around, and teasing. When you engage in these types of activities, you're sending the wrong message. These games teach puppies to challenge you and to clamp down hard on *any* object — a leash, the laundry, your shirt, or even your skin. For game alternatives, see Chapter 23.

- **Discourage all nipping, whether it's a bite on your arm or a nibble on your finger.** Teeth don't belong on human skin, period.

- **Put the leading applications in Chapters 13 and 14 into action.** It's time for you to start structuring your interaction.

- **Purchase a few weapons to use in defense, such as Binaca mouth spray, Bitter Apple spray, and a blaster or long-distance squirt gun.**

    Never stare at your pup while you spritz or spray him. Doing so turns an unpleasant result into a confrontational interaction.

✓ **Leave a leash on your puppy so you have something to direct him with and so you can avoid physical confrontation.** If your puppy's not wearing a leash, place a short drag lead onto his buckle collar.

✓ **If your puppy begins to mouth, turn to him and use a lead or collar to tug his head from your body, or spritz the region he's nipping with a mouth spray.** Don't glare at your puppy as you correct him — he'll perceive your actions as confrontational play.

✓ **If he continues to nip, ask yourself these questions:** Do I look convincing? Am I tugging or pulling? (Pulling encourages play.) Is my puppy taking me seriously? You may need more training before you earn his respect. Please reference Chapters 13 and 14 for good exercises to start you off.

Handling grabbing and chasing

Puppies, being puppies, are bound to chase and grab at things. If the thing being grabbed is a ball or squeak toy, you don't have a problem. But if it's the children or your clothing, well, that's a problem. Your next goal is to teach the puppy what's acceptable to grab and pull at and what's off-limits.

The bathrobe assault

If your puppy's a clothing grabber, dilute some Bitter Apple spray in a plant mister and carry it with you when you suspect an assault. Don't turn and face your puppy when he jumps after your clothes (he'll interpret your actions as confrontational). Without looking or responding, spray your clothing discreetly while your puppy is instigating this interaction, and continue walking.

If this problem persists, get help now. It can develop into postpuberty aggression. No joke.

The child chaser

Kids running around the yard, apartment, or house are a big temptation. If you were a puppy, you'd be jumping and nipping, too. Because you can't teach kids to stop being kids, you need to help your puppy control his impulses. Follow these steps:

1. **Put your pup on his leash and ask the kids to race around in front of you.**

2. **Anytime your puppy looks tempted to lunge, tug back and say "Shhh."**

3. **Repeat as often as necessary to gain control.**

After you've tamed your puppy inside, repeat the routine outside: first on the leash and then on a long line.

Grounding the Joyous Jumper

Everybody knows a jumper — a knock-you-over-when-you-come-in jumper, a muddy-paws-on-the-couch jumper, and a counter cruiser (the puppy who likes to sniff along countertops). Jumping is a surefire attention-getter for pups. The first step in solving your problem is to understand how it became a problem in the first place. Once again, your puppy's not to blame.

Puppies see us as other puppies, and eye contact is a big method of canine communication. Our eyes are above theirs, so to be gracious and greet us properly, puppies think they must jump. The first time this happens, you give your pup a hug because you think he's so cute. But after about the tenth jump, you realize that his jumping is not so cute. So the puppy usually gets a shove. But what's a shove to a puppy? You guessed it: confrontational play. The puppy jumps higher and harder the next time. So you try a little toe stepping, paw grabbing, and yelling — and, well, all of those reactions receive the same effect. After that hubbub, your puppy thinks jumping is very interactive and very fun.

Puppies who jump need to learn the *four paw rule,* which means that they receive no attention until all four paws are on the floor. That said, everybody in your household needs to respect this rule, too — friends and visitors alike. For your puppy to understand that the four paw rule applies everywhere and with everyone, consistency is a must! Soon you'll realize that your puppy isn't the most difficult one to train!

You're home! You're home!

The best way to remedy jumping when you arrive home is to ignore your pup. Try it for a week, using these suggestions:

- Come home and ignore your puppy until he's given up the jumping vigil.

- Keep a basket of balls or squeaky toys by the door. When you come in, toss one on the ground to refocus your puppy's energy.

- If your puppy's crated, don't let him out immediately; wait until he's calm.

If you have a big puppy or a super-persistent jumper, you have two options: Buy some Binaca mouth spray or a squirt gun and spray a boundary in between your bodies, or put on an overcoat to protect yourself (while you ignore his jumps). Whether it takes 2 minutes or 20, go about your business until your puppy calms down. The best lessons learned are the conclusions your puppy makes on his own: If sitting gets your attention, then sitting he will do!

If you have kids, when the puppy jumps up, tell them to "close up shop," and you do the same. Cross your arms in front of your chest and look to the sky (see Figure 16-3). Don't look down until the coast is clear. Remember that consistency is key. If one family member follows the program but the others encourage jumping, your puppy will jump-test all visitors.

Figure 16-3: Close up shop until your puppy calms down.

Puppies mimic their leaders' energy levels. If you come home to an excited puppy and you, too, get excited, you're sending the message that his excitement is acceptable. Instead, come in calm and wait until he's settled down to greet your puppy.

We have company!

The doorbell rings, and here's what happens: Your puppy runs to the door, paws flying everywhere, jumps all over the arriving guests, and because all eyes are on him, gets even more wound up — until, that is, you drag him to the basement. Then you apologize to your guests, who are no doubt wondering why you don't train your crazy puppy. Bummer.

It's a common scenario. Nobody's in control. Nobody's comfortable, except maybe the puppy. But even that passes if you have to isolate him. Fortunately, there's a better way. Remember the idiom "Good manners start at home"? Well, the same rule applies for puppies.

First, establish a routine regimen and train your company how to act around your puppy — and you thought training your puppy was tough!

✔ Practice doorbell setups.

✔ Do the reverse yo-yo.

✔ Create a greeting station.

✔ Designate a greeting toy.

Flip to Chapter 13 for details on each of these strategies.

If you're sitting down, anchor your puppy until he's calm enough to greet your guests. (Chapter 13 gives details on anchoring.)

Attention, please!

If you can ignore your puppy, the silent treatment is your most effective response to a pup who's begging for attention. If I kept bugging you for a game of Parcheesi and you didn't look up once, I'd go elsewhere for fun. After your puppy stops jumping, encourage him by saying "Get your toy!" and let him pay attention to that.

If your puppy's a real nudger, keep a lead (short or long) attached to his collar. When he jumps, grasp the lead and tug your puppy sideways quickly (this move is called a *fly flick*) as you continue to ignore him (give no eye contact, body language, or verbal corrections).

The fly flick says "How dare you" in the most passive manner; it's not tough or abusive. You just grasp the collar or leash with your thumb and forefinger and flick your puppy off to one side. You may need to perform the fly flick several times before your pup gets the message. When he finally sits down perplexed, give him a great big hug.

Also effective against a nudger is Binaca mouth spray as a boundary between your bodies. Spray your clothing as your puppy is approaching and then refocus his energy to a toy or game.

I wanna see what's on the counter, too!

Counter cruising is a bad habit that's difficult to break. Blatant corrections actually encourage sneaky behavior such as counter cruising behind your back. Even though you think your puppy's grabbing out of spite, he's not.

The reason your puppy grabs when your back is turned or you leave the room is so he can avoid a challenge: Your puppy sees your eyes and mouth (hands equal mouths in the puppy world) interacting with objects on the countertops all day. When he copies you, you bark (shouting is the same as barking to a puppy) and challenge him for whatever the prize is. Do you see the canine message? "Whatever is on the counter must be great, so I better grab it when all backs are turned or I'll have to give it up." Follow these steps to solve this problem with dignity:

1. **Place something tempting on the counter and bring your puppy into the room on leash.**

2. **The instant your puppy looks up to sniff the counter, tug the lead back, say "Nope," and shout at the counter "Bad counter!"**

3. **Continue to work in the kitchen, catching your puppy the moment he so much as looks longingly at the countertop. When you do catch him, repeat Step 2.**

If your puppy's already on the counter, you're too late to correct him. Instead, give him a good fly flick by curling your finger under his collar to tug him back or by tugging his leash sideways. Yelling or shoving your puppy after he's already on the counter or in possession of something will only reinforce his behavior. After all, a touch is attention.

If mealtimes are too distracting for your puppy, station him while you cook (see Chapter 13 for advice on stationing).

That couch sure does look comfy

Most people invite puppies on the furniture only to regret it later. If you have a puppy and you don't want him on your furniture permanently, do yourself a favor and discourage the behavior from the start.

Level training for young pups

If you have a delinquent furniture lover, the habit's not too difficult to break as long as you're consistent. Follow these steps to level train your young pup:

1. **Place your puppy on a leash and walk up to your couch or bed.**

2. **The second he prepares for the jump, tug back and say "Nope!"**

3. **Encourage him to sit and, when he does, pet him.**

4. **Walk back and forth until he sits automatically.**

After your puppy has these steps down, try the same setup with a family member on the couch or bed:

1. **Lead your puppy to the couch or bed and sit down yourself.**

2. **If he goes to jump, tug sideways and ignore him until he sits quietly.**

3. **Reward his cooperation with a chew toy.**

Young puppies should be level trained because their seeing you above them, whether on a couch or bed, communicates your authority passively. As your puppy matures, you can permission train him as detailed later in this section.

Be fair — set up a play station nearby to help your puppy feel welcome and directed when you're relaxing on the furniture. (See Chapter 13 for tips on setting up play stations.)

Permission training for older puppies

To tell you the truth, I enjoy cuddling with my dogs on the couch and sometimes even on the bed — especially when I'm sick. However, each of my dogs was taught to come up only when given permission. Sound confusing? It really isn't. Your puppy can learn anything if your rules are consistent.

Wait until your puppy is at least 6 months old to introduce the concept of "permission." Until this point, you should level train to ensure that he respects your authority and doesn't see you as a puppy.

Follow these steps to teach your puppy to join you on the furniture when he's invited:

1. **No furniture for one week.**

   This is an important step if you want to earn your puppy's respect and focus. For this step, follow the steps outlined in the level training section.

2. **Bring your puppy to the furniture and ask him to "Sit" and "Wait."**

   Sitting and looking to you is how your puppy should learn to ask permission to join you (see Figure 16-4).

3. **Next, tap the cushion and instruct "Up."**

   He'll freeze and look confused.

4. **Guide him up gently, and pet him lovingly.**

5. **After 5 to 10 minutes, lead him off the couch and say "Off."**

Figure 16-4:
Your puppy
should ask
permission
to join you
by sitting
and looking
to you.

Invite him up only once or twice each day. The rest of the time, direct him to his station by saying "Go to your mat."

If your puppy gets hyper on the furniture, he's too young to contain the excitement of being on your level. Wait a couple months before reintroducing permission training.

Remedying Leash Resistance

Whether your dog is pulling or just stopping dead in his tracks, the result is a no-win situation for everyone involved: Walking your dog becomes a downer and his social skills will be sharply limited.

The lunge and drag

A dog who drags you about at the end of the leash is a bear to control. This situation is no fun, it's rather unsightly, and you get all those comments from passersby like "Who's walking who here?" Permitting such a display communicates a message that transcends the walk itself. The dog perceives himself as in charge of the walk, and it's a worldview that may extend to the rest of his day.

Fortunately, if you're caught in this cycle, it's fairly easy to break. The first order of business is choosing a proper teaching collar. My top picks are in Chapter 5. Next, set aside times to reteach your puppy his leash manners. Start in a low distraction environment and gradually progress into more social situations. Follow these steps:

1. **Hold a 6-foot leash in your hand or tie it around your waist.**

2. **Walk in a straight line (see Figure 16-5a). If your puppy races out, call his name and quickly turn about and walk in the opposite direction (see Figure 16-5b).**

   In the likelihood that he doesn't follow, he'll get a quick unpleasant tug, reminding him to pay more attention the next time!

3. **Repeat these turnabouts until your dog is predictably focusing on you.**

4. **Now break out into a circle, holding the leash behind your bottom to push the leash back with the trunk of your body if your puppy starts his pulling.**

Figure 16-5:
Walk forward, turning as your puppy pulls, and then praise him as he catches up.

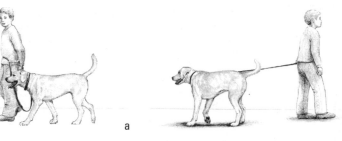

a   b

Mule wannabes

If your puppy plops down on the sidewalk and refuses to walk with you (don't you love walking a mule?), don't do the following two things:

- ✔ Drag him along (for obvious reasons)
- ✔ Turn to face him, run back, or lift him up

Acknowledging your puppy's resistance with coddling will create a dog who is plagued by learned helplessness. Coddling won't teach him how to follow along. You have a few options to stop your pup's resistance. Follow these guidelines:

- ✔ Let your puppy drag his leash about inside. Review the leash training techniques in Chapter 13, practicing them again if necessary.
- ✔ Lure him along with a favorite treat or toy. Gradually extend the distance between each reinforcement.

✔ Condition your puppy to the sound of a treat cup and/or a clicker. Use these combinations to encourage and reinforce your puppy forward.

✔ If he resists you, instead of turning to urge him forward, simply kneel in front of him (still facing forward) and tap the ground with your finger while you shake the treat cup or clap your hands to urge him along.

Refocusing a Runner

If your puppy is constantly running away from you, please ask yourself what he's running from. He may be running away from you personally, or he may be running after another creature, which is probably due to his instinctive nature.

If he's a breed that instinctively likes to chase other creatures, it's your responsibility to keep him safe from any harm that may come from getting caught up in his genetically driven impulse. This warrants your surveillance either on a leash or long line or in an enclosed area.

If your dog is clearly running away from you, your reaction to his behavior may be making matters worse. Yelling at him either when he's running or after you're reunited won't warm him to your calling. In fact, your stringency may be rather off-putting. Being with your puppy is like playing on a team: You're his captain. Wouldn't you want to have a captain who was positive and upbeat even when you made a mistake? Give your puppy this same respect.

Please review the skills in Chapter 14, which outlines the "Come" instruction as the human phrase equivalent to the huddle.

Methinks I Need Some Help!

Finding the right help for training, if you need it, is essential. Training is a joint effort for you and your puppy. My clients would be the first to tell you that training is a blend of the right actions — from how you hold the leash and the tone of your voice to the way you stand — that helps your puppy learn what you're trying to teach.

Free advice never pays. If you try a little of this and a little of that, guess who's going to suffer? That's right — your puppy. You'll make the poor guy crazy.

Professional trainers for your pup

A couple associations certify and list trainers in different parts of the country. The APDT (Association of Pet Dog Trainers) certifies and welcomes professional dog trainers and educators who are committed to their profession and who seek like-minded people to meet and exchange ideas with; it holds yearly conferences to promote ideas, educate, and reinforce the ideals of the dog-training profession. The APDT promotes dog-friendly training techniques and serves to educate the public, as well the veterinary professionals, about the benefits of a positive training approach. Here's how to contact the group:

The Association of Pet Dog Trainers
150 Executive Center Drive, Box 35
Greenville, SC 29615
Phone 800-738-3647
E-mail information@apdt.com
Web site www.apdt.com

The IACP (International Association of Canine Professionals) welcomes all professionals associated with dogs, including trainers, groomers, kennel owners, pet sitters, merchants, and veterinarians. They list members, and although they mindfully attest to high standards, a membership fee can buy association. It's still up to you to determine whether an individual is up to your standards. Of course, membership in a respectable association is a good sign. You can reach the IACP here:

International Association of Canine Professionals
P.O. Box 560156
Montverde, FL 34756-0156
Phone 877-843-4227 or 407-469-2008
E-mail iacp@mindspring.com
Web site www.dogpro.org

Finding the right puppy trainer

Finding a good trainer — one who is well-rounded in his or her knowledge of puppy behavior — can be a real lifesaver. Many of my clients call at their wits' end, only to discover a wonderful puppy who emerges after they (the people) modify their own behavior.

In my experience, it's usually the owner who's confused. So I train the owner, and the puppy behaves. Training is often just as simple as that. If you need help training your pup, scout out professionals in your area to get some good leads and call today. You and your puppy will be glad you did. The following sections look at a few of the training options that are available to you.

A personal trainer

I'm a personal puppy trainer. However, I train more than puppies — I train people, too. When looking for a personal trainer, you're looking for someone to train you (as well as your puppy).

Following are some of *my* training ethics, which I recommend you look for in any personal trainer:

- ✔ Put yourself in your client's shoes.

- ✔ Know that the client is trying to do the right thing.

- ✔ Understand the puppy's personality and listen to what the puppy is trying to communicate with his behavior.

- ✔ Know when you can't help. Be honest with your client.

- ✔ Help your client understand why the puppy is behaving inappropriately. Help the client think for her puppy.

- ✔ Teach the client to think like a puppy, enabling mutual communication. (Turn to Chapter 6 for info on speaking Doglish.)

- ✔ Help the client structure her home.

- ✔ Teach the client patience, tolerance, understanding, and sympathy. After all, she obviously loves her puppy.

Not all trainers are in this profession because they love puppies first and foremost. Some of them are in it for the money — I suggest you beware of those types. Other trainers are wonderful with puppies but don't excel in human communication skills. Look for someone who can train you as well as your puppy.

A group trainer

Group training classes can be a real blast. They can also be a puppy owner's worst nightmare. So what makes the difference? No, it isn't your puppy. No matter how badly behaved your pup is around other puppies, the instructor is the one who makes or breaks the class. When exploring different classes, talk to the instructor and get a feel for his or her style of training.

Here are some questions you can ask:

- ✔ **How many puppies are in the class? Are the classes divided by age or class levels?** The class size should be limited (I limit mine to six) and must be divided by age and experience. I offer Puppy Kindergarten classes for puppies who are less than 6 months old, Grade School for inexperienced pupils, and High School and College for advanced students.

- ✔ **Do you have a favorite breed of puppy, or do you have experience with a wide variety of breeds?** The answer can indicate a strong bias on the part of the instructor. Make sure your instructor isn't breed-biased. Your puppy should be seen as a unique and special personality, not a stereotype. Your instructor should be versed in breed-specific tendencies, however, and help you understand your puppy's individual character.

- ✔ **What do you teach in class?** Basic commands are necessary: Heel, Sit-Stay, Come, and Down. Find out whether the instructor spends time explaining how to integrate these directions in your life.

Which is better — private or group training?

People often ask me what the best way to train is: group or private lessons. Honestly, it depends on your individual situation, but often the best approach is to combine the two. Private lessons give you one-on-one attention and a complete focus on your frustrations and goals. A well-run class, however, exposes your puppy to a social atmosphere while at the same time organizing lessons that can be repeated at home.

- ✔ **Are the classes inside or outside?** Having access to both environments is best.

- ✔ **Are behavior problems discussed?** Bad behavior is often what encourages many people to train their puppies. The instructor should be as comfortable talking about problem behavior as he or she is with command training.

- ✔ **Do you have a make-up policy?** If not, can you speak to the instructor to find out what you've missed?

- ✔ **Is family participation encouraged?** Can the kids come? The instructor should help you understand how your puppy relates to your entire family and should encourage everyone to participate in the training.

Using books and videos

Are you a do-it-yourself type of person? I'm all for it as long as you follow the right advice. Obviously, because you're reading this book, you have some faith in my methods. However, not everyone suggests a positive approach to training, so be selective when choosing your reading material, and call for some help if matters don't improve. You train your puppy only once, so do it right.

Chapter 17

When Anxiety Strikes

*W*atching your household and yard get reconfigured by the paws of your puppy is never fun. But, before you set out to admonish her, you need to spend some time discovering the reasons prompting her reactions. For example, a puppy who shreds pillows when you leave, only to quake and look guilty when you return, doesn't have supernatural human powers — in other words, she doesn't know any better. But, if you dig deeper, you'll find that she's likely experiencing separation anxiety, which is something that will only increase if you have an exaggerated reaction.

So, in this chapter I show you the proper reactions you should have toward your puppy's behaviors. I give you an up-close and personal look at many of the behaviors that stem from anxiety — from excessive barking to digging and timidity. Just remember that calming your puppy's stress involves more than a one-step solution. After you've played psychiatrist and have successfully discovered why your puppy is having these reactions, you then have to modify both the environment and yourself in order to completely alleviate your puppy's stress. Read on to figure out how.

Quieting That Bark-Bark-Barker

A barking dog is a real headache. How you handle your puppy and her motivation depends on what's prompting her to bark in the first place. In the meantime, you need to watch your reaction.

The cardinal sin when rehabilitating your barker is to yell. When you yell, your puppy thinks you're barking too, which leads to — you guessed it — more barking. With all that barking, you have a full-blown barkalong. To solve your problem, stay cool and follow the advice in this section.

A few woofs from your pooch to announce new arrivals at the front door are appreciated, right? But, I'm guessing you agree that you get annoyed when the barking never stops. For tips on handling a puppy who barks incessantly at the door, flip to Chapter 13.

Barking at e-v-e-r-y-thing

Does your puppy bark at everything she sees and hears? If so, it's likely that nothing goes unnoticed at your home — bikers, the neighborhood kids, or little lively creatures passing through your yard. For some people, after a while, the puppy's barking can seem as much a part of their daily routine as the wind passing through the trees. For those who don't fall into that category, however, perpetual barking is a big pain.

Barking has an added lure for your puppy: Whenever she barks at something, whether from the window or the yard, that thing goes away. Sure, you and I both know that the mail carrier's going to keep moving, but don't tell your pup that. She thinks her strength and prowess drove the mail carrier away — talk about an ego boost.

To quiet your incessant barker, try these strategies:

- **Start training immediately.** Puppies who bark at everything perceive themselves (not you) as the leader, and one of the leader's duties is to guard her territory and her group from intruders. Your pup needs to understand that you're the boss. To teach your pup who's boss, follow the age-appropriate lessons covered in Chapter 14.

- **Avoid leaving your puppy alone outdoors for long stretches of time.** Unsupervised confinement often breeds boredom and territorial behavior. Put those two together, and you're likely to end up with a barkaholic.

- **Block off areas that your puppy uses as lookout posts, such as a living room couch or windowsill.** If she's a night guard, crate her or secure her on a lead in your room at night, giving her 3 feet of freedom — just enough to lie comfortably on her bed.

Remember that screaming at your puppy is translated into barking. When you yell, your puppy feels supported, and her role as leader (she barked first) is reinforced. Anytime you see (or hear) your puppy start to perk up, say "Shhht" (the extra "t" is critical for emphasis) and use a treat cup to call her back to your side. If she ignores you, place her on a drag leash so you can quickly gain control (see Chapter 5 for tips on using a drag leash). Use spray misters or penny cans to reinforce your verbal "Shhht!"

Many collars are on the market to help discourage the barking habit. Even though I've never tried the electrical stimulation collars (my dog would freak out), I have used the citronella collars with relative success. These types of collars work because the dog's barking immediately triggers a quick spritz of citronella, which is startling and smelly to your pooch. The chief complaints I get, though, are that they run out of juice, that the puppy learns to be quiet when the collar is on (smart puppy!), and that it's triggered by erroneous sounds and motions. In the end, I think this problem is best addressed by modifying both the environment and your temperament.

Barking in the car

Being locked in a car with a barking dog is my version of purgatory. The car creates an effect similar to the territorial situation I describe in Chapter 18. Your puppy barks, and the passing object disappears — only faster in the case of a moving car.

Yelling at your puppy isn't the thing to do, and pleading doesn't win you any brownie points either. This problem tends to disappear slowly as you progress through training. However, you can do the following things in the meantime to discourage this behavior:

- Enforce stillness while you drive by stationing your puppy in the car with a Seat Belt Safety Lead (SBSL), which is described in Chapter 5.

- Make your puppy pause before you let her enter or exit the car. Instruct "Wait" and give her permission to enter with "Okay." After all, the car is yours, not hers.

- When possible, ask someone else to drive so that you can sit next to your puppy and handle her while you ride.

- Play classical music and stay cool. Your puppy perceives any frustration on your part as backup, which increases her ferocity.

- Use a *head collar* (see Chapter 5). These restraints are quite calming and can be secured to a leash if your puppy is riding in the back seat.

- Ignore the barking if your car's moving — driving is a job in itself.

- If you're stationary when your puppy is barking, discreetly spray her (without turning and glaring — yes, this is quite a feat) or shake a penny can as you say "Shhht."

- If your puppy barks at gas station or tollbooth attendants, ask them to toss a treat into the car window from afar. Hopefully, this special treatment will help your puppy make a more positive association.

If you think your puppy is bordering on territorial aggression, refer to Chapter 18 and call for professional help.

Barking for attention or protest

All puppies go through a phase when they can't bear to be left alone. If you soothe a protest or attention barker, you end up with a real spoiled puppy. However, if you ignore the situation, your partner may threaten to leave you. Is there a happy medium? Well, not really, but I'll give it my best shot. Follow these guidelines:

- ✔ Ignore the barking if you can, and never yell because your puppy translates this as, you guessed it, more barking. Wax earplugs help.

- ✔ Avoid grandiose departures and arrivals because they're too exciting for your pup. (Chapter 13 gives tips for handling departures and arrivals.)

- ✔ Dogs like to be with you. Avoid problems in your home by keeping her nearby, leading or stationing her as described in Chapter 13.

- ✔ Place peanut butter in a hollow bone and give it to your puppy as you leave.

- ✔ Discreetly spray your pup from behind or toss a penny can toward (not at) her when she starts up. The goal is to have her think the reaction came from the environment, not you, and that stopping brings your immediate attention.

- ✔ Return to your puppy only after she's calmed down. If you must interfere with her barking tantrum, go to her quietly without eye contact or comments, place her on a leash, and either seclude her or lead her around for half an hour.

Getting Control of the Digging

Digging is often a puppy's favorite pastime — especially for puppies in the Terrier, Sporting, and Nordic Groups. Digging is a great way to alleviate boredom, is a reaction to stress (a move, a new baby, repair people in the home — see Chapter 9), and is a cry for company, especially with the 8- to 11-month crowd.

All puppies go through a phase when they can't stand being alone. They fuss, and fussy pups dig. Unfortunately, you can't teach your puppy not to dig. Instead, you must give her a digging place that's all her own. Here are some suggestions:

- ✔ Pick one area where your puppy can dig to her heart's content, whether that spot is around your house or in a park (if you live in an apartment or a condo). You can also buy your pup a sandbox to give her digging satisfaction a few times a week.

✔ Bring toys and treats to hide when you begin to dig. And don't forget the garden gloves.

✔ Go to your puppy's digging area with her each day, instructing "Go dig!"

✔ Have a dig-fest. Dig with your puppy and cheer her on.

✔ If you catch your puppy digging somewhere she shouldn't be, correct her with "No!" and then tell her (while escorting her to the right spot, if necessary), "Go dig!"

Spraying your puppy with a hose or setting mousetraps is cruel, and I don't encourage those correction techniques. A more-humane method that works is to place the puppy's own stool (provided she doesn't like it) in the hole with a dose of red-pepper flakes before covering it up.

Are you a gardener? Well, if you are and you let your puppy watch you garden, guess what? That's right — monkey see, monkey do. I suggest that you place your puppy indoors when you garden. It's just too tempting for her after seeing you dig in one area all day. Remember, only dig together at your puppy's designated digging spot.

Most puppies dig if you leave them outside while you're home. They love to dig while you're watching — it's a surefire way to get attention. Try to structure the indoor environment so that your puppy can be in the house when you're around.

How Embarrassing! Discouraging Mounting

Some puppies mount kids (and even adults) when they get too excited, feel a hormonal surge, or feel out of control. Don't be too embarrassed, though. Mounting is more a sign of misdirected impulse or dominance than sexual preference. Knowing this fact makes it no more acceptable, however. Mounting dogs are bossy dogs who get overstimulated in exciting situations. To rehabilitate yours, do the following:

1. **Leave a 4-foot lead on your puppy inside or out.**

2. **When the mounting starts, calmly grasp the short lead and tug down quickly and firmly.**

   Don't face off to a mounting puppy: She'll perceive this type of reaction as challenging or playful. Your attention will guarantee a repeat performance. For these same reasons, don't make eye contact or push her away.

3. **After your puppy is grounded, stand very tall, glare at her from above to clarify your height, and say "Shame on you!" in your most indignant tone.**

4. **Isolate or station your puppy for 15 minutes with no attention.**

If your puppy reacts aggressively at any point during these steps, terminate the corrections and seek professional help. Your puppy may react intensely because she perceives the situation as a power struggle.

In addition to these steps, devote more time to socializing your puppy away from your home (unfamiliar environments subdue even the most cocky puppies) and increase your dedication to training lessons. Puppies are a lot like kids — they need the structure of lessons to instill civility.

Those who say mounting is a male thing, don't know the half of it. Though there is a specific developmental window (4 to 9 months) when hormonal shifts may influence a boy dog's sexual drive, mounting is primarily used to displace tension or test rank. Don't go off the deep end if your female dog is scaling your pillows or your neighbor's Chihuahua.

Getting Through Separation Anxiety

Puppies hate separation. If they had their way, they'd follow you to the ends of the Earth. But, alas, they can't. Puppies suffering from separation anxiety may chew destructively, soil the house, bark excessively, or act out other destructive behaviors. However, they don't do these things out of spite — puppies just can't think that way. What you're seeing is instead anxiety, canine style.

A puppy who exhibits signs of separation anxiety falls into one of two categories:

- **Passive Puppies:** This puppy is sweet, but undirected and needy. No matter the amount of affection you offer her, it never seems to be enough. When you give her a direction or scold her she acts as though she's been shot.

    Her constant interaction speaks volumes: She loves you dearly, but she assumes that you're even more belligerent than she is and that you need constant direction. Because she thinks you need direction, she continually interacts and checks in with you. However, her constant vigil is brought to an immediate stop when you leave her alone. That's when the anxiety ensues!

- **Top Dogs:** This confident and bossy puppy likes to take charge. Headstrong and willful, she's unimpressed with you, until that is, you leave. In her mind, you have left without permission and it's her duty and responsibility to go along and serve as your protector. Believe it or not, when she's isolated, your puppy gets anxious for your safety and whereabouts!

Separation anxiety demands a multiapproach solution that starts with training. Training gives the Passive Pup a sense of identity and the reassurance that a competent leader is on the job. On the other hand, training places a Top Dog in a subordinate, carefree pack position. If you need help training, get it. In the meantime, follow these ground rules:

- ✔ Never correct your puppy after the fact. Never. Corrections aren't connected to the destruction; they're connected to your arrival, which makes your puppy more anxious the next time you leave.

- ✔ Avoid theatrical hellos and goodbyes. Lavishing your puppy with kisses, biscuits, and drawn-out declarations of devotion don't reassure her. Instead, they only stress her out.

- ✔ Leave a radio playing classical music to cover unfamiliar sounds.

- ✔ Place your puppy in a dimly lit area to encourage sleep.

- ✔ Leave a favorite chew toy. Rub it between your palms so that it smells like you.

If you're leaving for more than six hours, try to find someone to walk your puppy. If necessary, proof the house from destruction or buy an indoor pen (see Chapter 5). Indoor pens, which fold nicely for storage when you're home, can be expanded before you leave to give your puppy space when you're gone for extended periods. Puppies get cramped when left in small kennels for longer than six hours and can develop *Hyper Isolation Anxiety*. This type of anxiety results in a maniacal ritual once you return. In short, their isolation from you makes the pup anxious, which is displaced through hyperactivity.

When you're home, temporarily decrease the attention you give your puppy by 50 percent for two weeks while practicing the other exercises in this section. Don't give in to "pet me" solicitations. Even though petting her when she asks may relieve your feelings of guilt, it just makes being alone all day even more difficult for her. Going from lots of attention to no attention is too sharp a contrast for a pup. When she's alone, your puppy longs for companionship. Because watching the soaps or chewing fingernails isn't an option for her, she instead may settle for devouring your couch.

If possible, buy a kitten for your pup. Kittens are super companions, and they're great company for puppies if raised with them. Getting another dog is also an option, but I recommend that you wait until you've resolved the separation anxiety with this pup before you add another one to the mix.

Also try setting up practice departures by following these steps:

1. **Station your puppy in a familiar spot.**

2. **Instruct "Wait" and leave the room for 15 seconds.**

3. **Return and ignore her until she's calm and then praise her lovingly.**

4. **Repeat these steps ten times or until your puppy stays calm.**

Leaving your puppy at home alone

To be a good neighbor, you need to keep your puppy quiet when you're away from home. No puppy enjoys being left alone — she's sociable by nature. So, don't be surprised if she thinks of some activities to pass those lonely hours — digging, chewing destructively, or barking.

You have a lot of options when you leave your puppy alone. She can stay inside or outside. You can confine her in a room or let her roam around. You can tie her up or fence her in. What's best? Put yourself in your puppy's paws. Outside is okay — she'll have fresh air and sunshine. But being confined outdoors can be stressful because of all the activity that the puppy can't get to. Most puppies would rather remain inside with a cozy blanket and bone to chew.

Preparing for your departure has lasting benefits. Before you leave, do the following:

✔ Exercise your puppy for ten minutes.

✔ Follow playtime with a five- to ten-minute training session.

✔ Leave a couple of chew toys and scent them by rubbing them in your palms.

✔ If you leave your puppy indoors, leave her in a dimly lit, confined space with an old shirt or blanket and a radio playing soothing tunes.

✔ If you leave your puppy outdoors, provide her with access to a shaded area and plenty of fresh water.

Continue these short separations until she shows no anxiety. Then double the separation time and repeat the procedure. Continue doubling the departure time until you're able to leave the room for 30 minutes.

After your puppy's comfortable being alone for 30 minutes, go back to short separations, but this time leave the house. Gradually work your way up to being outside for 30 minutes. Start over once more, but this time get into and start your car. With patience, you'll be able to build your puppy's confidence and leave her for longer and longer periods of time.

Your veterinarian can prescribe your pup an approved drug to help alleviate her separation anxiety. These drugs, however, shouldn't be used without behavioral intervention, either from your veterinarian or from someone your vet endorsed. (If you seek help, make sure you avoid trainers who encourage discipline.)

If your puppy's prone to destruction when you leave, make her a party bag: Put a selection of treats, toys, and chewies in a brown paper lunch bag, crumple it closed, and place it in the middle of the floor just as you walk out the door. Even though it won't resolve her anxiety, the party bag will give her something to focus on, since most of the tension happens in the first five minutes after your departure.

Dealing with a Stimulated Tinkler

Do you have a tinkler? The most frequent question I've been asked about tinklers is "Do they grow out of it?" Well, yes and no. Yes, if you handle yourself properly, and no if you don't. Tinkling isn't a conscious thing — puppies do it because they're overexcited or anxious. And, discipline only makes the problem worse.

When you come home, ignore your pup until she's completely calm (see Figure 17-1a). Next, shake a treat cup to divert her mind (Figure 17-1b). Kneel down to pet her rather than leaning over.

If your puppy is timid around certain people, have everyone (including yourself) ignore her. When you soothe her, it only reinforces the fear. When your puppy approaches the person she's timid around, encourage the person to keep her back facing the puppy (no direct eye contact whatsoever) while you offer her treats, using a treat cup. When she's calm, have guests kneel and pet her chest. As her confidence improves, ask the company to offer her treats from her cup.

If your puppy piddles during greetings or play sessions, ignore her or stop the play until she has better bladder control.

Figure 17-1: Ignore your puppy when you come in; shake a treat cup to divert her focus.

a

b

Giving a Timid Pup Some Confidence

Timid puppies look so pitiful. Like shy kids, you want to soothe them. But, puppies aren't kids — they think your soothing is a sign of your fear, which means you're both afraid. That's a big problem.

To help your puppy, you must act confident when she's afraid. You're the leader. Stand up straight. Relax your shoulders. Breathe deep. Smile. Whether the fear-producing item is a bag blowing in the wind, a sharp noise (like thunder), or an unfamiliar face, act calm, face the feared object, and ignore your puppy until she starts to act more like you.

If your puppy shows aggression when she's fearful, call a professional and avoid knowingly putting her in threatening situations.

Chapter 18

Curbing Socially Unacceptable Behaviors

In This Chapter

▶ Handling an aggressive dog

▶ Resolving gulping, stool swallowing, and marking

*W*hat's socially unacceptable canine behavior? Aggression for one. Even though aggression is a normal form of canine communication that's similar to our anger, it's not cool. Other socially unacceptable behaviors include eating stool, marking, and ingesting socks. These behaviors are intense issues that require a greater commitment to modify and resolve. These transgressions have a common theme: Puppies do these things when they're frustrated, anxious, or vying for attention. This chapter identifies these problems and tells you how to resolve them.

Aggression

The word *aggression* strikes fear into the heart of dog owners. Yes, the occasional growl is a frightening sight but not as uncommon as most people think. Like humans, dogs get frustrated and defensive from time to time.

Remember, puppies aren't members of the human species, which means they're unable to articulate angry feelings through words. Puppies are canines, and canines communicate through vocal tones, eye contact, and body language. What humans communicate in words, some dogs communicate through aggression. How you cope and redirect this behavior determines how your puppy copes with these feelings as he grows into doghood.

Aggression is a serious topic. If you're having a problem, get help. Seek a well-known and respected animal behaviorist or trainer in your area. Your veterinarian may be able to help you find one. My recommendations are just that, recommendations. Don't follow them if you're unsure. Aggression, if approached incorrectly or with caution or fear, can result in a serious bite.

If your puppy has bitten, no one can guarantee you that he won't do it again. Your effort to remedy the problem can only help, however, and remedying the problem is your only option other than euthanasia. Passing an aggressive puppy onto another home or into a shelter is irresponsible. You'd ultimately be responsible if he bit someone or maimed a child. So get help if you need it.

Determining how serious the problem is

To determine how serious the aggressive behavior is, you need to consider these factors:

- **Breed:** Is your puppy a spatial or protective breed (for example, a Terrier, Nordic, or Guarding dog)? These breeds have a greater propensity toward aggression. Seeing a 17-week-old Golden Retriever, known for its passive nature, growling over his dish is more alarming than seeing a protective dog growl over his possessions. Neither should growl, but a growling Golden indicates that you may have a deeper problem than just a breed-inherent trait. Know your breed, understand its natural inclinations, and work through them at the earliest age possible.

  Research your breed. Understand your puppy's personality. An ounce of foresight can help you prevent problems before they arise.

- **Age:** A puppy under 20 weeks shouldn't show any sign of serious aggression. An occasional play growl is common, but if you witness any hard stares and belly growling, you may have a serious problem on your hands. Seek out a professional and call the breeder immediately, if applicable. Beyond 20 weeks, aggression usually coincides with the release of adult hormones. If this is the case, try not to be too alarmed. The information here can help you understand the problem.

- **Temperament:** Aggression is most commonly seen in puppies who are headstrong and bold. These pups determine early whether you're giving direction or taking it. If you're not considered "leadership worthy," your puppy takes charge. As he grows, he becomes more mindful of sounds and stimulation and may often show aggression in order to keep "his" group under tight surveillance. Of course, passive puppies can show a similar type of aggression. If you pamper a passive, fearful pup, he too will assume the leadership role (by default) and be cautious with any slight changes in his environment.

- **Early play patterns:** If you bring your puppy up on a play diet of rough wrestling and tug of war, he can become aggressive during adolescence. These challenge games set the stage for larger confrontations, which the puppy may not back off from just because you issue the word "No."

✔ **Corrective techniques:** If a young puppy is subjected to heavy-handed corrections early in his life, he learns self-control through fear, not through understanding. For example, if you slap your puppy for grabbing a sock, he may grab the sock less when he's with you, but he'll be more protective of the sock after it's obtained (known as *prize envy*). Read the upcoming section "Preventing various forms of aggression" and the problem-solving techniques in Chapter 16 to avoid these pitfalls.

If you have a puppy who shows aggression, keep him off your bed. This is a big deal because an aggressive dog thinks it's his duty to protect you or keep you in line. The first step in resolving this issue is to take over the high sleeping grounds. If you can't keep him off your bed, station him by attaching him to your dresser (see Chapter 13 for stationing tips).

Preventing various forms of aggression

Dogs display several different types of aggression. Understanding what may be developing enables you to react appropriately. This section identifies the various types of aggression and gives prevention advice.

If you meet up with an aggressive dog, don't run away. (Think about it: Have you ever seen a dog attack a post or a tree?) If you must approach the dog, move in sideways. Approaching from the front equals a challenge. You can extend a stick to distract the dog from your body.

The following descriptions and suggestions don't take the place of professional attention.

Dominant aggression

Do you have a dominant pup under your roof who steals clothing for fun, barks for attention, leans against you in new environments or around strangers, or successfully solicits attention whenever the mood strikes? Constant attention and dedication to his every need puts you at servant status. When you assert yourself, he has no other choice than to remind you to get back in line. To regain control, follow these tips for starters:

✔ Use the "Excuse Me" command when your puppy gets in your way. Using this command is the most passive way to communicate your leadership. (Chapter 14 covers "Excuse Me" and other training commands.)

✔ Ignore all his attempts to get your attention. Some of these attention-getting behaviors include barking, pawing, head butting, and whining.

✔ Practice two to five lessons each day (from five to ten minutes) and during those lessons, use each direction he knows. If he's growling when you ask him to lie down, skip that direction until you get professional help.

✔ If your puppy will obey the "Down" direction, repeat it throughout the day, positioning him rather than repeating yourself.

✔ Avoid stare downs unless you initiate them, in which case make sure your dog breaks eye contact first. Your puppy should watch you for direction, and you should be giving it.

✔ Regulate his feeding to twice a day. Don't free feed at this point.

✔ Once a day, enforce a 30-minute quiet time by stationing or anchoring (refer to Chapter 13).

If your puppy growls during any of these efforts, such as getting him to move out of your way, don't push it. Stop everything until you get professional help. Your problem is serious.

Spatial aggression (object guarding)

A puppy who shows aggression while eating, sleeping, grooming, or being medicated by a family member, stranger, or dog professional (veterinarian or groomer) is showing *spatial aggression*. Spatial aggression is usually tied in with dominant, territorial, or psychotic aggression.

If you see this type of behavior from your puppy, don't freak out, hit him, or scream. These reactions only reinforce his defensive notion that you've come to steal his prize or assert yourself.

To help your pup accept you as less threatening, follow these steps, which use the food dish as an example:

1. **Don't make a power struggle out of the feeding ritual.**

2. **Shake a treat cup or snap a clicker, always following the sound with a food reward (Chapter 11 goes over using these training aids).**

   Continue until your puppy connects the sound with a reward.

3. **Approach your puppy once a day with the treat cup or clicker and treat him while he's eating a meal.**

   If he growls as you approach him during a meal, you've entered his Red Zone (refer to Chapter 7). Stop where you are, and toss him a few treats before you leave. If this continues, seek professional advice immediately: Don't let your puppy become another dog-bite statistic.

4. **Repeat Step 3 until you can stand over him and drop treats into his bowl.**

5. **At this point, approach his bowl while speaking happy praises but without shaking the cup or clicking. When you get to his side, make the sound, toss a treat into the bowl, and leave.**

6. **Try kneeling down as you shake the cup or click and toss a treat into his bowl.**

7. **After your pup is comfortable with your kneeling and tossing a treat into his bowl, try placing the treat into his bowl with your hand.**

8. **After you offer your puppy a handful of treats, try stirring your pup's kibble with your hand.**

   If you're successful, continue stirring the kibble once every other day for a week.

9. **After offering a handful of treats, try lifting your pup's bowl. Give it back immediately and leave. Repeat once a month only.**

10. **Repeat this entire process for other prized objects, such as bones or squeak toys.**

Dogs notice fear. If you're afraid, your puppy knows it and will be suspicious. Call a professional immediately.

I can't guarantee that you won't get bitten in the process of training an aggressive pup, so be your own judge. Proceed as your puppy is comfortable, and seek help if you need to.

Territorial aggression

Dogs who act aggressively when strangers approach their homes are territorial. This problem is encouraged by the following:

- ✔ **When delivery people approach and leave the home territory.** Because the puppy thinks that he drove the people away, his aggression is reinforced.

- ✔ **When the owners are home and react to a territorial response by yelling or physical handling.** In this situation, the dog perceives the owners' heightened response as backup.

- ✔ **When a dog is allowed to react aggressively in a car or on a tie out.** When a dog acts aggressively in these situations, he's warning all intruders to stay away. Because they do, he considers himself victorious, which reinforces his territorial aggression.

- ✔ **When dogs are isolated during greetings or visits.** These isolated dogs may develop *Frustrated Territorial Aggression* (FTA). FTA isn't a good thing. In a normal group of dogs, the leader permits or denies entry to a visitor, who is then "sniffed out" by the rest of the pack. Isolation frustrates this normal process and encourages a more aggressive response the next time the doorbell rings.

To prevent territorial aggression, assert yourself by keeping your puppy off the furniture and by sticking to a regimented training program that includes the following commands:

- **Wait:** Have your pup "Wait" when going through thresholds and doors.
- **Heel:** Use this direction on walks in public spaces.
- **Sit:** Practice "Sit" for all greetings — inside the house and out.

Also discourage all marking behavior. (Your puppy should eliminate in one area.)

If your situation is already out of hand, purchase a *head collar* (described in Chapter 5), and leash or station your puppy during arrivals. This collar reduces the negative restraint around the neck and places the puppy's body in a submissive posture.

Handling an aggressive dog on a chain collar is like holding an angry man's arms behind his back. It creates fury. Using a head collar reduces this tension and communicates structure and discipline passively.

To make associations to visitors more positive, try the following tips:

- Use a treat cup or clicker to help your puppy associate outsiders with a positive reward.
- Eliminate all yelling and verbose or physical corrections because they add more negative energy to an already tense situation. To calm your puppy, you must set the example.

While guard and herding breeds are genetically prone to territorial aggression, this behavior can be found in any breed. So, if your puppy is threatening anyone, get help immediately. A territorial puppy, no matter the breed, almost always turns into a dangerous dog.

Protective aggression

Does your puppy feel responsible for you? Even outside his territory, does he react aggressively if anyone approaches? If your pup's acting like your guardian wherever you go, you have a serious identity crisis to deal with. He thinks it's his job to protect you. You must let your puppy know you're the captain here. Follow these tips:

- **Buy a head collar.** This teaching tool lies across your dog's muzzle like a halter on a horse. Laying pressure across your dog's neck and nose will tone him down considerably. See Chapter 5 for details.
- **Train yourself and your puppy.** Obviously your pup needs guidance, but don't forget that you, too, need to step up and assert dominance

over your puppy. For starters, keep your pup behind you at all thresholds and when meeting new people.

✔ **Call a professional if you need help.** Is your puppy giving you no respect? Get help before things get too out of hand.

It's not uncommon for dogs to develop a protective relationship with a young child or a passive, inexperienced owner. The dog perceives the owner — man, woman, or child — as weak and in need of protection.

Predatory aggression

Predatory aggression is another instinctive behavior from times when dogs were wolves and hunted for survival. Most dogs still possess a chasing instinct. Even though breeders have suppressed the drive to kill in most breeds, some instinctively chase and, in some instances, kill small game.

If you have a chaser on your hands, rehabilitating him will be quite the project. Instincts hold a powerful sway over behavior. Focused play gives chasers an outlet, but you need to correct their impulses with other animals or children to discourage interactive chasing rituals. (For focused predatory games, see Chapter 23.)

Fear-induced aggression

Every litter has its shy puppies. These mama's boys or girls depend on their mom's wisdom for safety. After these pups move into human homes, they continue to be needy. Their timidity, which surfaces in new situations, may turn into overwhelming fear if you don't give them proper direction and support. A puppy in this situation may react aggressively during adolescence.

Even though shyness is a temperamental trait, this behavior also has a learned element: Soothing a frightened puppy doesn't alleviate the fear; it reinforces it.

If your puppy shows the early signs of fear with company (such as flight, approach-avoid, or protective barking from behind your legs or furniture), you need to be understanding and patient. You can't correct a fearful puppy; doing so only increases his fear. You can't soothe him either because your attention just reinforces this behavior.

A large part of the problem is that the puppy feels like no one — not even you — has control of the situation. To help prevent this problem, you must assert yourself as the one who's calm, in control, and in charge of the situation. Here are some extra tips:

✔ Keep your puppy on lead when you expect company. Hold your puppy's lead while acting confidently in new situations. Look to him only after he's relaxed with the new situation.

✔ Encourage everyone to ignore your puppy until he approaches them. Ask them to shake a treat cup, click and treat, or extend a tasteful snack.

When strangers or caring professionals back away from a threatening dog, the dog gets the message that aggression works.

✔ Use your treat cup or a clicker and treats to encourage a more positive association to situations.

When seeking out a professional, find one who uses a soft and positive approach. Threatening this type of dog often creates more fear.

Dog-to-dog aggression

Aggression between dogs occurs when they perceive their territories as overlapping (which can happen anywhere because some dogs think that their territory is very extensive) or when there is a hierarchical struggle in a multidog household. This type of aggression is often exaggerated by well-meaning owners who scream or pull back when their puppies show aggression. Such a reaction only adds to the tension.

Overlapping territory disputes

Overlapping territory disputes usually result from a lack of early socialization. If your pup has limited socialization, you must assess how serious it is. A puppy class may be the perfect solution. You, as an owner, need to know how to assert yourself and act like a protective leader when you meet another dog.

In my puppy kindergarten classes, I allow ten minutes of off-lead play, which allows the puppies to socialize with each other and with other people. Socializing your puppy at a young age ensures that he will learn to interact and posture with other puppies and grow into a dog less reactive to the sight of his own species.

Hierarchical disputes

Whenever a home has two or more dogs, the dogs develop a hierarchical relationship. The lead dog dominates over toys or food and is the one pushing the other dog out of the way when attention is offered. In addition, your leader is the one racing to be out the door first.

Disputes arise when you undermine their organization by paying more attention to the underdog. The lead dog is frustrated, and the underdog is confused. To calm things down, pay more attention to the Top Dog. Feed, greet, and play with him first and most. Spend time training him. The other dog will follow. If they fight, praise the Top Dog and ignore the other. I know it sounds cruel, and it's difficult (I had to do it), but trust me — it works. If you're having difficulty, bring in a professional.

Psychotic aggression

I very rarely come across a psychotic dog or puppy, but they do exist. Most, although not all, dogs with this problem are the result of poor puppy-mill-type breeding. Psychotic aggression is identified by erratic or fearful aggression responses in atypical situations, and these traits are seen at a very young age. Following are the two categories of psychotic aggression:

- **Erratic viciousness:** At unpredictable intervals, a puppy in this category growls fiercely from his belly. This behavior may happen when the puppy's owner passes his food bowl, approaches when he's chewing a toy, or even walks by him. At other times, the dog is perfectly sweet — this Jekyll and Hyde personality is common.

- **Fear biting:** A puppy in this category shows dramatic fear or a startled bite response to nonthreatening situations such as turning a page of the newspaper or the sudden movement of an arm. These puppies, who are known as *fear biters,* may also act extremely confused or threatened when strangers approach.

  Many well-educated dog people use the term "fear biter" incorrectly. They don't realize the big difference between a puppy who bites out of fear and a fear biter. A puppy who bites because he is afraid feels trapped or threatened for good cause; a fear biter may suddenly fly off the wall and attack you when you turn a page in a book. Don't automatically assume the worst if someone labels your dog with this term.

Don't panic if your puppy occasionally growls at you or barks at the mail carrier. A lot of puppies growl when protecting a food dish or toy, and the guarding instinct is strong in many breeds. These are behavioral problems that you can cure or control with proper training. Even many biters can be rehabilitated. The situations I'm speaking of here involve *severe* aggression — bared teeth, hard eyes, a growl that begins in the belly, and a bite response you'd expect from a trained police dog. These personality disturbances are seen very early, usually by 4 months of age.

Psychotic aggression is both frightening and tragic because nothing can be done to alter the dog's development. Unfortunately, his fate was sealed by the people who ran the puppy mill he came from or bred him irresponsibly. In my career, I've only seen six psychotic dog cases, and all were purchased from unknown or suspicious breeders. If you suspect that your puppy is displaying erratic viciousness or fear biting, speak to your breeder and veterinarian immediately and call a specialist to analyze the situation. Most times these puppies must be euthanized.

Eating Indigestibles

Chewing sticks and socks and mouthing rocks are all perfectly normal activities for a pooch. Eating them, however, isn't. If your puppy is into swallowing everything in sight or has a difficult time passing up the kids' underwear or shoes, you're dealing with obsessive-compulsive behavior.

There are some breeds that show a propensity for this behavior, such as Bernese Mountain Dogs and Golden Retrievers. This behavior has an obsessive-compulsive quality to it, and though it's difficult to shake their focus, the action loses its thrill as puppies mature.

Most people react theatrically when their puppies grab forbidden objects. They make this big fuss hoping to discourage the puppy from doing it again. But to the puppy, this is a confrontational reaction, which I term *prize envy*. When your puppy grabs something he shouldn't, you think "Bad dog, give it back!" Your puppy, however, sees your body language from a puppy's perspective. He thinks you're racing forward to steal what he's found. If he wants to keep it, he had better split or gulp it — whatever "it" may be. Some split. Others gulp. To stop this behavior permanently, you may need to seek professional help. Until then, follow these guidelines:

- ✔ Don't chase angrily after your puppy for anything.

- ✔ Place treat cups or clickers and treats in several rooms around your home (flip to Chapter 11 for more on treat cups and clickers). If your puppy picks up something he shouldn't, grab your nearest rescue gadgets and encourage him to "Give." Exchange the object for a treat.

- ✔ If you both notice something tempting on the ground, don't dive for it. Remember, you're setting the example. Try to distract your puppy with another object or with a treat cup and then remove the object calmly.

- ✔ Don't think of your pup's behavior as a competition for your sock — your puppy is just showing a natural curiosity for items that carry your scent. Teach him to share and show, rather than grab and go (refer to Chapter 14).

- ✔ Pick up around the house. If your puppy can't find anything to steal, he has nothing to swallow.

If you own a puppy who has a problem with eating indigestibles, you have to keep a close eye on him. If you think your puppy has eaten something indigestible, call your veterinarian immediately, and then watch his bowel activity. Indigestible items can block your puppy's intestine, which would prevent him from eliminating. If left untreated, this situation can kill your puppy.

Marking

From the human perspective, marking is an unsightly, dirty habit that's a total bummer to have to deal with. To a puppy, marking is empowering: I scent-mark, therefore I am. And sex doesn't matter, both male and female puppies mark.

To resolve this habit, you need to look at life from your puppy's perspective. Your puppy is trying to communicate something. Decide which of the following your pup is trying to communicate:

- ✔ **Anxiety:** If a puppy is nervous when left alone or when he's within earshot (or eyeshot) of things out of his control, he may mark to settle himself. This puppy needs more socialization and training and should be isolated in a crate or small area when left alone to prevent pacing and marking.

- ✔ **Frustration:** If you have a strong-willed puppy who is suffering from Hyper Isolation Anxiety (see Chapter 17) from being isolated in a room or crate, don't be too surprised if he marks either in his enclosure or when given unsupervised freedom to explore. This pup needs a formal introduction to household freedom using the leading and stationing techniques listed in Chapter 13.

- ✔ **Territorial dominance:** A puppy who's given the message that he rules the roost will often mark to reinforce his position. If your home is run by your puppy, you must live with his rules. This puppy needs structured training lessons, including (but not limited to) these directions: Excuse Me, Wait, Heel, Stay, No, and Down (refer to Chapter 14).

Marking is more common in smaller breeds for two main reasons: Their tiny toy size often guarantees being coddled, and their normal dog posturing isn't taken seriously. Left untrained, their assumption is that they regulate their environment. Marking helps these pups feel empowered.

If your puppy is marking, review all the housetraining tips listed in Chapter 12, and follow a program to reinforce his bladder control and communication skills.

An unneutered puppy will be more prone to marking. It's nothing personal, just a hormonal urge to leave his scent all over! Another reason to make that appointment now!

Stool Swallowing

Stool swallowing is a delightful habit that involves a pup who eats stool — whether his or another creature's. Believe it or not, stool swallowing is a fairly common behavior. Though most puppies grow out of it within their first year, your reaction weighs heavily. If you're prone to dramatic outbursts, shouting and chasing your puppy from every pile, he will view your escapade as competition and gulp fast. What to do? Read on for some surefire tips!

Other creatures' stools

Stool from other creatures is actually quite a delicacy to your puppy. Deer duds, cat-litter logs, goose goblets — they're all candies to suit your puppy's delight. Most dogs outgrow this behavior if you feed them a balanced meal twice a day and ignore their stool fetish.

When you catch your pup stealing stool, try to refocus him on a favorite activity. If you're suffering from litter-box blues, put the litter box in an inaccessible area, buy a litter box with a lid, or correct the box rather than the dog (see Chapter 16).

If you have an outdoor issue, leave a long line on your puppy and redirect him by running in the opposite direction and calling out his name.

Puppy's own stools

Though eating stool is probably the most grotesque thing you could ever imagine, in dogland, it's just a handy way to keep the den clean. When your puppy was much younger, he watched his mother do it, and when he sees you cleaning up after him, he thinks — well, you get the picture.

To halt this habit, follow these tips:

- Never clean up messes in front of your pup.
- Don't correct your puppy when he shows interest in his stool. If you fuss, he'll gulp.
- If your puppy shows interest, refocus him on a favorite game: "Get your ball!"
- Ask your veterinarian to give you a food additive that makes his feces distasteful. I know, what could be more distasteful than dog poop? But, nonetheless, such things do exist.
- After your puppy finishes eliminating, spray the pile with something distasteful, like Bitter Apple, hot-pepper sauce, or vinegar.
- And last, but not least, keep the yard clean to reduce temptation.

Part V
In Sickness and in Health

The 5th Wave   By Rich Tennant

"I've got the salad spinner down here! I'm drying the dog."

In this part . . .

Most people are committed to their puppy the second their eyes lock and they call out: "I'll take this one!" In sickness and in health, for better or worse, and for richer or poorer, your puppy is dependent on you for everything from the food she eats to how you care for her when she's sick. Understanding your puppy from the inside out, and staying on top of everyday hygiene is the best insurance for a life well-lived!

In this part, you find everything you need on proper nutrition, fitness, preventative and emergency care, and how to deal with parasites (yuck!).

Chapter 19

Food and Fitness

*O*n a day-to-day basis, you can do so much — from feeding your puppy an appropriate diet to making sure she's getting the right exercise — to influence your puppy's health. A healthy puppy is a happy puppy, which, for you, means less chewing, more cooperation, consistent potty habits, and a calmer attitude overall.

In this chapter, I examine dog food labels, how much exercise is good for your specific pup, and various organized activities you and your pup can join together!

Puppy Nutrition 101: Making Sure Your Pup Is Well-Fed

Feeding your puppy the wrong diet affects her health *and* her behavior. The wrong diet can increase your puppy's susceptibility to disease, infection, and possibly nervous/aggressive disorders.

You have a myriad of choices when it comes to what to feed your pup: store bought or homemade, premium brand or run-of-the-mill, wet or dry. When nearly every brand on the market claims to be the best, how do you decide? Don't worry. I've done some investigative reporting to get the scoop on just what makes one puppy food different from the rest.

As your puppy ages, she'll need a different balance of nutrition to keep her healthy. Like humans, older dogs need less protein and fewer calories.

The origins of commercial dog food

Before World War II, dogs ate human leftovers — a tradition that had endured since the moment the first dog was domesticated from the wolf. With the war came economic strain and a weakened work force, which resulted in the development of commercialized dog food. Animal parts unfit for human consumption, which would otherwise be discarded as waste, were processed as dog food. Yum. The first commercial bags of dog food were sold in the grocery stores. Many of those same first brands can still be found today. In the early '70s, specialty pet stores were introduced, and with these stores came the study and preparation of higher-quality foods.

Essential ingredients — and how they differ from brand to brand

Broken down, aren't all dog foods basically the same? I'm afraid not. The only true similarity is in the percentage of organic components required to meet a dog's daily allowance, which is determined by the *Association of American Feed Control Officials* (AAFCO). Foods must contain six essential elements: protein, fat, carbohydrates, vitamins, minerals, and water. These elements make up the minimum daily requirement. But that's where the similarities end.

Even though the requirement is set by law, each company can choose whatever ingredients it wants to fill that requirement. For example, some foods include soy to meet the daily protein requirement, while other foods include meat or animal protein. Think of it this way: It's like the difference between eating ten soy burgers to get my daily requirement of protein versus eating a good, wholesome piece of chicken. Well, perhaps I'm exaggerating, but you catch my drift. For dogs, animal protein beats soy hands down.

You can find many brands of puppy food on the market, but they all basically fall into three groupings:

- **Pick-me-up-anywhere brands:** You can find these brand names just about anywhere. A segment on *60 Minutes* described how these widely commercialized food companies get their meats: They select from the Grade 4-D categories — meaning those animals that are dead, dying, diseased, or decaying. How's that for appetizing? In addition, much of the fat in these brands is indigestible, requiring greater amounts to meet daily nutritional requirements.

- **Premium labels:** Found in specialty pet stores and animal hospitals, premium foods originated to improve the quality control and ingredients offered to pets. A higher grade of meat is used, and the food contains a higher quantity of usable fats.

✔ **Holistic feed:** These foods can also be found in specialty pet stores. The word *holistic* translates into "human-grade everything." This means the food has human-grade meats, digestible fats, and a grain carbohydrate mix of the highest standard. Many are even hormone- and steroid-free. Even though holistic dog food often costs more and can be challenging to find, it's calorie-rich, requiring less bulk to meet the daily nutritional requirement. And theoretically, if you got really hungry. . . .

When searching for the right dog food, pay close attention to your dog's digestion. Foods with low-quality ingredients aren't absorbed as well and can give your dog loose stools. A good food should help your puppy produce two to four compact, inoffensive-smelling stools a day.

The following sections discuss each of the essential components in dog food and compare how the various grades of food meet these requirements.

Proteins (recommended 21 to 26 percent of the food)

Protein is the source that determines the quality of the dog food. When you read the label, you see one or more protein sources: meat, animal, and grain protein. Here's the translation:

✔ **Meat protein:** Meat protein consists of organ meat or muscle meat. This type of protein is the closest to human quality and is superior to other protein sources.

✔ **Animal protein:** Animal protein consists of any part of the animal that contains protein — hair, hoofs, lips, and eyelashes are included in this group.

✔ **Vegetable or grain proteins:** Reconsider foods whose ingredient list leads off with soy, meat byproducts, or *crude protein* (which includes everything crude on the body from hair to nails). First of all, you have to feed a lot of this food to your dog to meet her daily requirement, and of course, what goes in must come out. Second, unusable protein stresses the kidney. Anything that spells out "gluten" can be translated to mean a hard-to-digest, low-quality protein that is inexpensive for the manufacturer to produce.

Some puppies are allergic to grains found in dog food. The most common allergies are to corn, wheat, and soy. Certain grains also may contain fertilizer residue, which can cause an allergic reaction. If your pup refuses to eat her food or her digestion seems abnormal in any way, consult your veterinarian and bring along the labels from your puppy's food to help the vet identify any possible aggravating ingredients.

The crude protein measurement for a puppy food totals all protein obtained from the animal protein source, as well as the protein found in the grains.

Here are some interesting tidbits about protein:

- ✔ The need for protein changes throughout your puppy's life. Whenever she experiences a temperature change or any kind of emotional stress, her system will demand a certain amount of protein. When stress occurs, your puppy uses more protein (and therefore relies on you to feed her more protein). If your puppy leads a more sedentary existence or you've restricted exercise due to a recommendation or injury, speak to your veterinarian about reducing the ratio of protein in your puppy's diet.

- ✔ Ever wonder what the difference is between active, low-active, lite, puppy, and performance foods? You guessed it: the percentage of protein.

- ✔ More protein isn't always better. High-protein diets are used for show or working dogs. If you have a sworn couch potato or a dog who must spend hours alone, feeding her a high-protein diet (which, broken down, equals energy) makes her jittery and hyper.

Carbohydrates (recommended 42 percent of the food)

Some dog food manufacturers meet the minimum daily requirements for protein by primarily using vegetable matter, which contains high levels of carbohydrates. The problem here is that dogs don't digest carbohydrates the way people do. Human digestive systems are much more complicated. We start digestion in our mouths, where we chew and savor our food. Dogs, on the other hand, chew and gulp, causing their digestion to instead start later, when the food reaches their belly.

Understanding their digestive system is important because carbohydrate digestion is a slow process that's not cut out for gulping. Foods high in carbs can cause digestive problems in dogs, such as bloating, upset stomach, constipation, and too much stool. Make sure you provide your pup with a diet that contains more animal protein than vegetable protein by picking a food that has two or more animal sources of protein listed in the first five ingredients.

If your pup inhales her food, slow her down. Take a large pan, place heavy rocks in the bottom, and add her food to create an eatable obstacle course. Just be sure the rocks are too large to eat.

Fats and preservatives (15 to 20 percent of the food)

Fats are the costliest ingredient in dog food, primarily because they're harder to extract and preserve. The fat in the diet gives your puppy stable, even-tempered energy. In addition, fat keeps your puppy's skin and coat healthy, mobilizes digestion, and stabilizes temperature — keeping her warm when it's cold and cool when it's warm.

Sources of usable fats include chicken fats, sunflower or canola oil, fish oil, and lactose-free dairy products. I recommend lactose-free dairy products because after a puppy loses her baby teeth, she loses the enzyme needed to process the milk chemical lactose. Even though a dog doesn't know the difference between lactose and lactose-free, her stomach sure does — lactose in dogs produces gas and loose stool.

Here are some tidbits to keep in mind when researching fats and preservatives in your puppy's diet:

- Many food companies have begun adding *tallow fat* to meet the minimum daily requirement. Used in the production of candles, this fat is inexpensive and indigestible. When a brand claims a "new formula," make sure the change doesn't include this unusable ingredient.

- Supplementing fat in your puppy's diet is often unnecessary. However, if your vet encourages you to increase fat content, use pressed safflower oil drizzled over their meal — approximately 1 teaspoon for small dogs and 1 tablespoon for large dogs. This oil has a high concentration of linoleic acid and is least likely to cause an allergic reaction.

- In commercial puppy foods, check the label to see what preservatives are used. If you're unsure, speak to your veterinarian or other professional. For example, the preservative ethoxyquin is a recognized carcinogen.

Vitamins (1 percent of the food)

Vitamins do two things: They unlock nutrients from food, and they help the body use energy. That's it in a nutshell. There are two types of vitamins:

- **Fat soluble:** These vitamins, which include vitamins A, D, E, and K, are stored in fatty tissue and in the liver.

- **Water soluble:** These vitamins, which include vitamins B and C, are flushed through the body daily — either used up or excreted.

Should you supplement your pup's diet with vitamin C? Not everyone agrees on the answer to that question. Do an Internet search on "supplementing your dog's diet" and read the controversy. The arguments for supplementing with vitamin C are these: What's unused is washed from the dog's body, and in the best-case scenario, vitamin C can strengthen the elastic tissues, making them more resilient to stress. Although no formal studies prove this, negative effects don't seem to occur with supplements. However, opponents argue that dogs' bodies can produce all the vitamin C they need.

Water

Did you know that your dog can live three weeks without food but will die within days without water? Water is necessary for all digestive processes, as well as temperature regulation and nutrient absorption. Water acts as a transportation medium, shipping things between organs and out the body.

How much water your pup needs depends on the intensity of her physical activities and the type of food she eats. Panting is your dog's means of sweating. If your dog is panting, you know she needs a drink. Dry food also encourages thirst. Because dry food contains only 10 percent moisture, your dog needs about a quart of water for every pound of dry food she eats.

Canned dog food or home-cooked diets, on the other hand, contain more water (keep in mind, though, that the higher water content doesn't necessarily make them a superior food source).

If you're using water from the faucet, have it tested (or test it yourself) to ensure it's free of harmful contaminants. Faucet water has been known to contain bacteria, viruses, lead, gasoline, radioactive gases, and carcinogenic industrial components that can cause chronic health problems. Department stores, such as Wal-Mart, carry inexpensive water testing kits that test hardness and measure chlorine, pH, nitrate, and iron levels.

The need for vitamins varies, depending on your puppy and her lifestyle. If you're considering supplementation, speak with your veterinarian first. Vitamins are a rather unstable lot, easily destroyed by light and heat, so investing in a good vitamin supplement may be a smart decision. Ask your veterinarian for suggestions. If you're feeding your dog a high-quality diet, supplementation may be unnecessary and maybe even harmful.

Some foods have a long list of vitamins. Keep in mind that only 1 percent of the food should be sourced from vitamins. Though the list may look impressive, less is more.

Minerals (1 percent of the food)

Minerals are a lot like their vitamin cohorts. They help the body in its normal daily functions like circulation, energy production, and cell regeneration. A high-quality dog food should have an adequate balance. Oversupplementation can be harmful to your puppy's development and health. Speak to your veterinarian if you have more specific questions.

Though mineral deficiencies are more common than vitamin deficiencies, don't supplement your dog's diet unless your veterinarian directs you to do so. Adding minerals to your puppy's diet can cause an imbalance that's harmful to her health. (To discover more about how specific minerals affect your dog's health, refer to *The Holistic Guide for a Healthy Dog,* by Wendy Volhard and Kerry Brown, D.V.M. [Macmillan Publishing].)

The absorption of iron, a mineral necessary for good circulation, is decreased by a diet high in soy protein — yet another good reason to avoid dog foods that are high in soy protein.

Interpreting food labels to get more bang for your buck

When considering diets for your puppy, remember that each is monitored by the AAFCO and must meet specific nutritional standards. How each food arrives at those standards is what you need to evaluate.

To pick the right food for your dog, you need to figure out how to read ingredient labels. You also have to consider *your* puppy. Formulas that agree with one puppy don't necessarily agree with another. As you pay more attention to your puppy's diet, you'll discover that the most costly, aggressively marketed, or cleverly labeled food isn't necessarily the best. Speak with your veterinarian or another professional.

Figure 19-1 illustrates how the ingredient labels differ between low-quality and high-quality food.

Take a minute to read the ingredients listed in Figure 19-1. Compare the protein sources: The lower-quality food lists "soy" as the primary source. Soy is an inexpensive, though often poorly digested, protein source. I'll take the lamb meal, please, as listed on the high-quality food. Carbohydrate source is another apt comparison. Corn is an inexpensive source, as is wheat flour. Brown rice is just better for your puppy hands down. Fat source is another biggy: "Animal fat" is a generic term for a class of inexpensive fats. Sunflower oil is a better alternative. Again, if you're unsure, ask your vet for advice.

Even though some would argue that the high-quality foods cost more, that's arguable. Consider how much more you must feed your puppy to get her minimum daily requirements — almost double! And if that doesn't win you over, just remember the idiom "What goes in, must come out!" A healthy diet truly does affect your puppy's health, saving you loads in the long run as you get to enjoy your life together.

Lower Quality

	TOY	SMALL	MEDIUM	LARGE	X-LARGE
Cups a Day	½-1°	1¼-1¾	1¾-3¼	1¼-5	For dogs over 90 lb. feed 5 cups plus one cup for each additional 20lb. of body weight
Dog's Weight	2-10 lb.	10-20 lb.	20-50 lb.	50-90 lb.	

GUARANTEED ANALYSIS:

CRUDE PROTEIN...............................19.0% MINIMUM   CRUDE FIBER.....................................4.0% MAXIMUM

CRUDE FAT...8.0% MINIMUM   MOISTURE...18.0% MAXIMUM

INGREDIENCTS: CORN, SOYBEAN MEAL, GROUND WHEAT FLOUR, BEEF AND BONE MEAL, ANIMAL FAT (BHA AND CITRIC ACID USED AS PRESERVATIVES), CORN SYRUP, WHEAT MIDDLINGS, WATER SUFFICIENT FOR PROCESSING, ANIMAL DIGEST, DRIED CHEDDAR CHEESE, PROPYLENE GLYCOL, SALT, HYDROCHLORIC ACID, POTASSIUM CHLORIDE, CARAMEL COLOR, SORBIC ACID (PRESERVATIVE), SODIUM CARBONATE, CHOLINE CHLORIDE, MINERALS (FERROUS SULFATE, ZINC OXIDE, MANGANOUS OXIDE, COPPER SULFATE, CALCIUM IODATE, SODIUM SELENITE), VITAMINS (VITAMIN E SUPPLEMENT, NIACIN SUPPLEMENT, VITAMIN D SUPPLEMENT, D-CALCIUM, PANTOTHENATE, RIBOFLAVIN SUPPLEMENT, PYRIDOXINE HYDROCHLORIDE, THIAMINE MONONITRATE, VITAMIN D3 SUPPLEMENT, FOLIC ACID, BIOTIN VITAMIN B12 SUPPLEMENT), CALCIUM SULFATE, TITANIUM DIOXIDE, RED 40, YELLOW 6, YELLOW 5, BHA (PRESERVATIVE), DL-METHIONINE, ADO3.392

High Quality

Cups a Day	¼-⅓	½-¾	¾-1	1⅓-1⅔	1¾-2¼	2¼-2⅔	2½-3	2¾-3½	3¼-4½	3⅓-4¼	3⅔-4½	4-4¾	4½-5½	5-6
Dog's Weight	2 lb.	6 lb.	10 lb.	20 lb.	30 lb.	40 lb.	50 lb.	60 lb.	70 lb.	80 lb.	90 lb.	100 lb.	120 lb.	140 lb.

GUARANTEED ANALYSIS:

CRUDE PROTEIN...............................21.0% MINIMUM   MOISTURE...4.5% MAXIMUM

CRUDE FAT...11.0% MINIMUM   VITAMIN E...................................300 IU/KG MINIMUM

CRUDE FIBER......................................4.5% MAXIMUM   TAURINE*...0.19% MINIMUM

* NOT RECOGNIZED AS AN ESSENTIAL NUTRIENT BY THE AAFCO DOG FOOD NUTRIENT PROFILES

INGREDIENTS: LAMB MEAL, BROWN RICE, RICE, SUNFLOWER OIL (PRESERVED WITH MIXED TOCOPHEROLS, A NATURAL SOURCE OF VITAMIN E), TAURINE, POTASSIUM CHLORIDE, CHOLINE CHLORIDE, CALCIUM CARBONAE, VITAMINS (A-TOCOPHEROL ACETATE, BETA CAROTENE, NIACIN, D-CALCIUM PANTOTHENATE, THIAMINE MONONITRATE, PYRIDOXINE HYDROCHLORIDE, RIBOFLAVIN, VITAMIN D3 SUPPLEMENT, VITAMIN B12 SUPPLEMENT, FOLIC ACID, BIOTIN), MINERALS (ZINC PROTEINATE, IRON PROTEINATE, COPPER PROTEINATE, MANGAESE PROTEINATE, CALCIUM IODATE).

CALORIE CONTENT:
(METABOLIZABLE ENERGY)
3990 KCAL.KG (108G=1CUP)
430 KCAL/CUP (3.8 OUNCES=1 CUP)

Figure 19-1:
Label-by-label comparison — commercial versus holistic brand.

Feeding your pup a homemade diet

Yes, you can still feed your dog a human-food diet, but you have to make sure it's balanced. Followed responsibly, the home diet can be modified for your puppy's age, breed distinctions, and individual needs. Some dogs, regardless of breed, suffer when they eat commercialized dog foods. The natural homemade diet can solve problems related to this condition. The drawback to feeding your dog naturally is that you *must* commit yourself to prepare balanced meals and to shop for products regularly to ensure freshness.

If you want to try a homemade diet, refer to *The Holistic Guide for a Healthy Dog,* by Wendy Volhard and Kerry Brown, D.V.M. (Macmillan Publishing).

Understanding food allergies and special needs

Dieting allergies are being diagnosed with increased frequency. Symptoms include itchy face and paws and vomiting and diarrhea.

Allergies to your food and theirs

Your puppy's system is simply not set up to handle the variation that's present in our diet. Processed foods are especially problematic because they have chemicals that are neither recognized nor absorbed by her body. If you're determined to share your plate with your pooch, keep the additions unprocessed. For example, fruits, veggies, or meats are best for your pup.

Avoid giving your puppy dairy products. She's unable to break down the enzymes, which leads to indigestion, diarrhea, and gas — and I mean loads of gas.

To detect what's causing an allergy, your vet may begin your puppy on a hypoallergenic diet. Hypoallergenic diets use novel protein and carbohydrate sources that your puppy hasn't been exposed to. The protein chosen is usually one that isn't in other types of dog food (such as lamb, venison, rabbit, or fish); rice is often the carbohydrate of choice. (Your veterinarian can provide you with a specialized diet or ingredients to blend.) In addition to all flavored treats, chews and medicines are eliminated. You then reintroduce familiar food groups one at a time to determine your puppy's allergies.

Special nutritional situations

All puppies are different. One formula just can't suit everyone. Find out as much as you can about the nutritional needs of your puppy — by talking to your veterinarian, breeder, or educated pet-store professional — to determine the diet that best suits your pup's needs.

If you have a large-breed puppy who's prone to growing quickly, don't be surprised if your breeder or veterinarian suggests feeding her an adult food.

Some puppies have specific ailments, such as sensitive stomach or allergy issues, that require a prescription diet. Your veterinarian can guide you in your selections and provide appropriate foods to keep your dog well.

Keeping Your Puppy Fit

In addition to a healthy diet, your puppy needs exercise to keep her system in balance. One common misconception about dogs is that leaving a dog outside all day is good for her. "She needs fresh air" is a statement that couldn't be further from the truth. If you leave your puppy out all day, you end up with a neurotic creature who digs in the yard and barks until the neighbors complain. Proper exercise outside does lead to a calmer dog inside, but "proper exercise" is the key phrase. Proper exercise involves planning age- and size-appropriate activities and setting aside time to join in the fun.

Making the activity age-appropriate

A puppy's tissues are soft and her bones are growing. She's as awkward as an infant trying to take her first step. Not to mention that the stairs frighten her. Even though taking your brand-new companion with you on your 5-mile jog would be nice, it wouldn't be safe. Too much exercise stresses your puppy's growing body. Your puppy would get distracted and quit or she might demand to be carried. Sure, you want to keep your puppy in shape — an obese puppy is an unhealthy puppy — but puppies aren't born ready to run endless miles. You have to let her develop first.

Until a puppy is 4 months old, you should play with her (preferably on a long line; see Chapter 5) instead of walking her. Walking directly away from your home confuses her perception of your territory, and extended walks can stress her growing muscles. *Note:* Short walks in town or at a park in order to socialize her are encouraged!

Play on grass or dirt surfaces. Keep pups off the pavement, except for when they're going out to potty. Hard pavement is too stressful on their bones and tissues. Tile and linoleum floors are also a real nightmare for puppies because they're so slippery. Lay carpet strips down on these types of surfaces until your pup gets older.

Don't just watch — be an exercise companion

Puppies don't like to exercise alone. They need a companion to frolic and play with. Unless you have a couple of dogs, you need to exercise your puppy two to four times a day for 5 to 20 minutes, depending on her age and breed. I know this sounds like a lot of exercise, but after you get into a groove, it'll feel like recess in the third grade.

When you bring a young puppy home, she has five needs: food, water, elimination, sleep, and *exercise*. Yes, exercise is a need. When it's time to play, you have no choice: You must get involved. Because a walk down the street can be frightening to a new puppy (because of cars, big dogs, and so on), games (see Chapter 23) are the best way to tire her out.

Avoid games like tug of war, wrestling, chasing, or teasing. These games frustrate pups, communicate confrontation, encourage nipping (especially on clothing), and make you look more like a playmate than a leader.

Factoring in size, breed, and energy level

Size and breed are other factors in determining how much and what kind of exercise your pup needs. A German Shorthaired Pointer — a large puppy bred to run around in fields looking for birds — needs more exercise than a teacup-sized Poodle. Yes, common sense would tell most people that, but I'm surprised how many people buy a breed for its looks without realizing the amount of exercise their new puppy needs. See Table 19-1 to find out the energy level of your breed (for more information on breed groupings, flip to Chapter 2).

Table 19-1	Breeds and Their Energy Levels	
Breed	*Bred To*	*Energy Level*
Pointers	Course fields all day, point, and retrieve	Very high
Retrievers	Stay by master's side and retrieve on command	High
Spaniels	Flush and retrieve birds	High
Setters	Run in the fields, point, flush, and retrieve fowl	High
Sighthounds	Pursue fast-moving game	High in spurts and then low

(continued)

Table 19-1 *(continued)*

Breed	Bred To	Energy Level
Scent hounds	Follow and trail game	High
Large game hunters	Challenge large game	Medium
Sled/draft dogs	Pull sleds long distances and pull carts to market	Medium to high
Guarding	Guard territory	Medium
Personal protection	Protect home and master	Medium
Rescue/water dogs	Rescue humans	Low (in general)
Portuguese Water Dog	Retrieve nets from water	High
Sheep herders	Herd sheep	Medium to high
Livestock driving	Move sheep and cattle from field to field	High
Terriers	Hunt barn pests	Medium to high
Fighting breeds	Originally bred to fight each other or other species	Medium
Non-Sporting	All vary historically	Medium
Dalmatian	Currently bred for companionship	Very high
Toy Group	Companionship	Low

Your breed's energy level determines the amount of interaction needed and how often. See the following table:

Energy Level	Amount of Interaction Needed	How Often
Very high	20 minutes	2 to 4 times daily
High	15 to 20 minutes	2 to 3 times daily
Medium	10 to 15 minutes	2 times daily
Low	5 minutes	1 to 2 times daily

If your puppy doesn't work off her energy outside, she'll work it off inside. Along the same lines, if you don't run her, she may demolish your couch. No, it's not spite. It's just energy coupled with boredom.

Fun and games

Do you have a high-energy dog who's only interested in high-speed fun? The following sports are open to dogs of every persuasion. The only requirement: energy — and plenty of it.

Agility

Agility is the Grand Prix sporting event in the dog world. At first sight, an agility course looks like a gigantic playground. The course obstacles include long open and closed tunnels, a tire frame for the dog to jump through, an A-frame for her to navigate across, a see-saw, weave poles, jumps, and much, much more.

Agility fever is very catchy. To find an Agility Club in your area, call or write to the American Kennel Club's Agility Department (American Kennel Club, Attn: Agility Dept., 5580 Centerview Dr., Raleigh, NC 27606; phone 919-816-3559; e-mail agility@akc.org, Web site www.akc.org/events/agility) or the United States Dog Agility Association (USDAA, P.O. Box 850955, Richardson, TX 75085; phone 972-487-2200; Web site www.usdaa.com). The USDAA Web site includes a Group Locator directory under General Information.

Flyball

Flyball is a real heart-pounder. This game is unlike anything else in the dog world. Although the majority of enthusiasts remain in Canada and the north Midwestern United States, I have a strong feeling its popularity will continue to grow.

To play the sport of Flyball, you need a team of four spirited dogs with a slight obsession for tennis balls. The team races together on a relay-type system. The goal of each dog is to run 51 feet to the Flyball box, clearing all four jumps along the way. Once at the Flyball box, the dog picks up a tennis ball and runs back over the jumps to the start-finish line. As one dog returns, another is sent until all four dogs have run.

Freestyle

Swing your partner round and round! This activity choreographs dance routines between dogs and humans. Now you're really going to feel like you have two left feet. Some groups meet to prepare for competition where both the choreography and the performance are rated. Other groups meet just for fun, bringing training to a new level of fun and aerobic activity.

Frisbee

To play Frisbee with your puppy, she has to know how to catch (the *fly*) and retrieve (the *return*), and *you* have to know how to throw.

To see whether your puppy has any interest, try the following steps:

1. **Treat the disk as a dinner plate.**

   It looks like one anyway, right? For a week, feed your dog on the disk, picking it up after each meal to prevent chewing. Wash and hide the disk until the next feeding.

2. **Practicing inside initially, teach your dog playfully with the disk, saying "Get it."**

   When she grabs the disk, tug *lightly* to ensure a secure grip before you get her to release it by offering food or tremendous praise.

3. **Now play keepaway.**

   Show your dog the disk and run a short distance before allowing her to grasp it. To see whether your dog is sufficiently in love with the new object, turn it upside down and slide it a short distance away from you on the floor. When your dog grasps it, praise her tremendously. (Initially, your dog probably won't want to give the disk back to you. That's okay, though. Worry about the good retrieving skills after you've nailed the grab.)

4. **Try the keepaway game with a new disk that hasn't been used as a dinner plate.**

   Your dog may react differently. Keep the praise high every time she grasps the disk.

5. **Now roll the disk; don't throw it just yet.**

   Your puppy will learn to follow and chase and snatch it while in motion. Once she's addicted to this game, showing her how to catch it on the fly is all that awaits!

Are you sure she loves the disk now? Then you're ready to teach her to catch and fetch:

1. **Place a 10-foot light lead or rope on your dog during Frisbee time; circle your body as you simulate the motion of a flying disk.**

2. **When your dog shows interest, give a very light toss or simply fly the disk into her mouth and release it as she grabs hold.**

   Progressively increase the length and distance of your tosses.

3. **When she grabs the disk, encourage her to come back.**

   If she returns with or without the disk, praise her wildly. If she decides not to, tuck quickly on the lead and reel her in. Again, you're concentrating on the return, with or without the disk.

4. **After your dog is cooperating, try the return off-leash.**

   If you practice outside, stay within an enclosure to ensure your puppy's safety.

5. **Next, practice with five or six disks, encouraging your dog to return to you before you toss the next one.**

Chapter 20

Preventative and Emergency Care

. . . .

In This Chapter

▶ Keeping your puppy healthy with daily care, grooming, and regular checkups

▶ Relieving your puppy's allergies

▶ Getting your puppy spayed or neutered

▶ Treating your pup in emergencies

. . . .

*I*n this chapter, I cover everything from how to gussy up your puppy to how to prevent illness through daily maintenance. Prevention really is worth a pound of cure. I also address how to handle emergencies and how to do CPR and artificial respiration on your puppy. Hopefully you won't need this information, but do read it over just in case. Knowing how to handle situations from cuts and burns to skeletal injuries can save your pup's life.

Staying on Top of Good Hygiene and Health

Staying on top of good health can prevent a lot of disease and heartache. One way to accomplish this task is to keep your dog clean and groomed. Not only does regular grooming make your puppy look and feel good, but it also helps you discover any ailments before they become serious. Brushes, nail clippers, toothpaste, cotton balls — these are just some of the items you may use to keep your puppy in tip-top shape. Of course, the other way to stay on top of your pup's good health is to make sure you join forces with a caring vet who can help your puppy grow into a healthy adult dog. (For more on grooming as your pup grows up, check out *Dog Grooming For Dummies,* by Margaret H. Bonham [Wiley].)

Making bath time lots of fun

I remember dog baths back when I was a kid. I had a big Husky-Shepherd mix named Shawbee. To say she hated her bath is an understatement. She dug her heels in the minute we'd turn her down the hall. Restraining her in the tub was no picnic, either. Four hands had to be on her or else she was hall-bound, shaking suds as she ran down the stairs and out the door. It was quite entertaining.

Here's a way to prevent this scenario of having your dog bolt during bath time: Make "Tub" a direction and practice tub exercises long before you give your puppy a bath. The trick works so well that your puppy may start jumping into the tub on command. Use the following steps:

1. **Say "Tub," run to the tub, and treat your puppy (without actually putting him in). Repeat often.**

2. **Next, lay a towel on the bottom of the tub for traction, place some toys around it, and rub a tasty spread (like peanut butter) onto the basin at your puppy's nose level to keep him content and occupied.**

   You're doing a practice run without water.

3. **Help your puppy into the tub, play for five minutes, and then take him out.**

   While sitting on the tub's edge, love on him and treat him calmly. Remember that at this step you have no bath and no water.

4. **Repeat Step 3 until your puppy looks forward to tub togetherness.**

5. **Next, run the water as you're playing but let it drain (don't fill the tub).**

6. **After your puppy allows the water to run while he's in the tub, let the tub fill to hock (ankle) depth.**

   If your dog squirms, stop the water, sing softly, and offer some treats as you scratch his back lovingly.

7. **Proceed gradually until you're able to fill the tub and bathe peacefully (see Figure 20-1).**

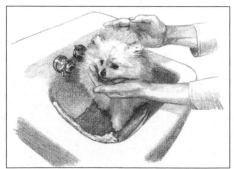

Figure 20-1:
This puppy loves bath time.

I know these steps sound extensive, but think of it as one week's adventure. After all, it's a training exercise — and a relatively small effort for a lifetime of easy bathing.

Stick with one bath a month at the most. The reason? Dogs don't have pores to produce oil. If you bathe them constantly, their coats become dry, dull, brittle, and full of dandruff.

Brushing made easy

Grooming can be a complete nightmare or a delightful, interactive time with your dog. Whether grooming is a chore or a treat is determined in puppyhood. Keep the first brushing episodes fun, and always end on a positive note by giving your pup a treat or his favorite toy.

Following are some suggestions to make your puppy's first associations with grooming pleasant ones:

- **Use a soft-bristle human or puppy brush.** You can eventually work toward using the brush of your choice, but for now, avoid the wire-bristled brush. Also keep in mind that as your puppy matures, he'll shed his puppy coat and will require a more sophisticated brushing tool. To discover which brush is best for your pup's needs, speak to a groomer or pet-store professional.

- **Spread peanut butter or chicken broth in your puppy's food bowl or provide a delectable chew for distraction.** Show your puppy the seasoned bowl when he's in a quiet mood, and as he enjoys the diversion, softly draw the brush over his body.

If you follow the preceding suggestions, your puppy will take the experience in stride, and soon you'll both be looking forward to the time together.

If your puppy growls fiercely at any point while you're brushing him, stop everything and call a professional right away.

Performing daily care and spot-checks

Any mindful puppy owner knows that a puppy can't articulate discomfort or dismay. Establishing daily routine checkups not only conditions your puppy to handling but also keeps you aware of anything that runs amiss.

Eyes

Soulful, sweet, comic — your puppy's eyes express it all. It's up to you to keep them healthy, bright, and clear. If you notice that your puppy's eyes are tearful, full of mucus, swollen, or itchy, see your veterinarian. Your puppy could be suffering from conjunctivitis (which is very contagious to other dogs), a cold, an internal parasite, or an allergy.

Your puppy has a third eyelid. If you lift the lower lid carefully, you see a pinkish lid that closes independently. This lid protects your puppy's eye from dust and other particles that are picked up near the ground. This third lid can become infected, so note its healthy color and take your puppy to the veterinarian if you notice it becoming inflamed.

If your veterinarian prescribes eye medication, administer it carefully by swiping something tasty on the refrigerator (peanut butter or broth) at a 30-degree angle above your dog's eye level. Stand behind your dog or to his side and pull back the upper lid until you see the white of your dog's eye; carefully drop in the medication.

Ears

Different dogs require different cleaning schedules ranging from every couple weeks to daily. As a general rule, floppy ears require more care than uprights because of limited air circulation. If you have a hairy-eared breed, you may be instructed to pluck the hair out of the way because excess hair can trap wax and make one big mess that cries out for parasites. Talk to your veterinarian or groomer for personal instructions. (Refer to Chapter 21 for information regarding ear mites.)

Following is some general information about caring for your puppy's ears:

- ✔ **Clean the outer ear flap.** Ask your veterinarian to recommend a commercial ear solution that helps prevent infection. Using a cotton ball soaked in the solution, swipe the outer flap. Use caution when cleaning because the ear is very tender and going in too deep can be painful. Repeat this process until the cotton comes up clean.

   Don't use cotton swabs or poke into your puppy's ear canal. You can cause irreparable damage by doing so.

- ✔ **Prevent water from entering the ear.** If you're bathing your pup, put a cotton ball in the opening ahead of time and wipe the ears out with a dry cotton ball when you're finished.

Ear infections are quite common. Signs of infection include a red or swollen ear, discharge, head shaking, ear itching, or bad odor. If you notice any of these symptoms, get your puppy to his doctor immediately. Left untreated, infections can cause fever, depression, irritability, and loss of balance. Your veterinarian may prescribe an ointment that you administer at home. Here's how to use it:

1. **Wait until your dog's a little sleepy.**

2. **Bring him to the refrigerator and swipe some peanut butter or broth at his eye level.**

3. **As he's licking the refrigerator, gently squeeze the amount of ointment specified by your veterinarian into his ear canal.**

4. **Massage his ear as you praise him warmly.**

Taking your puppy's temperature

Now here's a fun activity your whole family will enjoy. Okay, maybe not. With all the technological improvements of late, your puppy will still have to endure the old thermometer-in-the-bottom style of preventative care. It's best to occupy his mouth with something tasty (peanut butter or treats top my dog Whoopsie's list) while you dip a rectal thermometer in petroleum jelly and slide it in. The time varies on the individual thermometer: Read the instructions for use. Note that a resting dog's temperature is between 100.5 degrees and 102.5 degrees, which is much warmer than the 98.6-degree normal for humans. A good idea is to take your puppy's temperature when he's well so you can gauge an illness when symptoms show.

Nose

There's not too much to say about the nose, though it is helpful for tipping you off to the fact that your puppy's not feeling well. A warm nose can be caused by an elevated temperature (see the sidebar "Taking your puppy's temperature"). However, weather conditions also can lead to dryness or fluctuation in temperature. If you suspect your puppy has a fever, touch his other body areas without fur (belly, paws, or the inside of his ears) or take his temperature. Did I mention you have to do that rectally? What fun!

Dogs' noses can become discolored. One potential cause is the sun. When your puppy hangs in the sun, protect his nose with a sunblock with an SPF of 45. Another reason a pup's nose may become discolored is an allergic reaction to a plastic food dish or household detergent. In such cases, use stainless-steel bowls for your dog's dishes, and clean with environmentally safe products.

Mouth

You must take care of your puppy's teeth. Though dogs are less prone to tartar buildup than humans are, they're not immune, and poor dental hygiene can also lead to heart disease and kidney disease.

Sure, dogs have more-concentrated saliva and they chew bones and things, but these preventatives don't take the place of dental care. Without a little help from friends (that means you!), your pup may suffer from tooth decay, cavities, abscesses, periodontal disease, and tooth loss. To keep your puppy's teeth healthy:

- ✔ **Include dry food in your puppy's diet.** The saliva involved in chewing kibble helps clean your puppy's teeth.

- ✔ **Start brushing your puppy's teeth once a week.** Use special dog toothpaste instead of human toothpaste because fluoride and dogs don't mix. If your dog is adverse to the brush, use your finger or a finger brush. If your dog growls at you, quit immediately and call a professional.

If you have a young puppy, acquaint him with this procedure early on. Rub your fingers along his gums throughout the week and praise him calmly as you brush.

✔ **As your dog gets older, you may opt for professional cleaning.** To clean your dog's teeth, your veterinarian needs to anesthetize him. Then she scales each tooth separately and finishes with polishing.

Some puppies put up an enormous struggle when getting their teeth brushed. For these critters, your veterinarian may suggest an oral spray that breaks down tartar.

Nails

If your puppy's nails grow too long, they can force his foot out of position, and the nails can crack or break if they catch on something. To keep your pup's nails healthy, you need to clip them about once a month.

The best kind of clipper looks like a guillotine. Seriously. I can't explain it any better than that. This clipper is ideal because it isolates the nail and steadies your cut. Ask your veterinarian or groomer or pet-store employee about this tool.

When clipping your puppy's nail, you want to clip the very tip, just at the point it starts to curl (see Figure 20-2). You may notice that your pup's front nails grow faster than the hind ones due to the amount of surface he exercises on. If your dog has dewclaw (a nail that rides high on the back or front paw), don't forget to trim it.

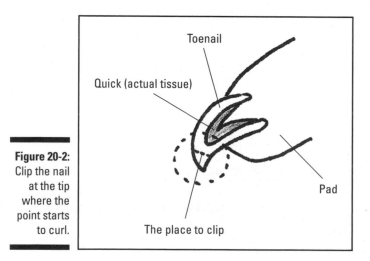

Figure 20-2:
Clip the nail at the tip where the point starts to curl.

If you're reading this section before you've had the chance to cut your dog's nails, consider yourself blessed. To avoid having a clipper-phobic dog, make paw handling part of every positive interaction, from petting to treating, by following these steps:

1. **Initially, just handle your puppy's paws — nothing fancy.**

   If you're in the car and come to a red light, turn to your puppy, handle his paws, and tell him "Good boy." Have as much hand-on-paw contact as possible for a week or two. Perform no clipping at this step.

2. **Next, take out your peanut butter (or broth) and swipe some across the refrigerator at your dog's eye level. As he licks, rub his paws with the clipper.**

   Don't cut the nails just yet. Open and shut the clippers to acquaint him with the sound.

3. **Now try one cut — just one. Place the edge of the clippers over the top of the nail and squeeze the handle quickly.**

   White nails show the nail bed, which you must avoid. If your puppy has dark nails, you need to take extra precaution. If you're concerned, ask your veterinarian or groomer to give you a lesson.

4. **The next day, try two nails and then three.**

Don't correct your dog if he protests. Be understanding and slow down. Again, nail clipping sounds like a production, but in the long run, you'll be glad you took the time to do it right. Anyone who has cut her dog or frightened him by being too rough can tell you that having a clipper-phobic dog is a nightmare.

God forbid you cut into your puppy's *quick* (the tissue part of the nail). Aside from being excruciatingly painful, the cut will bleed for hours because the quick has lots of veins. To prevent excess bleeding, purchase a clotting solution like styptic powder from your veterinarian. It works like magic.

An Apple a Day: Taking Your Pup for Regular Checkups

Puppies, like kids, need vaccinations and regular checkups. After you've found a veterinarian you're comfortable with, get out your appointment book and schedule regular visits to ensure that your puppy gets all the protection he needs.

First vaccines should be given as the puppies are weaned off their mother's milk. Unless a puppy is orphaned, which would require more medical intervention, a puppy's first vaccine should begin at six weeks. If a series is recommended, follow-up shots are given two to three weeks later. These shots are called *boosters*. After the puppy reaches doghood, vaccines generally need to be given annually.

Vaccines aren't guaranteed 100 percent. Some dogs are allergic to them. In others, antibodies don't build up enough of a defense. Postvaccine illnesses are tragic. Keep your puppy at the animal hospital for 30 minutes after he receives his initial vaccines, and find out the signs and symptoms of each illness so you can recognize them.

When possible, spread the vaccines out so that your puppy isn't exposed to many on the same day. This plan may cost you a little more in veterinarian visits, but in the long run it may prevent your pup from having an adverse reaction.

Achoo! Dealing with Allergies

Dogs with allergies suffer from swollen paws, itchy skin or gums, sneezing, and eczema. The worst part is that dogs can't articulate what's wrong, so pinning down the culprit is difficult. Canine allergens include wool, dust, molds, pollen, cedar chips, propylene glycol (a rawhide treat preservative), pesticide chemicals, house and garden plants, weeds, and food products. If you suspect your dog has allergies, talk to your veterinarian. She can test to determine what's bugging your puppy and can give him medication to relieve his symptoms.

Here's a checklist to follow if you suspect your puppy suffers from allergies, noting all seasonal and environmental changes:

- ✔ Use detergent soap designed for babies' diapers when washing your puppy's bedding.

- ✔ Check out the sprays used in your home, yard, and garden. Don't use any products toxic to your pet. Imidacloprid and fipronil are nontoxic.

- ✔ Because many dogs are allergic to commercial disinfectants, use bleach and water (¼ cup of bleach per gallon of water) to clean your dog's areas.

- ✔ Don't overuse cleaning or parasite products. Flea sprays, powders, and dips can be very toxic.

Many dogs also have or over time acquire food allergies. Corn and wheat are common culprits, but your puppy may also be sensitive to the base meat in his food. If you suspect a food allergy, speak to your veterinarian. She'll likely suggest a dietary change and may want to narrow your pup's diet fundamentally to pinpoint the cause.

Spaying or Neutering Your Puppy

A female dog is prevented from reproducing by an operation commonly called *spaying*. Her ovaries (the egg-producing sacs) are removed. This operation requires that your gal be anesthetized, and recovery takes 5 to 14 days. A male dog is prevented from fathering puppies through an operation called castration, or *neutering*. Basically, his testicles are removed from a small incision and his sac's sewn up before you can say "Boo." Your dog is anesthetized for the procedure and is back on his feet in 5 to 10 days.

If you're not planning to breed your dog, have your dog spayed or neutered. Here's my argument for why you should spay or neuter your pup: Dogs have three needs. They need to eat. If humans didn't feed them, they would hunt and kill for survival. They need shelter. If humans didn't provide shelter, they'd need to find it. Finally, they need to reproduce. Hormonal drives can override all else. A dog will leave the warm, safe perimeters of home to go out and look for a mate. This could lead to catastrophe and bring about great frustration if you were to place your dog under lock and key. Think about telling a human child he or she could never leave home and find a mate!

I've loved every dog who lived under my roof, but none were intended for show or breeding, and consequently all were either spayed or neutered. It didn't change their personalities, and they didn't get fat. Trust me: Altering isn't like a lobotomy — it simply removes the need to scope out and fight for mates. Here's a list of some other, more scientific arguments for altering your dog:

- According to the book titled *The Adoption Option* (Howell), approximately 4 million to 6 million dogs are euthanized in animal shelters each year. Don't add to the problem. If you're not breeding your dog responsibly, have him or her altered.

- Having your dog fixed reduces the chance of breast, ovarian, uterine, and cervical cancer in females and testicular cancer and prostate infection in males.

- Male dogs are less likely to mark your home or fight with other male dogs and are more likely to stay close to home when they're neutered.

 If you adopt your puppy from a shelter, you may be required to neuter him. Some shelters offer to do the procedure for you, and others direct you to a low-cost facility. Altering can cost anywhere from $50 to $250, depending on the individual dog's sex and health.

Accidents Happen: Preventing and Treating Puppy Mishaps

Nobody wants an accident to happen, and no one wants to see his puppy get hit or cut, be poisoned, or suffer from the heat. But things can happen, and you need to be prepared. Knowing what steps to take before you get your puppy to the animal hospital can save his life. This section covers the steps you need to follow in an emergency. Remember, though, that none of the suggestions in this section take the place of seeing your veterinarian immediately.

Knowing how to puppy proof your home

Puppies are insatiably curious creatures. Take a look at your house from your puppy's point of view: "Plants, cords, and dropped items get a giant reaction from my parents if they're within hearing distance. What fun!"

Try to prevent as many emergencies as possible by puppy proofing your home and restricting your puppy's freedom to enclosed or puppy-proofed environments.

Hunting for household dangers

Walk (or better yet, crawl) around your house and look at it from your puppy's perspective. What looks tempting? You can use duct tape to secure wires, and you can clean off coffee tables and clear bookshelves for the time being. I know that you don't want to rearrange your living space, but remember that puppies are like babies: They get into everything for the sheer fun of discovering something new.

Hanging there like a snake, an electrical cord or a telephone wire can be quite tempting to attack and chew. The damage can range from a sharp to lethal shock or a mild to third-degree burn. If you notice a severed cord, check your puppy's mouth for burns (and then see "Treating burns," later in this chapter).

Prevent lamp-cord electrocution! Tape all cords hanging 4 feet from the ground to the wall, and pin floor cords to the baseboard. Also, keep a bottle of Bitter Apple spray handy, and each time you see your puppy nosing a wire, spray it immediately.

Taking care of small indigestibles

Though it may seem odd to you, some puppies love to swallow what they chew — especially if you're trying to take the object away from them forcefully (this behavior is known as *prize envy*). The problem is that not all things pass through a puppy's intestines. Some get stuck there, initially causing vomiting, gagging, dry heaves, and coughing, which can go on for days. If that's not cause enough for alarm, the puppy's loss of appetite will be. If the intestine is blocked and nothing is done to remove the obstruction, the intestine ruptures, which can be a fatal condition.

Treatment depends on how soon you get your puppy to the veterinarian. That's because you don't know whether the object is sharp or could break (thereby rupturing the intestines), if it's small and likely to pass, or if it's large enough to block digestion. Unless your veterinarian can induce your puppy to vomit the object up (which she may or may not be willing to do to guard your dog's safety), an X-ray will be needed to identify what he swallowed. To remove the foreign object, the doctor may order surgery.

Keeping poison control numbers on hand

Put all dangerous substances out of the reach of your pet, just as you'd put them out of the reach of children.

You can call the 24-hour National Animal Poison Control Center if your puppy has swallowed something poisonous: 900-680-0000. (Because this is a 900 number, your phone bill will be charged or they will ask for a credit card. However, their immediate and professional assistance is worth a pot of gold when your puppy is in distress!) Keep the label of the ingested matter on hand or describe what was swallowed; the operator is trained to talk you through the incident, translate symptoms, and tell you exactly how to handle each incident.

Also keep your veterinarian's number on hand (or in speed dial) and phone her immediately after an accident. Even if your dog seems okay, it's good to speak with your veterinarian and discuss the issue and possible preventative tips. Additionally, have a backup plan if your veterinarian is out of the office or on vacation. Ask her to recommend a respected clinic for emergencies.

Avoiding poisonous plants

Inside or out, plants can entertain your puppy for hours. However, not all plants are dog-friendly. In fact, some are deadly. Check out the Cheat Sheet for a list of harmful plants.

If your puppy is carrying a plant in his mouth, don't race toward him. If you do, he perceives your actions as prize envy and may gulp the evidence. Approach calmly and stare at the floor, not into his eyes.

Puppy first aid 101: Knowing the basics

If your puppy has an accident, stay cool. If you lose it, he'll get nervous and go to pieces. Be a rock of confidence. Be mentally tough. Organize. Think. If necessary, get him to the hospital as quickly and efficiently as possible. If you've prepared, you'll be fine.

Restraining a hurt pup

Even the most beloved pet may bite when he's in pain or confused. If he doesn't bite you, he may go for the vet or one of the technicians, so restrain your puppy for their sakes. The simplest restraining technique requires a bandana or a rope (the bandana is more comfortable).

To restrain your puppy, follow these steps:

1. **Fold a bandana into a long band.**
2. **Drape the center of the band across the top of your dog's nose.**
3. **Cross the two ends underneath your dog's chin.**
4. **Tie the ends securely behind your dog's ears.**
5. **Check the crossing point underneath.**

    If the crossing point is too loose, your dog may paw it off; if it's too tight, you may choke him.

Transporting a hurt pup

Transporting a dog who has internal injuries is tricky business. He'll be restless and want to move. It's your job to make sure he doesn't. If you suspect a broken bone, spinal injury, or internal bleeding, transport your puppy on a firm surface, such as metal or plywood. Otherwise, placing your puppy on a sheet or towel is acceptable. Don't cover his face or he may panic.

Be ready for an emergency anytime by having a dog-sized board in your home or garage.

Puppies can't articulate pain. They can't intellectualize it, meditate on it, or separate themselves from it. Pain is pain. It's an intense feeling and a state of being. Pain puts dogs in a vulnerable state. It confuses their thought process and their physical organization. Their only drive is to protect themselves and alleviate their distress. Add that state of mind to your puppy's natural temperament, and what you get is a fairly unpredictable reaction. Though dogs experience pain in the same way, they deal with it differently.

Helping a choking pup

Choking usually occurs when your puppy is chewing or playing with a toy and is suddenly challenged, is startled, or takes a deep breath. If you're not around or you don't react quickly, choking could be fatal. One way to prevent choking in the first place is to think smart: Don't give your puppy toys that are smaller than his face.

If your puppy chokes on something, stay calm and focused while following these steps:

1. **Bring your puppy into a standing position, even if someone must hold him there.**

2. **Try to reach in and dislodge the object.**

   Be careful — you could jam the object in farther or get bitten if your dog's panicking.

3. **If you can't dislodge the object, try a modified version of the Heimlich maneuver.**

   If your puppy is able to stand, clasp your hands together underneath him and pull up into his abdomen — just behind the sternum. Repeat this action five times vigorously.

   If he's unable to stand or is wiggling, steady him into an upright position and continue as described before.

4. **If all else fails, get your dog to the veterinarian immediately.**

Performing artificial respiration and CPR

As horrible as it is to see your puppy lying there after a fire or a car accident or after choking, ingesting poison, or being electrocuted, it may not be too late to save him. So be quick, stay calm, and think clearly when performing the following steps for performing artificial respiration:

1. **Check for a heartbeat and breathing.**

   If your pup's heart is beating but he isn't breathing, proceed to the next step. If you also don't feel a pulse, see the instructions that follow for administering CPR.

2. **Check for any obstructions in the mouth and clear his mouth of any blood or mucus.**

3. **Pull his tongue out to make sure the airway is clear.**

4. **Shut his mouth gently.**

5. **Pull his lips over his mouth and secure them by wrapping one hand under his chin.**

   For breeds that have pushed-in noses, wrap your mouth around the nose.

6. **Create an airtight funnel to his nose with your free hand.**

7. **Inhale, and then exhale air smoothly into your puppy's nose.**

8. **Repeat every five to six seconds.**

If you can't feel your puppy's heartbeat, you must pump his heart for him by performing CPR (cardiopulmonary resuscitation), which means doing chest compressions in addition to the artificial breathing method described earlier. To give CPR, follow these steps:

1. **If you have a large pup, lay him on his right side. If you have a small pup, place a hand on either side of his chest.**

2. **Compress the heart area of the chest in short bursts, one compression per second.**

3. **Exercise one breath every six seconds.**

   You'll know when you've saved your dog because he'll come back to life.

Stopping your pup's bleeding

Bleeding comes in three forms:

- ✔ **The everyday cut and scrape:** This injury is no big deal. Twice a day, wipe the area with hydrogen peroxide to keep it safe from infection, and it should heal just fine.

- ✔ **A continuous or oozing stream:** This type of bleeding requires medical attention immediately. Raise the body part above the heart if possible and apply bandages one on top of the other to soak the blood as you press down on the area to slow the flow.

- ✔ **A gushing spurt and flow:** This type of bleeding is serious — very serious. Your puppy can go into shock quickly and die if he loses too much blood. Place bandage on top of bandage, elevate the limb if possible, and put constant pressure on the incoming artery. Drive to the nearest animal hospital.

If you suspect internal bleeding, get your puppy to a hospital immediately. Internal bleeding is a life-threatening situation. White gums, a distended abdomen, a bloody cough, or vomiting spells are indications of internal bleeding.

Find your puppy's pressure points. While he's sleeping, feel for the pulse near the hip and elbow joints. These arteries regulate blood flow, and in an emergency, you can press them to slow it down. You can also use ice packs to slow the flow of blood from oozing cuts and scrapes.

Treating bug bites and stings

Most bug bites are no more of an annoyance for a dog than they are for us. A bump, scratch, and a bit of swelling won't alter the day too dramatically. However, if a dog is allergic to the bite or sting, the reaction can be severe or even life-threatening. Symptoms of an allergy include facial swelling, hives, fever, joint pain, muscle ache, swelling, vomiting, and diarrhea.

A severely allergic dog goes into respiratory failure, which can be fatal within minutes. This reaction is called anaphylaxis and requires immediate veterinary attention. If you know your puppy is sensitive to insect bites, ask your veterinarian to prescribe a bee sting kit that can counteract the reaction in an emergency.

Treating snake bites

Although most snakes issue pressure bites when they feel threatened, most bites aren't poisonous. How can you tell? Poisonous snakes have fangs that make holes in the skin. Here are some other general guidelines for telling whether a snake is dangerous:

- ✔ Most native North American snakes that are solid colored or have stripes running the length of the body are nonvenomous.

- ✔ Be careful of snakes with diamond backs, stripes running around the body, or those with blotch patterns. In North America, poisonous snakes include rattlesnakes, water moccasins, cottonmouths, coral snakes, and copperheads.

A puppy who tangles with a poisonous snake usually doesn't have long to live. The first thing that happens physically is he swells up like a balloon. Then, within hours, he'll go into seizures, fall into a coma, and most likely die.

If your puppy is bitten by a poisonous snake, get him to his veterinarian immediately, phoning her as you're en route so that she may prepare an antidote.

Treating burns

Curiosity strikes again. Puppies can get burned from a variety of chemicals and household appliances.

Your reaction should be calm and immediate when treating burns. Here are some things to keep in mind:

- ✔ Take your puppy to a quiet area and calm him.

- ✔ Steadily pour cool water over the area. If it's a chemical burn, continue to pour water on the burn for five to ten minutes.

- ✔ If the burn is superficial, keep it clean and rub it with an antibacterial ointment twice a day. More-serious burns demand immediate medical attention.

If your puppy gets burned by chewing on electrical cords and is in pain, apply ice to the burns and give him ice water. Then take him to his veterinarian, who may prescribe antibiotic oral gel to prevent infection and may recommend a dietary change until his mouth is back to normal.

Treating and preventing heatstroke

Because dogs don't have pores, they can't sweat. The only way they can release heat is through the pads in their feet and by panting. Dogs can suffer from heatstroke if left in poorly ventilated areas, such as a car or kennel, or if tied out or overexercised on a humid day. If you notice that your puppy has shallow breathing, a rapid heart rate, and a high temperature, cool your puppy gradually with wet towels, a cool bath, or ice around his neck, head, and groin. After cooling him off, take him to the veterinarian.

Heatstroke is preventable. Never leave your puppy in a poorly ventilated environment, and make sure water is always available on warm days. If an emergency necessitates leaving your puppy in the car, contain him in a kennel or seat-belt harness and leave the car running with the air conditioning on and doors locked. For cases like these, keep an extra set of keys in the glove compartment to take with you so you can get back in your locked car.

The best solution is never to take your puppy with you on hot days. A car, even with all the windows down, can overheat within an hour. What a horrible way for a dog to die — locked in a hot automobile just wanting and waiting for his caretaker to come back.

Chapter 21

Bugged In and Bugged Out: Internal and External Parasites

In This Chapter

▶ Tackling your blood-sucking parasite problem

▶ Recognizing the signs and symptoms of internal parasites

Gee whiz. How can I make this chapter fun and entertaining? It's a difficult task, considering that I'm completely bug phobic. Thinking about any bug — flea, worm, tick, or otherwise — nesting on or in my dog really gives me the creeps.

In this chapter, you find out more than you want to know about parasites, including how to recognize them. (A *parasite* is a creature that lives off of another animal. Parasites can feast on skin and blood, or they can leech off your puppy's intestinal tract.) In addition, I discuss methods to annihilate these critters from your puppy's body, and I offer some handy prevention tips.

You're Buggin' Me: Understanding External Parasites

External parasites live for blood — your dog's, to be precise, although some settle for a human snack if the mood strikes them. The following sections go through these suckers (pun intended) one at a time.

Fleas

Fleas are an age-old problem, and they generally hang out in the lower portion of your puppy's body, behind the shoulder blades.

Puppy hot spots

Dogs can be allergic to flea saliva, a condition veterinarians call *flea allergy dermatitis*. The itching from this condition is so intense that it can lead to hair loss and self-mutilation. Sometimes the itching gets so bad that your dog creates a *hot spot* (officially known as *acute pyoderma,* which is not due to a single underlying cause), and a bacterial infection develops.

Go to the doctor immediately and treat the problem before the condition gets any worse.

If your puppy gets one, you'll recognize it right away: A hot spot is a bright-red, hairless patch that looks scaly, and it may ooze pus if badly infected. It's also painful and hot to the touch.

One surefire way to detect a problem is to buy a flea comb and brush your dog's rear with it. If you pull out some "dirt," put it on a paper towel and add a few drops of water. If the dirt turns a reddish color, you're holding flea excrement. Oh joy.

Contrary to popular belief, fleas don't live on dogs — they only feed on them. Fleas live in carpets and grass, so treating the problem involves all-out war.

Treating your puppy

Talk to your veterinarian about safe options for treating your puppy. Your vet may recommend collars, oil pouches, or other products during flea season. Be sure to use these remedies only as frequently as the label instructs.

Don't spray, rub, or squeeze flea prevention products near your dog's face or bottom regions, because most products are toxic. Not all products are created equal. Pet stores sell many flea and tick preventions that aren't as safe as some of the newer products. The flea product's active ingredient and its mode of action are the most important things to know. Talk to your veterinarian first to discuss safe treatments.

Ask your vet about flea tablets or preventative powder. Although these remedies don't take care of the fleas you have now, they do sterilize the fleas, putting a cramp in their reproductive cycles.

Treating your home and yard

Home isn't so sweet when you share it with fleas. A full-blown flea infestation is like a scene from a horror show — bugs hopping onto your skin from every direction faster than you can bat them away. Treat your home the second you discover a flea problem. Following are some suggestions:

✔ **Ask your veterinarian for advice.** He will likely recommend two treatments repeated in ten days to two weeks in order to kill the pupae that have turned into adults. No flea treatment can kill flea pupae.

Talk about the pros and cons of different products. Select a product that treats all life stages and repeat the treatment as suggested. Don't forget to check the flea product label to ensure that it's EPA approved. Follow the label instructions for personal safety.

✔ **Vacuum, vacuum, vacuum.** Not only do you pick up the adults, but you also scoop the eggs and larvae from their nests. Make sure you toss the bag after you vacuum, though — adult fleas are wonderful acrobats and may escape from the bag.

✔ **Treat your dog's bedding by washing it with an anti-flea detergent from the pet store or by simply throwing it out.**

✔ **Treat all rooms in your house with the recommended product and don't forget to vacuum (but don't suck up all the product you just applied — vacuum first).** Fleas love to travel.

✔ **Open all windows when you get home.**

✔ **Exterminate fleas in the yard.** A good freeze usually takes care of them, but if you can't wait — or if you have mild winters — talk to your veterinarian about your options. Your entire yard should be treated (it can get costly if you own a large parcel), and your dog should be kept from surrounding environments that may be infested.

Ticks

A tick is another blood-sucking parasite. Like fleas, ticks prefer furry creatures, but they settle for humans in a pinch. Unfortunately, ticks are found all over the world and can carry blood-borne diseases.

Ticks, like fleas, develop in stages: egg, larva, nymph, and adult. The eggs are laid in a damp, shady environment, and as ticks develop from stage to stage, they have several hosts and can pick up bacterial infections from any one of them.

Removing a tick

Ticks love to climb, so their favorite area is naturally around your puppy's head. Removing a tick is no picnic. When ticks feed, they insert barbs into the skin like fish hooks. If you try to pull a tick out, you end up with a headless, blood-filled sac, and your puppy ends up with a nasty bump on her head.

To remove a tick, follow these steps:

1. **Stun the tick for 30 seconds with a cotton ball soaked in mineral oil.**

2. **With special tick-removing tweezers you can buy from a pet store, press down on the skin on either side of the tick.**

3. **Squeeze the skin surrounding the tick tightly and grasp the head.**

4. **Lift up and out.**

This step can be painful, so you may want to give your puppy a spoonful of peanut butter or some biscuits while you take care of the removal business.

5. **Dispose of the tick.**

It's hard to kill these (blood) suckers. They're drown-proof, squish-proof, and squeeze-proof. I find the best way to kill ticks is to burn them or drop them into a jar of bleach, rubbing alcohol, or vodka (for lower toxicity). If you have children, keep the jar out of their reach.

6. **Wash your hands when you're done.**

Deterring ticks in the first place

You can do a lot to prevent ticks from feasting on you and your puppy:

- **Walk your puppy in the open sunshine.** Walking in the sunshine is safer because most ticks prefer to hang out in shaded, woody areas instead.

- **Inspect yourself and your puppy during and after every walk in the woods or a field.** If you're with a human partner, take turns looking each other over from head to toe. If traveling alone, bring a mirror. Ticks can latch on at any level — they fall from trees, attach to the undergrowth, and crawl on the ground. (How delightful!)

  To check your puppy's coat, run a flea comb (which you can purchase at any pet store) over her coat after every outing. Ticks take awhile to burrow, so a flea comb usually picks them up.

- **Wear protective clothing.** To protect yourself, wear light colors and tuck your pant legs into your socks. To protect your head, wear a cap.

- **Speak to your veterinarian about recommending a good topical treatment to prevent ticks.** Many products on the market are less toxic and highly effective tick repellants. With topical spot treatments, you put a drop of the product on the puppy's skin; the repellent moves through the pup's oil glands and hair follicles to cover the whole body.

  If you prefer a spray repellent to a topical one, remember not to spray repellent around your puppy's eyes. To treat her forehead and ears, place the product onto a glove and massage into those hard-to-reach areas. Don't forget her paws.

  Tick products are toxic. To prevent your puppy from licking herself after treatment, keep her occupied with her favorite game until the product dries. Discuss safe treatments with your veterinarian.

The quick scoop on tick diseases

Because ticks feast on blood from birds and others on up through the food chain, they often carry diseases. Here are the four most common:

Rocky Mountain spotted fever: Ticks carrying this disease (*Dermacentor ticks*) are most common in the southeast United States. However, Rocky Mountain spotted fever has been diagnosed as far north as Long Island, New York. It causes failure of blood-clotting mechanisms, rash, fever, loose and bloody stools, bloody urine, nosebleeds, and respiratory difficulty.

Canine ehrlichiosis: This nasty condition is transmitted by a brown dog tick (although deer ticks are also in question). Canine ehrlichiosis causes severe anemia, fever, bruises, and bleeding disorders by attacking the white blood cells.

Canine babesiosis: This disease is more common in Europe than in the United States, though the number of cases in the Gulf states is growing. This organism attacks the red blood cells, causing severe anemia.

Lyme disease (canine borreliosis): Lyme disease has spread to over 47 states. It can affect most mammals and is transmitted through the common deer tick. (Nearly 50 percent of all adult deer ticks carry the disease.) After the disease gets into your dog's system (or yours, for that matter), it seeks out joints, causing painful inflammation, fever, loss of appetite, and lameness. Left untreated, your dog's kidneys, heart, and neurological processes may be in danger.

Your veterinarian can run a *titer,* which measures levels of antibodies or immunity, to determine whether your dog has been infected with any of these diseases and needs treatment.

Mites and mange

Mites and mange, which live on skin, hair, and blood, are quite content hanging around on or in the skin or coat of your puppy. Before treating for these parasites, make sure you get a diagnosis from your vet to ensure the treatment is parasite-specific (infections can cause some of the same symptoms).

Ear mites

Ear mites nestle in your dog's ear and feed on the outer layer of skin. The first sign of ear mites is your puppy's behavior — she'll scratch her ear intently, shake her head, and walk funny. Why? Because these eight-legged buggers crawl into your puppy's skin to reproduce.

You can check for ear mites by examining your dog's ear canal. If the canal is filled with brown wax and is crusty around the edge, take your pup to the vet. Your veterinarian can determine whether it's mites or another sort of infection and can quickly get your pup on the road to recovery. After your puppy gets a professional flushing from her doctor, you need to follow up with daily drops and cleaning procedures. (Check with your vet — some newer products need only one or two applications a month apart.)

Mange mites

Mange mites are nasty little creatures that are related to ear mites. However, they're more free-ranging than ear mites and often localize along the spine, legs, head, or underside. Here are the three different types of mange mites (talk to your vet for a diagnosis and treatment):

- **Cheyletiella or "walking dandruff":** These critters hang out along your puppy's spine and create a lot of flaking as they munch the skin. The surest sign is intense scratching and nibble-biting along the spine.

- **Demodectic mange:** Demodex mites are usually transferred from a mother dog to her pups during nursing. Under normal conditions, these mites exist at a harmonious level. However, if a puppy gets stressed or is malnourished, they can multiply and create either a localized infection (the infected area loses hair and becomes itchy, red, and bald) or a widespread infection (creating large, inflamed, bald patches).

- **Sarcoptic mange:** Otherwise known as *scabies,* these crab-shaped bugs burrow into your puppy's skin and tunnel around laying eggs and sipping blood. Their favorite spots are the head region, legs, and underside. The surest sign is a dog who literally can't stop itching all over.

As much as you want to control your pup's itch with anti-inflammatories, don't. Anti-inflammatory drugs, such as cortisone, lower an already weak immune system.

Below the Surface: Internal Parasites

Internal parasites are much more of a health hazard to dogs than external parasites. These parasites are especially dangerous to puppies because they can really mess with the pup's developing systems and can deplete the necessary balance of nutrients.

If you have young children, take extra precaution with the internal parasites. Some of these parasites can be transmitted to humans. Walk your puppy in an area where your children don't play and carry a poop bag for immediate cleanup. Enforce good hygiene habits with your children, too, encouraging them to wash their hands before they eat.

Heartworms

This nasty worm is transmitted by mosquitoes (and therefore is more prevalent in warmer climates) and lives in the chambers of the heart and in the lungs. If left untreated, heartworm disease is fatal. This disease is much better to prevent with medication than to cure after your puppy is affected.

Look into once-a-month preventative pills. These medications are prescribed according to weight. If you have a pup, be sure to ask your veterinarian how to accommodate for her growth. Though these pills are more expensive than daily pills, busy people often prefer them. They also have the added advantage of preventing and treating many common intestinal parasites.

Follow your veterinarian's prescription. If he says to use the heartworm prevention year-round, you should do so. Also, you must still have an annual heartworm test done on your puppy because prevention doesn't work 100 percent of the time.

Other internal critters

Following is a list of other nasty but fairly common internal parasites (see your vet for the diagnosis and treatment options):

- *Coccidia* lay their eggs in stools, and dogs become infected by eating other dogs' stools. Intestines playing hotel to these creatures become inflamed, which leads to loose, watery stools; bloating; vomiting; weight loss; and strained elimination. Diagnosis and treatment is easy when the puppy's mildly affected and the stool checked shows coccidian eggs; however, this isn't always the case. If you suspect an imbalance in your puppy's system, you may need to have her stool checked more than once because the adult parasite isn't recognizable under the microscope. If the puppy has an extreme case, the procedure to eliminate the invader can be detailed and costly.

- *Giardia* are water-loving creatures found in most outdoor water sources, especially in warm climates. After being ingested, they feast on the inner lining of the small intestine, creating inflammation, which leads to loose, mucus-coated stools, bloating, and weight loss. These parasites are easy to detect, but early prognosis is key.

- *Hookworms* not only feed off your dog's food but also suck her blood. Dogs pick up hookworms by eating an infected animal's feces. A pup can become infected by nursing on her mom or coming in contact with worms that creep through her tender skin. Symptoms include bloating; excessive gas; smelly, loose stools; a skinny dog with a large appetite; bloody stools; a dry, brittle coat; and even severe anemia and death.

✔ *Roundworms* float inside a dog's body — in the liver, through the heart, and into the lungs. In their final stage, roundworms settle in the small intestine, where they feast on your dog's dinner. Many dogs who have a case of roundworms are plagued with an insatiable appetite or no appetite and vomiting, smelly diarrhea, gas, and bloating. Often, dogs with roundworms have a very pot-bellied appearance. Make an appointment with your vet if you suspect your dog has roundworms.

Puppies are infected with roundworms in utero or from nursing on an infected mom. Older dogs can become infected by ingesting roundworm eggs, which are shed in another dog's stool and contaminate the environment, often surviving for years. Lovely.

✔ *Tapeworms* leave evidence when they inhabit your pooch. I remember once asking my brother why a piece of rice was crawling out my dog's rear end. Turns out it wasn't rice after all. It was a tapeworm. Yuck. Truth is, most people discover their dog is infected with tapeworms by using the "white rice" diagnosis. Other subtle signs include an increased appetite accompanied with weight loss, rectal itching, abdominal pain, and indigestion. Dogs pick up this parasite by eating fleas, which serve as the tapeworms' intermediate hosts. See your vet if you, too, find "rice" in your puppy's bedding or around her potty spot.

✔ *Whipworms* live and reproduce in a dog's large intestine, causing inflammation and the following symptoms: bloating and cramps; bloody or mucus-coated stools; a dry, brittle coat; smelly diarrhea; and a major appetite. Also, some puppies may have vomiting, anemia, and/or no appetite. Dogs become infected with whipworms by eating worm-ridden stools (an especially popular activity among pups!) or by stepping in feces and licking their paws.

Hookworms and roundworms aren't strangers to humans. Children can fall victim to these parasites if their play area is frequented by free-ranging pets (cats as well as dogs). These parasites are usually transmitted in a fecal-oral fashion, but they can also enter through the skin. Plus, it's not unheard of for a responsible owner to forget to wash his hands after cleaning up after his dog or for a child to play with dog poop. If you suspect you or a child has hookworms or roundworms, call your doctor immediately. To prevent these problems, clean up after your puppy, wash your hands after cleaning, and check your child's play area twice a day. Have your pet routinely screened for intestinal parasites, and use monthly heartworm prevention that includes intestinal parasite control. Though not common, a roundworm infection in humans can cause blindness or neurological damage.

Part VI
The Part of Tens

The 5th Wave   By Rich Tennant

"Okay, before I let the new puppy out, let's remember to be real still so we don't startle him."

In this part . . .

Top Ten lists: You can't get through a day without seeing one somewhere — whether it's on TV, at the grocery store checkout lane, or in the morning paper.

In this part, I give you my own Top Ten lists, canine-style. You get ten of my favorite games and ten crowd-pleasing tricks. Enjoy!

Chapter 22

Ten Crowd-Pleasing Tricks

Tricks are a real delight and can be fun for your pup to learn if you have the right approach: Training doesn't have to be all work and structure. After your puppy knows the basic directions and shows that he enjoys the process of learning, teaching a trick or two spices up the normal routine. This chapter gives you ten favorite tricks that the two of you can learn together. You don't have to teach every trick — just those your pup picks up easily. For example, if your puppy is paw expressive, he'll definitely get into the Paw or Wave tricks.

Never practice tricks during lesson time. Otherwise, you turn serious work into a game.

Bow

Does your puppy love a good stretch? Betcha didn't know you could turn this one into a trick. Just follow these steps:

1. **As your puppy's stretching, bow toward him and say "Bow!"**
2. **Praise your puppy like he just invented the puppy biscuit.**

Repeat these steps each time he stretches. Soon you'll have him bowing on cue.

Paw

Teaching your puppy Paw is easy and fun. Have your pup start from a sitting position and follow these steps:

1. **Say "Paw" or "Shake" as you extend a treat in front of his nose with one hand and extend the other in front of your puppy's leg.**

2. **If he looks puzzled, press his shoulder muscle with your other hand.**

3. **Take his paw the instant he lifts it off the ground and praise him (see Figure 22-1).**

   Soon he'll be reaching out for you.

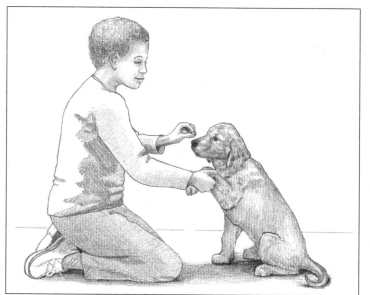

Figure 22-1: "Paw" is always a crowd-pleaser.

A puppy can learn many tricks from one action. With pawing, for example, you can teach your puppy to shake your hand, wave a big hello, or give you a high-five.

Wave

All my dogs have mastered the Wave. It's a real charmer, especially for kids.

1. **Have your puppy sit. Hold a treat inches from his nose and say "Wave" as you wave your hand in front of him.**

2. **Praise and treat him the instant he lifts his paw.**

3. **Encourage more enthusiastic waving as he catches on.**

If your puppy is conditioned to cooperate when given a treat, phase out the treats gradually. However, always praise enthusiastically!

High-Five

Now your puppy's going to learn the High-Five. This trick is too cool. Follow these steps:

1. **Do two Paw exercises. Be enthusiastic.**

2. **Hold your hand up and out for the High-Five. Say "Paw, high-five!"**

3. **Lower your hand if your puppy makes an attempt.**

   Soon, he'll be bringing that paw up with gusto.

Roll Over

Everybody loves the Roll Over routine. Some puppies are into it, but others would rather hibernate in Alaska than roll over. Does your puppy roll over on his own? Does he shift from side to side with ease? If you answered yes to either of these questions, your pup will likely be excited about this trick. Follow these steps:

1. **Get a handful of treats and encourage your puppy into a "Down" position.**

2. **Scratch him until he rolls to one side.**

3. **Take the treat and circle it from your puppy's nose, under his chin, and around behind his ear over the back of his neck (see Figure 22-2a).**

4. **Say "Roll Over" as you circle the treat around his nose toward the opposite side of the floor (see Figure 22-2b).**

   Imagine a string tied from the treat to your puppy's nose. Basically, you're trying to pull his body over.

5. **If he seems to lean into it, praise him, and flip his paws over.**

   When he's rolled over, treat and praise him (see Figure 22-2c) and encourage him to jump up.

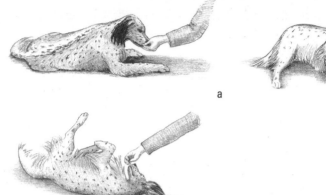

a

b

c

Figure 22-2:
Teaching
"Roll Over"
is as easy
as 1-2-3.

Over

Create your first jump out of a broom and two rolls of toilet paper. A low jump builds your pup's confidence and looks less scary.

Puppies younger than a year should not jump at heights above their elbows — too much development is going on under the skin. Forcing high jumps could cause serious developmental damage.

Follow these steps to teach your pup how to jump:

1. **Place your puppy on-lead for control.**

2. **Let him sniff the jump, and show him a couple of times how you jump the obstacle.**

   Discourage any chewing with a leash tug.

3. **Give your puppy at least five strides of runway space and say "Over" as you trot toward the jump. Jump ahead of your puppy and cheer him for following you.**

   If your puppy refuses to jump, stay calm. Don't pull him over. Walk over the jump several times while your puppy watches. Then try to walk over it together. Although it may take a few tries, your puppy will soon overcome his fear and be more excited for succeeding.

4. **After your puppy takes the jump with pride, put him on a short lead. Drop the lead just before the jump to let your puppy take it alone.**

Bravo. Enthusiastically praise your pooch.

5. **Slowly fade out your approaching run but keep saying "Over" as you point to the jump.**

"Over" can also be a game for the kids. Jumps placed in thresholds encourage jumping to fetch toys and balls. The kids can set up a course, inside or out, and jump with the puppy.

Through the Hoop

Purchase a hula hoop at a local variety store and then follow these steps:

1. **Set up your original jumping pole across a threshold or between two pieces of furniture.**

   Put your puppy on a short lead and let him sniff the hoop as you position it on the floor in the center of the jumping pole (see Figure 22-3a).

2. **Ask someone to hold the hoop or prop it up securely.**

3. **Instruct your puppy "Over" as you run toward the hoop, letting go of the lead as you get close (see Figure 22-3b).**

4. **After your puppy cooperates, combine the "Through" and "Over" directions as you start for the jump, like this: "Over-Through."**

5. **Hold the hoop higher so that it's even with the height of the original jumping pole and say "Over-Through" (see Figure 22-3c).**

   Your puppy may hesitate because the hoop looks, well, like a hoop, not like a level jump. If he hesitates, walk over to the hoop slowly and allow him to walk through it a couple of times. Use food to encourage him.

   After he successfully completes Step 5, you're ready for the solo hoop.

6. **Prop the hoop at floor level, encourage "Through" as you trot toward the hoop, and allow your puppy to go through alone.**

   Praise him and encourage him back through by running backward as you cheer.

7. **Gradually raise the level of the hoop.**

If you want to be really clever (and you have a puppy who won't grow too big!), you can practice Through the Hoop with your encircled arms. Repeat the preceding steps with the assistance of a close friend, this time using your arms in place of the hoop.

a

b

Figure 22-3:
Have your puppy jump through hoops for you for a change!

c

Ask Nicely

Good balance is a requirement for the Ask Nicely trick. You're asking your puppy to tilt back from a sitting position and balance on his hind paws, like the old begging routine. (Unless your puppy is a natural, wait until your puppy is 9 months old before you teach this routine. You don't want to put undo pressure on developing muscles and tissues.) Follow these steps to teach the Ask Nicely trick:

1. **Break up five of your pup's favorite treats.**

2. **With your pup in a sitting position, place a treat a few centimeters above his nose.**

3. **Direct "Ask Nicely" as you bring the treat back toward his ears.**

   If he tilts back for a split second, treat and praise him. Encourage the slightest effort initially, and then slowly increase your expectations.

If your puppy's trying, but can't seem to balance himself, stand behind him with your heels together near his tail. Draw the treat back and catch his chest, leaning his body against your legs. Repeat the direction, teaching him how to balance as you hold and treat him. Don't forget to praise him.

For complicated tricks like this one, praise each step toward the goal. If at first your puppy tries to lean back, praise that. After leaning back becomes a snap, praise the next step your puppy attempts, such as lifting his paws off the ground.

Play Dead

I've always thought that the trick Play Dead was a little depressing. It's clever, though, so I suggest switching the direction to something more creative like "chill, take a nap, or bang," depending on the situation. This trick's easy if you have a calm puppy, and it's good practice for high-energy pups:

1. **Direct "Down." Encourage your puppy to rest on one side.**

2. **Kneel next to your pup, but don't look at him. Then tap the floor near his head and say "Play Dead," "Nap Time," "Chill," or "Bang."**

3. **Gently apply pressure to his shoulder and help him rest his head on the floor.**

4. **Keep his head in place by stroking it gently while saying "Stay."**

After your pup cooperates, take your hand off his head slowly. Eventually, stand up. Make sure you do everything gradually, and remind him "Nap Time, Stay" as needed. Soon you'll be able to drop the "Stay."

Speak and Shhh!

If you've got a dog who loves to vocalize, this trick is a surefire guarantee. Not only can you teach him to bark on cue, you also can teach him the meaning of "Shhh," and silence him cheerfully at a moment's notice.

Consider for a moment how you might urge your dog to bark. Does he clamor if the doorbell rings, if you tease him with a toy, or if you play an instrument? Now follow these steps:

1. **Organize this situation, and as he's getting stimulated (see Figure 22-4a), get excited with him as you flash a snappy signal and say "Speak" (see Figure 22-4b).**

2. **Praise him for cooperating — even bark with him, especially if he seems confused.**

3. **Initially break his concentration with a toy, treat, or praise.**

After you're able to encourage him to bark without a stimulus, you're ready for the second part of the equation, "Shhh!" Follow these steps:

1. **Encourage him to bark. Praise him and bark along — make it a good old time.**

2. **Suddenly, stand tall and say "Shhh" as you wave your arm diagonally across your body up to your mouth (see Figure 22-4c).**

   He's likely to be taken by surprise — and may step back too.

3. **The instant he stops barking, treat him (preceding the food with a clicker if you're using one) and praise him well.**

   You may also use a treat cup to encourage him to follow you simply by shaking the cup and running away from him the moment he quiets. This method is especially useful if your goal is to have him bark when people come or if he hears a noise.

a

b

Figure 22-4: Everyone loves a dog who speaks and quiets down on cue.

c

Chapter 23

Ten Fun Games

In This Chapter

▶ Playing games that encourage cooperation

▶ Mixing games and obedience

*P*uppies learn best through playing. How you play together, especially in those first few months, influences your relationship more than my mere words can convey. This chapter presents ten groovy games for you to play with your puppy. Read them over, try them out, eliminate what doesn't work, and invent your own.

The games you play with your pup should encourage cooperation and focus.

Soda Bottle Soccer

Soda Bottle Soccer encourages your puppy to follow you and to fetch.

Players: Any number of people and a puppy of any age.

To play: Get several plastic bottles (with the caps and labels removed). Place a few on the ground or floor. Let your puppy check the bottles out. When she's comfortable, start kicking. No matter how many bottles are on the playing field, your puppy will want the one you have. Kick it to her only if she's standing calmly (to discourage confrontational play, avoid challenging your puppy for one bottle). Then go off and play with another and another and another, until you've tuckered out your pup.

Rules: Play with your feet, not your hands (it's soccer, after all). Always kick the bottle your puppy's not chasing.

The Two-Toy Toss

The Two-Toy Toss helps your puppy focus on what you have, not the other way around. It also reinforces the "Come" and "Give" directions, as well as the grab-'n-show concept found in Chapter 16.

Players: One puppy and one person. This game is good for pups over 12 weeks. However, younger pups may show interest for a couple of tosses.

To play: Gather two or more toys or balls. Toss one toy, and when your puppy races to get it, cheer her on. As she turns to you, say "Good puppy," and then produce a different toy and start playing with it. When she wants the toy you have (and she will), make sure she sits politely before you toss it.

Rules: Never chase your pup or wrestle a toy out of her mouth because these actions are puppylike and will encourage confrontational play. You may exchange a toy for a treat by exchanging another toy or popping a treat into your puppy's mouth.

The Squeak Toy Shuffle

The Squeak Toy Shuffle encourages following skills and can be played inside or out. This game is a great diversion for ankle-happy nippers.

Players: One person with one puppy. This game is good for pups under 12 weeks.

To play: Tie a squeak or rope toy onto a 4-foot leash or line and attach the other end of the line to your shoelace or ankle. Walk around, doing whatever you do. Puppies love to wrestle moving objects: Better the toy than your ankle.

Rules: Don't move too quickly or snap the object out of your puppy's mouth. If she starts to tug assertively, either ignore her or remove the toy from your ankle and clip it onto an immovable piece of furniture.

Fishing for Fido

Use Fishing for Fido to provide an outlet for your puppy's chasing instincts. Because this game can be used to divert your puppy from attacking your legs, it's great for morning foot traffic and outside runs.

Players: Good for puppies under 12 weeks and their people.

To play: Tie a squeak toy onto a 2- to 5-foot string and attach the other end of the string to a rod (anything can pass for a rod: a stick, an umbrella, and so on). By holding and moving the rod, bounce the toy in front of your puppy.

Rules: Let your pup grab the toy often to keep her interested. Avoid tug of war. If your puppy insists on tugging, look away until she gets bored, and then resume the animation.

If your puppy insists on tugging, slather the opening of a ½-gallon jug (cap and label removed) with a creamy spread. Instead of tugging, she will tackle and lick the jug. This tip also works well for the upcoming Extended Rope Toss game.

The Extended Rope Toss

The Extended Rope Toss is a great game for energy release. It also helps to relieve predatory energy (better to chase a bottle in a field than a biker on a busy street).

Players: One person and one puppy of any age.

To play: Tie an empty soda bottle (cap and label removed) or your pup's favorite toy onto a 20- to 30-foot rope. In a yard or field, swing the object around so that your puppy chases it. If the yard or field has tall grass, use it as cover to hide the object from your puppy's view — doing so will be much more exciting for her!

The Treat Cup Name Game

The Treat Cup Name Game encourages positive association to the direction "Come" while teaching your puppy name identification (her name and yours!).

Players: Start with two people and eventually add more as your pup masters the game. Any age puppy can play.

To play: Make a treat cup as described in Chapter 11. Shake the cup until your puppy associates the sound with a reward. Stand 6 feet from a friend and, using the other person's name (John, for example), tell your puppy to "Find John!" as you point to John. When John hears his name, he shakes the cup and calls out your puppy's name. When the puppy is at John's side, John can send her back to you in the same way.

Rules: As your puppy gets better, increase your distance, eventually moving to different rooms and playing outside. Avoid correcting your puppy if she loses interest; limiting game time ensures fun.

After your puppy catches on to this game, play hide-and-seek. Either alone or with a partner, hide in gradually more concealed spots and call to your puppy as you shake your treat cup. Play this one inside and outside to encourage your puppy's focus — whether she can see you or not!

Give (Or Drop)

The goal here is to get an automatic "spit out" reaction whenever you say the word "give." Aside from being a handy playing skill, it has safety features that can't be argued against. If your puppy has something you value in her mouth or an object that might endanger her, "Give" covers all bases. After you make "Give" less of a demand and more of a direction, your puppy will be eager to share her treasures.

Players: "Give" can be taught from the start, so it's good for puppies of all ages.

To play: When your puppy is chewing on something (whether appropriate or not), approach her with a treat cup (or just a treat from your pocket) and say "Give" as you put the treat in her mouth. If she's chewing on a puppy toy, don't take it away from her. After you say "Give" and offer the treat, go away calmly.

If your puppy runs off with excitement, you can practice in a small bathroom to keep her confined. Or, leave a leash on her around the house to enable a calm catch.

Rules: If your puppy is growling or clamping the object too tightly, call a professional. Aggression is no joke.

Take

If your puppy loves to carry things in her mouth, you have all you need to teach Take.

Players: Practice this game one on one with a puppy who's at least 14 weeks old.

To play: Start with a toy or ball and go into a small room or hallway. Wave the object in front of your pup, tempting her for a few seconds before instructing "Take." Cheer when she takes the object, letting her hold onto it for varying amounts of time. Encourage "Give" by using a treat or another toy if necessary.

Rules: Repeat this sequence no more than three to five times. Always quit while you're ahead.

The Four-Footed Fax

The Four-Footed Fax game encourages interaction and responsibility.

Players: Two people (a sender and a receiver) and a puppy who's at least 6 months old. Make sure your puppy has mastered the preceding three games.

To play: Ask your friend (John, for example) to stand 10 feet across the room. Encourage your puppy to "Take" a toy or other object (such as a folded newspaper) and send her to John, saying "Take it to John!" Have John kneel down and call to your puppy. When your puppy trots over, John rewards her with a treat.

If your puppy won't carry the object all the way, have John stand right next to you and slowly inch back. With encouragement and love, your puppy will become everyone's favorite fax machine.

Rules: Don't discipline your puppy if she won't cooperate. This game takes a lot of concentration.

Wiggle Giggle Freeze

The Wiggle Giggle Freeze game is a fun way to work on a challenging command such as "Sit," "Wait," or "Down."

Players: Several people and, of course, a pooch. Someone who has practiced training with the puppy is chosen to give the directions. The puppy must be older than 12 weeks and must have mastered the direction that's introduced.

To play: Pick one direction. Have everyone jump around and act goofy. Then suddenly have everyone freeze on cue. The chosen director calls out a direction. Whoever is closest to the puppy can position her calmly and then offer her a food reward or a hug. Resume goofing off. Repeat this sequence no more than five times.

Rules: Don't repeat your direction. If your puppy doesn't listen, help her into position before releasing her toy or treat. She'll catch on soon enough.

Index

urine, sample collection, 176
USDAA (United States Dog Agility
    Association), 305

• V •

vaccinations
  proof of, 148
  receiving, 313–314
vermin hunters, 47
veterinarian
  checkups, 313–314
  choosing, 158
  emergency care, 158
  impressing with pup's behavior, 206
  teeth cleaning, 312
videos, 268
vinegar, 185, 290
vitamins, 297–298
Volhard, Wendy (*The Holistic Guide for a
    Healthy Dog*), 301
vomiting, inducing, 158

• W •

Wait (command)
  function and when and where to use,
    17, 116
  practicing with distractions, 235
  reinforcing with retractable leash, 240
  teaching, 218
  use in car travel, 197, 198
  use in doorway etiquette, 193
  use in entering buildings, 206

use in stationing, 192
use in territorial aggression
    prevention, 284
use while leading, 190
walker, dog, 143, 158–159
walking dandruff, 328
wands, targeting, 172–173
Warning! icon, 5
water
  diet effect on need, 298
  faucet, 298
  intake effect on housetraining, 186
Wave (trick), 334–335
weather patterns, conditioning puppy to,
    119–120
Web site
  American Kennel Club (AKC), 22, 305
  Association of Pet Dog Trainers
    (APDT), 266
  dogperfect.com, 79, 188
  International Association of Canine
    Professionals (IACP), 266
  United States Dog Agility Association
    (USDAA), 305
Westminster Dog Show, 39–40
whipworms, 330
Wiggle Giggle Freeze (game), 345
Working Group, 43–44

• Z •

zipper tug, 82
Zuchon (designer breed), 39

BUSINESS, CAREERS & PERSONAL FINANCE

0-7645-5307-0

0-7645-5331-3 *†

Also available:
- Accounting For Dummies †
  0-7645-5314-3
- Business Plans Kit For Dummies †
  0-7645-5365-8
- Cover Letters For Dummies
  0-7645-5224-4
- Frugal Living For Dummies
  0-7645-5403-4
- Leadership For Dummies
  0-7645-5176-0
- Managing For Dummies
  0-7645-1771-6

- Marketing For Dummies
  0-7645-5600-2
- Personal Finance For Dummies *
  0-7645-2590-5
- Project Management For Dummies
  0-7645-5283-X
- Resumes For Dummies †
  0-7645-5471-9
- Selling For Dummies
  0-7645-5363-1
- Small Business Kit For Dummies *†
  0-7645-5093-4

HOME & BUSINESS COMPUTER BASICS

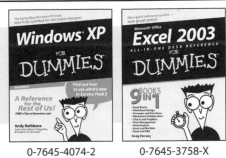

0-7645-4074-2

0-7645-3758-X

Also available:
- ACT! 6 For Dummies
  0-7645-2645-6
- iLife '04 All-in-One Desk Reference
  For Dummies
  0-7645-7347-0
- iPAQ For Dummies
  0-7645-6769-1
- Mac OS X Panther Timesaving
  Techniques For Dummies
  0-7645-5812-9
- Macs For Dummies
  0-7645-5656-8

- Microsoft Money 2004 For Dummies
  0-7645-4195-1
- Office 2003 All-in-One Desk Reference
  For Dummies
  0-7645-3883-7
- Outlook 2003 For Dummies
  0-7645-3759-8
- PCs For Dummies
  0-7645-4074-2
- TiVo For Dummies
  0-7645-6923-6
- Upgrading and Fixing PCs For Dummies
  0-7645-1665-5
- Windows XP Timesaving Techniques
  For Dummies
  0-7645-3748-2

FOOD, HOME, GARDEN, HOBBIES, MUSIC & PETS

0-7645-5295-3

0-7645-5232-5

Also available:
- Bass Guitar For Dummies
  0-7645-2487-9
- Diabetes Cookbook For Dummies
  0-7645-5230-9
- Gardening For Dummies *
  0-7645-5130-2
- Guitar For Dummies
  0-7645-5106-X
- Holiday Decorating For Dummies
  0-7645-2570-0
- Home Improvement All-in-One
  For Dummies
  0-7645-5680-0

- Knitting For Dummies
  0-7645-5395-X
- Piano For Dummies
  0-7645-5105-1
- Puppies For Dummies
  0-7645-5255-4
- Scrapbooking For Dummies
  0-7645-7208-3
- Senior Dogs For Dummies
  0-7645-5818-8
- Singing For Dummies
  0-7645-2475-5
- 30-Minute Meals For Dummies
  0-7645-2589-1

INTERNET & DIGITAL MEDIA

0-7645-1664-7

0-7645-6924-4

Also available:
- 2005 Online Shopping Directory
  For Dummies
  0-7645-7495-7
- CD & DVD Recording For Dummies
  0-7645-5956-7
- eBay For Dummies
  0-7645-5654-1
- Fighting Spam For Dummies
  0-7645-5965-6
- Genealogy Online For Dummies
  0-7645-5964-8
- Google For Dummies
  0-7645-4420-9

- Home Recording For Musicians
  For Dummies
  0-7645-1634-5
- The Internet For Dummies
  0-7645-4173-0
- iPod & iTunes For Dummies
  0-7645-7772-7
- Preventing Identity Theft For Dummies
  0-7645-7336-5
- Pro Tools All-in-One Desk Reference
  For Dummies
  0-7645-5714-9
- Roxio Easy Media Creator For Dummies
  0-7645-7131-1

* Separate Canadian edition also available
† Separate U.K. edition also available

WILEY

SPORTS, FITNESS, PARENTING, RELIGION & SPIRITUALITY

0-7645-5146-9

0-7645-5418-2

Also available:
- Adoption For Dummies
  0-7645-5488-3
- Basketball For Dummies
  0-7645-5248-1
- The Bible For Dummies
  0-7645-5296-1
- Buddhism For Dummies
  0-7645-5359-3
- Catholicism For Dummies
  0-7645-5391-7
- Hockey For Dummies
  0-7645-5228-7

- Judaism For Dummies
  0-7645-5299-6
- Martial Arts For Dummies
  0-7645-5358-5
- Pilates For Dummies
  0-7645-5397-6
- Religion For Dummies
  0-7645-5264-3
- Teaching Kids to Read For Dummies
  0-7645-4043-2
- Weight Training For Dummies
  0-7645-5168-X
- Yoga For Dummies
  0-7645-5117-5

TRAVEL

0-7645-5438-7

0-7645-5453-0

Also available:
- Alaska For Dummies
  0-7645-1761-9
- Arizona For Dummies
  0-7645-6938-4
- Cancún and the Yucatán For Dummies
  0-7645-2437-2
- Cruise Vacations For Dummies
  0-7645-6941-4
- Europe For Dummies
  0-7645-5456-5
- Ireland For Dummies
  0-7645-5455-7

- Las Vegas For Dummies
  0-7645-5448-4
- London For Dummies
  0-7645-4277-X
- New York City For Dummies
  0-7645-6945-7
- Paris For Dummies
  0-7645-5494-8
- RV Vacations For Dummies
  0-7645-5443-3
- Walt Disney World & Orlando For Dummies
  0-7645-6943-0

GRAPHICS, DESIGN & WEB DEVELOPMENT

0-7645-4345-8

0-7645-5589-8

Also available:
- Adobe Acrobat 6 PDF For Dummies
  0-7645-3760-1
- Building a Web Site For Dummies
  0-7645-7144-3
- Dreamweaver MX 2004 For Dummies
  0-7645-4342-3
- FrontPage 2003 For Dummies
  0-7645-3882-9
- HTML 4 For Dummies
  0-7645-1995-6
- Illustrator CS For Dummies
  0-7645-4084-X

- Macromedia Flash MX 2004 For Dummies
  0-7645-4358-X
- Photoshop 7 All-in-One Desk Reference For Dummies
  0-7645-1667-1
- Photoshop CS Timesaving Techniques For Dummies
  0-7645-6782-9
- PHP 5 For Dummies
  0-7645-4166-8
- PowerPoint 2003 For Dummies
  0-7645-3908-6
- QuarkXPress 6 For Dummies
  0-7645-2593-X

NETWORKING, SECURITY, PROGRAMMING & DATABASES

0-7645-6852-3

0-7645-5784-X

Also available:
- A+ Certification For Dummies
  0-7645-4187-0
- Access 2003 All-in-One Desk Reference For Dummies
  0-7645-3988-4
- Beginning Programming For Dummies
  0-7645-4997-9
- C For Dummies
  0-7645-7068-4
- Firewalls For Dummies
  0-7645-4048-3
- Home Networking For Dummies
  0-7645-42796

- Network Security For Dummies
  0-7645-1679-5
- Networking For Dummies
  0-7645-1677-9
- TCP/IP For Dummies
  0-7645-1760-0
- VBA For Dummies
  0-7645-3989-2
- Wireless All In-One Desk Reference For Dummies
  0-7645-7496-5
- Wireless Home Networking For Dummies
  0-7645-3910-8